The Governance of England

General Editor A.L. Brown

LLL/SJC

3

The Governance of England

The Governance of Late Medieval England 1272–1461

A.L. Brown

Professor of Medieval History
University of Glasgow

Edward Arnold
A division of Hodder & Stoughton
LONDON MELBOURNE AUCKLAND

© 1989 A.L. Brown

First published in Great Britain 1989

British Library Cataloguing in Publication Data

Brown, A.L., *1927–*
    The governance of late medieval England
    1272–1461.—(The governance of England; 3)
    1. England. Governance, 1272–1461
    I. Title II. Series
    354.42′0009

ISBN 0–7131–6380–1

Typeset in 11/12 pt English Times Compugraphic
by Colset Private Limited, Singapore
Printed and bound in Great Britain for Edward Arnold, the
educational, academic and medical publishing division of Hodder
and Stoughton Limited, 41 Beford Square, London WC1B 3 DQ by
Richard Clay, Bungay, Suffolk

Contents

Abbreviations

BIHR	*Bulletin of the Institute of Historical Research.*
EHD	*English Historical Documents*: vol. iii, 1189–1327, ed. H. Rothwell (1975); vol. iv, 1327–1485, ed. A.R. Myers (1969).
Eng. Gov. at Work	*The English Government at Work, 1327–1336*, ed. J.F. Willard, W.A. Morris, J.R. Strayer and W.H. Dunham, 3 vols. (Cambridge, Mass, 1940–1950).
English Parliament	H.G. Richardson and G.O. Sayles, *The English Parliament in the Middle Ages* (London, 1981).
EHR	*English Historical Review*
Foedera	*Foedera, conventiones, litterae*, etc., ed. T. Rymer, 20 vols (London, 1704–35).
Hist. Studies	*Historical Studies of the English Parliament.* ed. E.B. Fryde and E. Miller, 2 vols. (Cambridge, 1970).
Parl. Writs	*Parliamentary Writs*, ed. F.W. Palgrave, 2 vols. in 4. (Record Commission, 1827–1834).
Paston Letters	*The Paston Letters, 1422–1509*, ed. J. Gairdner, 4 vols, (Edinburgh, 1910).
Procs. & Ords.	*Proceedings and Ordinances of the Privy Council*, ed. H. Nicolas, 7 vols. (Record Commission, 1834–1837)
Rot. Parl.	*Rotuli Parliamentorum.* (1777 and index volume, 1832).
Rolls Series	*Rerum Brittanicarum Medii Aevi Scriptores*, or *Chronicles and Memorials of Great Britain and Ireland in the Middle Ages* (London, 1858–1964).
Select Charters	*Select Charters and Other Illustrations of English Constitutional History*, ed. W. Stubbs (9th ed., revised by H.W.C. Davis, Oxford, 1913).

Select Documents	*Select Documents of English Constitutional History 1307–1485*, ed. S.B. Chrimes and A.L. Brown (London, 1961).
Stat. R.	*Statutes of the Realm*, vols. (Record Commission 1810–1828)
TRHS	*Transactions of the Royal Historical Society.*

Medieval English Money

The common English currency in the late Middle Ages and until decimalization in 1971 was the pound containing 20 shillings (20s.) and 240 pence (240d.) One penny equalled two half-pence or four farthings. For example £1 11s. 6d. was the equivalent of £1.575 in decimal currency.

A mark was two-thirds of a pound or 13s. 4d. or 66.66p.; a half mark was one third of a pound or 6s. 8d. or 33.33p.

It gives better sense to cite money in the old terms rather than use approximate modern equivalents or use three decimal places!

Introduction

By 1272 England and its king possessed a remarkably extensive and sophisticated form of government, built-up, as the two previous volumes in this series have shown, over eight centuries. This volume discusses how this government worked and changed over less than 200 years and at relatively greater length. The precise period, it must be admitted, is a convenience. The accession of Edward I in 1272 did not break the continuity of government though the late thirteenth century was a time of significant change in many areas of government, in part because of Edward's own aggressive kingship. The usurpation of Edward IV in 1461 led to better government but not to new government and, frankly, was chosen because 1485 or 1529 carry with them too many preconceptions. Nevertheless, though the years 1272 and 1461 have no absolute significance, the period as a whole, the late Middle Ages, does have a significance in the history of government. It was a time when government expanded considerably and became more institutional and more professional; it was the time when the representative parliament became the centre of the political life of the kingdom; and it is striking how many of the ideas and institutions of government of this period survived, often further developed, for centuries – many of them into the nineteenth and often in name at least into the twentieth century. This is true also of much of the late-medieval social structure which is integral with its government. This is the theme of this book, developed in ten analytical chapters and a Conclusion which seeks to characterize the changes that took place.

The chapters are not chronological as in the two earlier volumes because government was now so extensive and documented and because the time-scale is shorter. The order reflects what I see as the characteristics of government. The first three chapters discuss the executive part of government which became normally government from Westminster. The point is worth stressing; this is the time when London became the capital city and Westminster the home of government. The first chapter considers, as it must, the king and his Household because England was a kingdom and the initiative in government was largely in the hands of the king himself. This was not a fiction as it is today; the king personally did govern; and his prestige and personality were essential parts of his authority. The great kings of the period, Edward I, Edward III and Henry V, largely created their own success and the personal inadequacies of Edward II, Richard II and Henry VI largely brought about their own downfall. The government of the kingdom required a king to have good sense, political judgement, ideally military ability, and considerable application to the everyday matters of government which flooded in upon him. The king personally was the mainspring of government and because of this the place where he lived, his Household, and the senior officers and clerks there had a part to play in government. It is however a fundamental mistake to consider late medieval government 'Household' government. If one must coin a phrase it was 'personal government', government directed by the king personally. The Household played a part but a decreasing part. Court and courtiers become more relevant terms and concepts to consider. The king had to rely increasingly on a new type of royal Council and on the great officers who headed the three main administrative departments at Westminster to assist him to bear the burden of government. Chapter 2 discusses the Council which in 1300 seems to have been a gathering rather than an institution, a gathering of smaller or larger numbers of councillors, with or without the king, to advise or decide on issues as each occasion demanded. By 1400 and probably from mid-century the Council was an institution. It could meet at Court but normally it met at Westminster without the king on several hundred days in the year to take decisions in the king's name and to offer him advice. It is the ancestor of the later Privy Council and ultimately of the Cabinet. Government at the highest executive level becomes a matter of an active king and a busy Council. The busiest councillors were the chancellor, the treasurer and the keeper of the privy seal who headed the three great Westminster offices discussed in Chapter 3. These offices can justifiably be described as bureaucratic and their officials (anachronistically) as 'civil servants'. They kept voluminous records in files of loose documents, copies of documents on parchment rolls and carefully written and audited financial records – often in triplicate! The greater problem in studying late medieval government is not lack of sources but quantity and technicality of sources. The 'civil servants' who worked there, still mostly clerics but increasingly career laymen, knew all about 'proper channels' and authorizations, due caution, precise accuracy of statement and all the trappings of a literate, professional administration.

Chapters 4 and 5 discuss two fundamental areas of government, finance and military force, in both of which there was enormous though not unprecedented change during the period. For centuries kings had needed coin to govern and had taxed to obtain it, but it was in this period that regular and heavy taxation first became normal. It was necessary because the king often could not meet even the expenses of his Household and Court without taxation and because military forces, save for local or temporary needs, could not be raised without payment. The English victories in the Hundred Years War, Crécy and Agincourt for example, were won by paid troops fighting for honour and for profit. The king's dependence on taxation which comes to be the prerogative of parliament to grant is a fundamental factor in the politics of the period.

The acid test of government is its ability to maintain order and respect in the localities and to ensure that justice is done. Chapter 6 discusses this in terms of the legal system and Chapter 7 in terms of royal authority in the localities. In 1272 there was already a substantial structure of royal, communal and private courts, ancient custom and the newer law common to all England described in a great book by a judge, Henry de Bracton, in the 1250s. This has tended to overshadow the achievement of the next two centuries when the two great central common-law courts, King's Bench and Common Pleas, became settled at Westminster, served by professional judges and lawyers trained in law schools with a legal literature; when the Council and chancery began to provide a companion jurisdiction; and when in the localities the new Justices of the Peace took over a considerable part of the duty of maintaining law and order in the counties in co-operation with the Westminster judges and serjeants who came down on regular visits to hold the assizes and deliver the gaols. The older communal courts, feudal courts, manorial and other courts continued to exist but in a subsidiary role. It was a fine new system but the fundamental question is how far was it capable of providing justice and order when the king had to rely so much on the co-operation of local people to operate it.

The final three chapters are concerned with parliament. Contemporaries would have been surprised by this and the history of late medieval government has certainly been unduly concerned with parliament. But there are good reasons for doing so. First, there is an illusion among students that the history of parliament is beyond comprehension because historians have made it a battlefield and no adequate history of it has been written. Second, the development of the representative parliament with so many of its classic rights and procedures was one of the greatest and probably the greatest governmental achievement of this period. The obvious danger is to see it with too much hindsight, to see it in terms of the post-medieval parliament. The development of parliament is also important because it mirrors fundamental social and political change. Chapter 8 tries to give a perspective to this development and to escape from the controversies of the past about its early history. Chapter 9 analyses the composition of parliament. Chapter 10 discusses the development of its procedures and its rôle in government and politics. Finally, there is a Conclusion which seeks to bring together the major achievements in government during the period and place them in an historical perspective.

This is a book about the 'governance of England'. It is a personal impression of how government worked within a framework of description of institutions. It is not an account of 'constitutional' incidents nor of every institutional development, and a number of topics hotly debated in the past are mentioned only in the passing, sometimes only in the footnotes. A deal of cross-referring has been used, though some repetition is deliberately included. There is a critical bibliography at the beginning of each chapter and of some sections within chapters but none at the end of the volume. This is intended to direct readers immediately to the authorities on each topic and, with the footnotes, enable them to pursue problems or issues for themselves. Sources are often cited because the original words speak louder than any commentary on them.

I am most grateful to Professor Alan Harding who read Chapter 6 and saved me from a number of misjudgements; to Mary Brodie, Sue Quigley and Claire Spence, three secretaries who struggled with the changes in the text, and the publishers who waited patiently while I practised university governance through the lean eighties.

1

Kingship and the King*

[handwritten: × King was its heart & driving force.]

Any discussion of the government of England must begin with the
king because he was its heart and driving force. Government was *his*
government; it was conducted in his name and he personally took
most of the important and surprisingly many of the less important
day-to-day decisions. He governed almost in the manner of a great
lord whose estates were the kingdom. But he was much more than any
lord. He was God's vicar, anointed like a priest, crowned, exalted
above all his subjects and held in reverence by them. He was an
emperor in his kingdom with prerogative and majesty – but he could
not rule as he pleased. He was bound to observe the law, to do right
and justice and in some matters to act only with the counsel or consent
of his subjects. Informed Englishmen knew and accepted these ideas.
Both the documentary and the literary sources contain many references to them but there was little sustained political thinking and no
'constitutional law' of kingship as we know it today. Late-medieval
Englishmen had deep-rooted assumptions about kingship but they did
not probe them deeply nor enunciate them logically and they were
distinctly pragmatic when the need arose. The germ of many Tudor,
Stuart and indeed modern concepts of government were present but
they must not be exaggerated with hindsight.

Monarchy clearly seemed the proper and traditional form of government. There had been a succession of kings for many centuries;
indeed the popular contemporary legend of the origin of Britain told

[handwritten: Monarchy – proper & traditional form of government]

* There is an extensive literature on many aspects of medieval kingship but no synthesis. The
most direct account of contemporary English assumptions (mainly from governmental
sources) is S.B. Chrimes, *English Constitutional Ideas in the Fifteenth Century* (Cambridge,
1936) and two very different and important studies are M. Bloch, *Les Rois Thaumaturges*
(Strasbourg, 1924, trans. J.E. Anderson as *The Royal Touch*, London 1973) and E.T.
Kantorowicz, *The King's Two bodies: A Study in Medieval Political Theology* (Princeton,
1957). Two judges, Henry de Bracton (d. 1268) who wrote *The Laws and Customs of
England*, ed. S.E. Thorne, 4 vols. (Cambridge, Mass., 1968–77) and particularly Sir John
Fortescue (d.c. 1479) whose writings include *The Governance of England*, ed. C. Plummer
(Oxford, 1883) and *De Laudibus Legum Anglie*, ed. S.B. Chrimes (Cambridge, 1942) con-
vey contemporary ideas about kingship though neither wrote extensively about it.

of a king, Brutus the Trojan, and of a succession of kings after him. Monarchy, as distinct from the king for the time being, was never in danger. It scarcely needed to be justified though educated men knew the standard texts and ideas of political theory and were aware that there were forms of government other than monarchy. Chief Justice Fortescue in the mid fifteenth century explained monarchy briefly in conventional terms as both God-made and man-made.[1] It was the product of God's providence and at the human level created either by force or, as in England, by agreement out of the need for a head to govern and protect the people – and he cited Brutus. He did not go on to speculate about the nature or the implications of this agreement; there is for example no theory of social contract or right to restrain the king. The divine and the human elements in kingship are frequently to be found together, for example at the coronation in the anointing and the recognition by the people. Potentially they were conflicting but neither was pursued to its logical conclusion, to Divine Right kingship or to kings who were answerable to their subjects.

The divine element in kingship was frequently mentioned. The Bible, the great source of texts and examples on every subject, was full of stories of kings empowered by God. It was the source most quoted by Fortescue. All formal royal letters began Edward or Richard or Henry 'by the grace of God king of England . . .'. The most impressive sign of God's grace – as it is still – was the coronation, a service which in spite of papal attempts to deny this, resembled the sacrament of Holy Orders. In this period it did not make the king (pp. 7–8) but it did make him a man set apart, the Lord's anointed, priest and king, the words used in the Old Testament of Melchizedek, a *mixta persona*, both clerk and layman. English and French kings enjoyed the advantage of being anointed with chrism, the holy oil used at the consecration of a bishop. French kings enjoyed the further advantage of a special oil said to have been brought from heaven at the baptism of Clovis in 496 and contained in the Sainte Ampoule, and a drop was added to the chrism. In the fourteenth century the English kings also acquired a miraculous oil said to have been given by the Virgin Mary to Thomas Becket and contained in a phial within a small eagle of gold.[2] This was 'found' during the reign of Edward II, rediscovered by Richard II, used for the first time at the coronation of Henry IV in 1399 and apparently for all sovereigns thereafter down to James I. It sounds the contrivance of kings who needed all the divine sanction they could muster but, even so, it is significant that it was thought

1 Fortescue. *De Laudibus*, pp. 28–33.
2 T.A. Sandquist, 'The Holy Oil of St. Thomas of Canterbury' in *Essays in Medieval History Presented to Bertie Wilkinson*, ed. T.A. Sandquist and M.R. Powicke (Toronto, 1969), pp. 330–44.

worthwhile to use it, though surprisingly the oil did not excite much continuing comment. Long before this Englishmen had come forward in hundreds each year to be 'touched' by the king in the hope of being cured of scrofula. Precise figures are known for some years in the reigns of the first three Edwards because each sufferer received a penny in alms; the largest number was 1,736 in the twelve months from November 1289. An additional element was apparently introduced in the reign of Edward II, the making of 'cramp' rings from the royal gold and silver offerings on Good Friday as a cure for cramps and epilepsy. There is a good deal of evidence of this sort of belief. I like the story told to the Doge of Venice in 1340 by an envoy of Edward III that his master had offered to settle the dispute with Philip VI of France over the French throne by a personal duel or by a group duel or by 'exposing himself to hungry lions; for lions never attack a true king; or let him perform the miraculous healing of the sick, as all other true kings are wont to do.[3] The paradox is that Englishmen deposed or restrained their sacred kings.

The Succession

God's choice of king was revealed by hereditary right, a principle that came to be more clearly recognized in this period though never defined with precision. King John like most twelfth century kings had owed his throne both to heredity and election. He was chosen king in 1199 in preference to Arthur, the son of his elder brother Geoffrey, and his reign was held to begin only on the day he was crowned. The succession of John's elder son as Henry III in 1216 at the age of nine was some vindication of primogeniture but he had no English rival and his reign did not begin until his coronation, ten days after John's death. When Henry III died in 1272 his eldest son, Edward, succeeded without question but he was in Sicily returning from Crusade and the conventions had to change. After Henry's funeral on 20 November the magnates took an oath of fealty to Edward and his reign began on that day while the coronation took place almost two years later. The proclamation of his peace declared that governance had come to him by hereditary succession and the will and fealty of the magnates (*proceres*) of the kingdom.[4] In 1307 his eldest son, Edward II, succeeded – 'par descent de heritage' declared the proclamation of his peace;[5] his reign began on the day after his father's death and the coronation followed seven months later. This was the normal pattern

3 Bloch, *The Royal Touch*, p. 1.
4 *Foedera* (Record Commission ed., 1816–69), ii. 1.
5 *Ibid.*, iii. 1.

[handwritten margin note: Reign began on the day after his predecessor's death]

thereafter – a king succeeded by hereditary right; his reign began on the day after his predecessor's death – from 1547 on the day, at the moment of his death; and the coronation followed at whatever interval was convenient. The implications of this were not, however, pursued. It was not stated explicitly that the throne was never vacant nor that the king never died – though the royal peace was considered to be continuous. The king began to rule immediately but the coronation was required to make his power complete; for example, according to Fortescue he could not 'touch' until he was anointed. *[handwritten margin note: Coronation to make power complete]*

In most cases the succession was straightforward, the eldest son succeeded his father. Edward III was the obvious heir when his father was deposed in 1327. Edward III's eldest son, Edward, the Black Prince, died in his father's lifetime, during the parliament of 1376, and his son was honoured there as true heir apparent and duly succeeded as Richard II in 1377. At this point, however, definition ended and force ruled – four times between 1399 and 1485. The outstanding case was in 1399 when Richard II was deposed and another grandson of Edward III, Henry of Lancaster, succeeded. It is still far from clear what happened then and why. It was usurpation and the official Lancastrian version of events contains deliberate falsifications and obscurities; contemporary chroniclers were confused and historians have debated it at length.[6] Richard had no children and no full brothers or sisters, but his father had had six brothers. The eldest, William, had died young. The next, Lionel, duke of Clarence, had only one child, a daughter, Philippa, who married Edmund, earl of March; and their grandson and heir, another Edmund, was almost eight when Richard II was deposed. The third brother, John of Gaunt, duke of Lancaster, had died early in 1399 leaving one legitimate son, Henry of Lancaster. A table makes this clear.

In principle the choice lay between the heir general, Edmund, and the heir male, Henry, but the principle was not decided. According to one chronicle, Richard in 1385 caused parliament to recognize Roger, Edmund's father, as his heir but this is not confirmed in any source

[handwritten margin note: male line, elder son succeeded father]

---

6 The more important articles are G.T. Lapsley, 'The parliamentary title of Henry IV', in *Crown, Community and Parliament*, ed. H.M. Cam and G. Barraclough (Oxford, 1951), pp. 273–340 (from *EHR*, 1934) and B. Wilkinson, 'The deposition of Richard II and the accession of Henry IV', *Hist. Studies*, i. 329–53 (from *EHR*, 1939). Important recent articles on the sources are J.J.N. Palmer, 'The authorship, date and historical value of the French chronicles of the Lancastrian Revolution,' *Bull. J. Rylands Lib.* 61 (1978), 145–81, 398–421 and G.O. Sayles, 'The deposition of Richard II: three Lancastrian narratives', *BIHR* 54 (1981), 27–70.

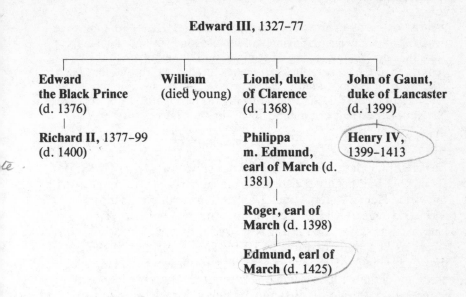

Genealogical table showing the succession after Edward III

and it is unlikely because Richard at the age of 18 had no need to do so.[7] In practice the issue in 1399 was how to find an acceptable procedure and justification for the succession of Henry of Lancaster, the leader of the rebellion against Richard. This proved difficult and the methods employed show how far contemporaries were prepared to overlook deception. Briefly, Richard came into Henry's control in mid August and writs dated 19 August were issued in Richard's name for a parliament to meet at Westminster on 30 September. A commission was meanwhile appointed to consider how Richard could be replaced by Henry and it probably advised that Richard be deposed and Henry chosen to succeed in the parliament. Late in September Henry rejected this advice, probably because he wished to succeed in a more traditional way, perhaps also because it was suggested that Richard's parliament would be dissolved when he ceased to be king. The method adopted was to cajole Richard into abdicating. He did so on 29 September, and his reign was held to end on this day. On the 30th his abdication was accepted and he was deposed in a gathering of 'the estates', not a parliament but the prelates, lords and commons who had assembled for parliament. (p. 15) Henry then and there claimed the throne in carefully chosen words – in English.[8]

7 *Eulogium Historiarum*, ed. F.S. Haydon (Rolls Series, 1858–65), iii. 361.
8 *Rot. Parl.*, iii. 422–3 – *Select Documents*, p. 191.

> In the name of Fadir, Son, and Holy Gost, I Henry of Lancastre chalenge this rewme of Yngland and the corone with all the membres and the appurtenances als I that am disendit be right lyne of the blode comyng fro the gude lorde Kyng Henry therde, and thorgh that ryght that God of his grace hath sent me with helpe of my kyn and of my frendes to recover it, the which rewme was in poynt to be undone for defaut of governance and undoyng of the gode lawes.

This was a deliberately imprecise claim based upon hereditary right and God's vindication by conquest to rescue the misgoverned realm. The hereditary claim implied but did not state that Henry III's rightful heir in 1272 had been not Edward I but his brother, Edmund, earl of Lancaster, Henry's great-great grandfather through his mother. This reflected a legend which the commission of 1399 had rejected and Henry of Lancaster, one presumes, used it in preference to his direct descent as heir male of Edward III because the claim of the English kings to be kings of France passed through a woman. This specious hereditary claim with its touch of conquest was accepted, according to the record, 'without any difficulty or delay' by the lords spiritual and temporal and all the estates present with the whole people, and Henry's reign began that day, presumably there and then. There were several rebellions in subsequent years in support of the March claim, but Henry died as king, his son and grandson ruled until 1461 and it is difficult to identify much honest soul-searching about these events in 1399 or to prove that Henry suffered any significant loss of royal dignity.

It used to be said that Henry was 'made' king by parliament and became in some sense a 'constitutional' king, but it seems that he deliberately avoided the use of parliament, not because of 'constitutional' fears but out of a sense of kingly propriety. In fact he was the first king to use parliament to affirm the succession. In February 1404 the estates in parliament affirmed their loyalty to Henry's eldest son as heir apparent, to the heirs of his body, that is male and female and, if he had none, to his brothers and their children successively. This had been Edward I's view of the right succession. In 1406, the succession was twice defined in parliament by the king with the advice of the lords at the request of the Commons. In June it was stated in a 'statute' and in a particularly solemn patent sealed by the lords and the Speaker of the Commons to lie with his eldest son and his heirs male and then successively with his three other sons and their heirs male. In December this was changed and the succession declared to lie with the heirs of their bodies, not only their heirs male, and the subsequent statute (7 Henry IV, c.2.) governed the succession until it was repealed by parliament in 1460.[9] The reasons for this muddle are not clear but the

9 *Rot. Parl.*, iii. 525, 574–6, 580–3 and *Select Documents*, pp. 225–6.

incident does underline the uncertainty of succession customs and also that there were no qualms about defining them with the consent of all in parliament. On the contrary, in the fifteenth century parliament was the proper place to determine succession issues.

The succession again became an issue in the 1450s when Richard duke of York, who had inherited the March claim, began to consider displacing the well-meaning but incapable Henry VI. In October 1460 York presented a written claim to the throne before the lords spiritual and temporal in parliament, basing it solely on hereditary descent through Lionel, duke of Clarence, from Edward III.[10] The lords sought the opinions of the justices and then the serjeants-at-law and the king's attorney but they prudently declined to advise on so high a matter which they said was for the lords of the king's blood and the peerage. The lords prepared objections to the claim but concluded that York's title could not be defeated. They were not however prepared to dethrone Henry, their king for almost 40 years to whom they had sworn loyalty, and a foolish but not unprincipled compromise was made. Henry was to retain the crown until he died and York would succeed him, ignoring the right of Henry's son. This was done in parliament with the agreement of the three estates but on the initiative of the lords alone who had a pre-eminent status in matters affecting the succession. The statute of 1406 governing the Lancaster succession was repealed but no new statute was enacted; York indeed held it a sign of Henry IV's weakness that he had used a statute. York never became king for he was killed two months later, but two of his sons did so as his true heirs, Edward IV as his eldest son and heir in 1461 and Richard III in 1483 at the expense of the children of his two elder brothers, the children of Edward IV declared illegitimate and those of the attainted George, duke of Clarence. Both relied solely on hereditary right declared, accepted and acclaimed by the lords and the 'people' in contrived gatherings when parliament was not in session.[11] Even more blatantly, with a poor hereditary claim vindicated by God in battle, Henry VII assumed the throne in 1485. It would be fair to conclude that though hereditary descent in the male line was the normal manner of succession to the English throne, another male member of the family might, given the right political circumstances, vindicate a claim by force and some appropriate 'constitutional' proceedings. Fortescue wrote tracts justifying first the Lancaster claim and then, after it had succeeded, the York claim, but he admitted that the law had little to say about the succession to kingdoms.

10 *Ibid.* v. 375–80 – *Select Documents*, pp. 313–18; *EHD*, iv. 415–19.
11 C.A.J. Armstrong, 'The Inauguration Ceremonies of the Yorkist Kings', *TRHS* 30 (1948), 51–73.

King and People

Increased emphasis on hereditary right did not extinguish the popular, elective element in kingship and did not make the king more free to rule as he pleased. Kings were created for the benefit of their people. Fortescue said this and the royal instructions given to English envoys to treat with the French in 1439 expressed it unusually clearly.[12]

> God made not his people. . . . for the princes, but he made the princes for his service and for the wele and behove of his people, that is to say to reule theim in tranquillite, namely by the mene of deue ministracion of justice. So that they so reuled shalle mowe restfully and peasible serve hem.

The coronation proceedings were the best and most cited expression that the people had a hand in making a king and of his obligations to them.[13] At least from 1308 they began with the prelates and lay lords meeting in Westminster Hall to 'treat regarding the consecration of the new prince and the confirmation and firm enactment of the laws and customs of the realm', and from 1377 this was expanded to 'consecration *and election*'. The king sat on the marble bench in the Hall where the Chief Justice of the King's Bench normally sat in what amounted to an inauguration. The service in Westminster Abbey then followed and it began with the king standing to face the people on all four sides while they were asked for their consent to his consecration. Their reply 'Fiat, fiat et vivat rex' was an acclamation, a formality, not a genuine election, but it was a symbol of the king's bond with his people. This was made more explicit, still before the anointing and crowning, in the coronation oath. Traditionally this had been in the form of three questions and royal promises, but it was re-written with a fourth question added for Edward II's coronation in 1308 and the new form was used with only slight modifications until 1689. The questions are worth quoting in full.[14]

> Sire, will you grant and preserve, and by your oath confirm to the people of England the laws and customs granted to them by former kings of England, your predecessors, righteous and devoted to God, and especially the laws, customs and liberties granted to the clergy and the people by the glorious king Saint Edward, your predecessor?
> Sire, will you preserve for God and Holy Church, and for the clergy

---

12 *Procs. & Ords.*, v. 357.
13 P.E. Schramm, *A History of the English Coronation* (Oxford, 1937, trans. L.G. Wickham Legg) is a good, brief guide. L.G. Wickham Legg, *English Coronation Records* (Westminster, 1901) prints and translates some of the sources.
14 *Select Documents*, pp. 4–5; *EHD*, iii. 525. The oath of 1308 has been the subject of much comment, see H.G. Richardson, 'The English Coronation Oath', *Speculum* 25 (1949), 44–76.

and people, entire peace and accord in God, according to your power?

Sire, will you act in all your judgements with equal and right justice and discretion, in mercy and truth, according to your power?

Sire, will you grant to hold and preserve the laws and righteous customs which the community of your realm shall have chosen (*aura esleu*), and defend and strengthen them to the honour of God, according to your power?

The first three promises were the ancient obligations of a king; the fourth was new and seems to go much further. It has been much debated and certainly given too much 'constitutional' significance. It was not a promise to accept legislation made by subjects; that would have been at odds with contemporary ideas about legislation (p. 218); it seems rather a response to Edward I's failure to observe the promises *he* had made to his subjects rather than an anticipation of the troubles of Edward II. It was important because it made clear that kings were bound by promises made to their subjects. Edward II respected it and even when victorious over his enemies he did not repudiate the Ordinances forced on him in 1311 but had them revoked in parliament, by a statute, the Statute of York of 1322, which also laid down how such provisions should be made in future (p. 16).

The promises to the 'people' in the coronation oath were expressed in general terms, but this had the advantage that they could be and often were cited when misgovernment was alleged. There were also several principles, already ancient in 1300, which restricted the king's freedom in particular areas. Magna Carta had enshrined the principle that the king must observe the law and it had became a symbol of this which all kings confirmed. Clause 39 of 1215 had stated that the king must use lawful means not force against his subjects and in the fourteenth century this was redefined to mean that he must proceed against them only by 'due process' of law, by presentment or indictment. True, this was evaded and legal proceedings could be manipulated but there was a strong belief in law reinforced by a procedure that was increasingly formal and by lawyers who were increasingly professional, legally trained men. There were also ancient principles that the king should not change the law nor impose taxes without counsel and consent and in this period these became defined as the consent of lords and Commons in parliament and by recognized procedures. Fortescue expressed this clearly.[15]

Nor can the king there, by himself or by his ministers, impose tallages, subsidies, or any other burdens whatever on his subjects, nor change their laws, nor make new ones, without the concession or assent of his whole realm expressed in his parliament.

15 Fortescue, *De Laudibus*, p. 87.

These were the classic principles which protected the subject for centuries, expressed in legal terms by lawyers. In Fortescue's terms England was a *dominium regale et politicum*, a dominion regal and political, where the king could be likened to God but ruled for the benefit of many and was bound by these principles. The language used became more populist. In the thirteenth century it was feudal; 'earls and barons', and in practice a small number of them, gave consent and could act for the community of the realm. In the fourteenth century the Commons, normally in parliament, came to represent the community. Fortescue wrote of the 'whole kingdom' in the king's parliament. All men were held to be represented there, and though in practice parliament represented directly only some thousands of the 'better' people, in principle the recognition was of considerable significance. It was only in the mid seventeenth century that the rights of the people were expressed in political terms and only in 1832 that the county franchise of 1430 was enlarged and even then not in terms of the representation of the people. The late-medieval mould of thinking about government was not outdated for centuries.

In practice kings in England were subject to much greater restraint than this because they were free to govern (subject to the principles just outlined) only as long as they did not antagonize their greater subjects. The extreme examples of what could happen if they did so were the depositions of Edward II in 1327 and of Richard II in 1399. Both kings were considered threats by many of their subjects and members of the royal family led risings to depose them. The proceedings were revolutionary and backed by force but consciences were calmed by a cloak of legality. In January 1327 a parliament summoned in Edward II's name met at Westminster while he remained a prisoner at Kenilworth.[16] In this assembly, for some historians have doubted if in the circumstances it could be a parliament, Edward's insufficiency and breaches of his coronation oath were rehearsed and it was agreed that he should be removed and his eldest son succeed. The Londoners played a vocal part and the archbishop of Canterbury preached on the dangerous text 'Vox populi, vox Dei'. Edward meanwhile was persuaded by threats to renounce the throne and a commission, perhaps consisting of two each of bishops, abbots, earls, barons, justices and barons of the Cinque Ports, four London citizens and four knights, was sent to him. The social balance is significant. A procurator on behalf of all renounced the homage and allegiance of all in the

16 The truth about the events of the deposition are obscured in contemporary sources; even the numbers on the commission are uncertain but deposition 'by the clergy and the people' was certainly the aim. See Wilkinson, 'The deposition of Richard II', M.V. Clarke, *Medieval Representation and Consent* (London, 1936) and Natalie Fryde, *The Tyranny and Fall of Edward II, 1321–1326* (Cambridge, 1979).

kingdom and the steward of the Household broke his wand of office as he did when a king died. This was probably on 20 January, the day Edward's reign was held to end. The proceedings were reported to 'parliament' on 24 January, Edward III's peace was proclaimed and his reign was held to begin on the 25th. In 1399 Richard II was a prisoner in the Tower and a parliament was summoned in his name for 30 September. On the 29th however he was persuaded to renounce the throne and all allegiance sworn to him, and to state this before a group including two each of bishops, earls, barons, abbots, justices, doctors of law, knights and notaries empowered by what must have been a meeting of his enemies, and his reign was held to end. On the 30th this was reported to a gathering of the estates of the realm, most of them no doubt the members assembled for parliament; they accepted it but went on to agree a series of charges against Richard; a bishop, an abbot, an earl, a baron, two knights and a justice, through the mouth of the bishop facing the empty throne then solemnly deposed Richard. Henry of Lancaster then claimed the throne and became king on that day; and on 1 October the same group visited Richard to make a formal renunciation of homage and allegiance. A deal of thought went into these proceedings to ensure that contemporary beliefs were respected, though awkward theocratic and legal issues were avoided. Both kings renounced the throne – under threat; their failings were declared for all to see and homage and allegiance were renounced by delegations representing all the grades and estates of the realm so that all bonds with the king were broken. Monarchy meant mutual obligations. The inner story was of course less neat; force ruled and for example Richard II certainly did not surrender with a smile on his face as the official record states; there were doubters and opponents but there was remarkably little fuss or apparent damage to monarchy.

Most kings, even the successful kings, found their freedom of action at times restrained in less dramatic ways. Edward I had to concede a confirmation of Magna Carta and the Charter of the Forest with additional clauses in 1297; Edward II had to concede authority in 1310 to a group to make ordinances about his Household and the realm; Edward III had to agree to four limiting statutes in 1341; Richard II had to accept a reform commission in 1386 and was apparently deposed for a few days in 1387; and there were many other occasions when royal ministers were attacked, commissions of enquiry and reforming councils introduced and lesser limitations on the king's freedom of action introduced. It was common to disguise the issue by blaming the failings on the king's ministers or by declaring his free assent, as when Edward II empowered the Ordainers 'of his free will', but the truth was that while the king was expected to rule, if he did not rule well he was likely to be faced with outspoken criticism and if necessary with enforced changes. Force was not uncommonly used but it became common in this period for political issues to be aired in parliament – with the Commons playing an active role if the issues were common grievances, and not merely magnate politics – and for 'paper' solutions to be provided in the form of commissions, councils and administrative arrangements. The contrast with earlier periods is striking. In feudal law it had been legitimate to use force against a lord or a king who had failed in his duty as long as he had first been formally 'defied' but this was now archaic and the provision in the Statute of Treasons of 1352 that it was treason to wage war against the king was not an innovation.[17] Kings resented 'paper' restraints imposed on them but in general they wisely reacted with caution. After Edward II's recovery of authority in 1322 the Statute of York revoked the Ordinances of 1311 because they restrained royal power against right and damaged royal lordship, adding that such restraints in the past had led to trouble and violence; it then declared such restraints by subjects in future to be null but that matters concerning the king and the kingdom should be determined by the king and the others in parliament.[18] Edward III simply revoked the statutes of 1341 later that same year, saying that he had 'dissembled' when he agreed to them and that they were 'contrary to the laws and usages of the realm and to his rights and prerogatives'. Several times kings agreed to restraints saving their prerogative. Only Richard II took a stand on it. In 1387 he asked the judges a series of questions about the restraints imposed on him in 1386 and they agreed or were forced to agree that they were derogatory to his 'regality and prerogative' and the perpetrators worthy of death, and in 1397 he had a clerk, Thomas Haxey, condemned to death (but not executed) for presenting a 'bill' to the Commons in parliament concerning his Household, an act which Richard considered derogatory to his regality, royal majesty and liberty. Richard had a case because a king had a right to rule, but in terms of practical politics his actions were foolish and his reign ended with deposition and accusations of absolutist ideas.[19]

Kings were certainly often restrained but the justification for restraint was not much pursued. Bracton in the mid thirteenth centrury had written that 'the king ought not to be under any man but

---

17 J.G. Bellamy, *The Law of Treason in England in the Later Middle Ages* (Cambridge, 1970) is now the standard work on treason.

18 *Select Documents*, pp. 31–2; *EHD*, iii. 543–4. The precise meaning of parts of this document have been the subject of much erudition, but is still unresolved. See G.T. Lapsley. 'The interpretation of the statute of York' in *Crown, Community and Parliament*, pp. 153–230 (from EHR, 1941).

19 S.B. Chrimes, 'Richard II's Questions to the Judges, 1387', *Law Quarterly Review* 72 (1956), 365–90. R.H. Jones, *The Royal Policy of Richard II* (Oxford, 1968) argues that Richard had a policy of absolutist monarchy.

under God and the law, because law makes the king' but either Bracton or another added that his court, namely his earls and barons, had a right to bridle a lawless king.[20] This idea was repeated by several writers at the turn of the century but the context was always the law. A king was bound to observe the law; a lawless king was not a true king; he could not make law of his own will; if he broke the law an appeal to him, but not of course litigation against him, in his court, in parliament his highest court, ought to be maintained by the earls. A right to correct a foolish as distinct from a tyrannical king was never formulated but repeated criticism in parliament in practice imposed a degree of restraint on kings and with the theory that parliament represented *all* the people, was of revolutionary potential.

One avenue of justification, the distinction between the king and the crown, was briefly opened in the reign of Edward II. A declaration by magnates begins[21]

> Homage and the oath of allegiance are more by reason of the crown than by reason of the king's person; and this is evident because, before the estate of the crown has descended, no allegiance is due to the person . . . (If the king is not guided by reason) . . . the lieges are bound by oath made to the crown to lead the king and the estate of the crown back again by reason . . . (Should this be by law or force? The judges are the kings) . . . So when the king will not right a wrong and remove that which is evil and hurtful to the people at large (*le commun poeple*) and to the crown, it is adjudged that the evil must be removed by force.

This line of thought was not however pursued at the time and did not reappear during this period. The word 'crown' was often used but it was only in the early modern period that the legal and political implications of the distinction were explored.

The King in Government

The rôle of the king in day-to-day government was equally undefined by contemporaries. Treatises on kingship were written but they were concerned primarily with the qualities expected of a king; they exhorted him to be humble, merciful, charitable, to seek advice, beware of flattery, protect poor men – with an array of biblical and other exemplars.[22] A king had the governance (*gubernaculum*) of his realm. He had prerogative, a term much used to mean the power inherent in a king to govern, but only his prerogatives were listed and these were merely his rights as supreme feudal lord, rights such as the

20 Bracton, i. 33 and 110.
21 *Stat. R.*, i. 182 – *Select Documents*, p. 5.
22 *Four English Political Tracts of the Later Middle Ages*, ed. J-P. Genet (Camden Fourth Series, 18, 1979) and other treatises cited there.

forfeit of felons' goods and over royal fish. The king's duty was often said to be to defend the realm, maintain the law and do justice. Fortescue summed this up in the sentence 'Lo! to fight and to judge are the office of a king.'[23] The king was certainly expected to fight. Like any nobleman or gentleman he was trained to do so. The most admired kings were successful warriors, Edward I, Edward III and Henry V, and kings still fought in the midst of battles, they were not commanders in the rear. Every king in this period fought in battle or campaign save the incapable Henry VI and ironically he was wounded at the civil-war battle of St Albans in 1455 while standing by his banner. A change was taking place however; the ideal of the warrior king was maintained but the long campaigns of the Hundred Years War made it impossible for him always to be present and civil government was taking up more of his time. Campaigns were therefore often led by noblemen. Fortescue's remark on civil government is archaic and narrowly legal. Judgements were for the courts and judges were supposed to ignore royal interference with legal process though in practice justice was riddled with favour. What a king had to do was to maintain the law and justice. He had for example to send commissions into the counties to enquire into disorder and if necessary go himself to ensure that the law was enforced. Even Henry VI, who conspicuously failed to keep order, undertook extended visitations with magnates and justices in 1452 and 1453 (p. 152). A king and increasingly his Council had to hear and remedy complaints of injustice to individuals where force denied them a fair hearing in the courts or where no remedy was available and the king himself received a continuous stream of requests for pardons.

A greater burden on a king was the day-by-day drudgery of government. This is apparent in broad terms in the importance of the character and personality of individual kings. The wars of Edward I and Henry V for example were very much their own personal choice and the personal failings of Edward II and Richard II had disastrous consequences. A king gave his own character to a reign, chose his own ministers and advisers and to a large extent made his own policies. Unfortunately discussions in the king's presence and the moment of major decisions are rarely recorded but from Edward I's reign onwards there are letters between the king and the Council which tell of business before the king, lists of items and draft documents for him to consider and decide and the occasional narrative account though nothing equivalent to the series of Tudor State Papers to record business being done. Sometimes the king sat on a throne under a cloth of estate surrounded by his ministers and councillors and took

23 Chrimes, *Constitutional Ideas*, p. 14.

decisions – as he is depicted in miniature paintings. Most decisions were taken in less formal circumstances. On 13 October 1398 for example, Richard II conceded a petition 'in a little chamber beside the major chamber in the Bishop of London's house in the presence of the duke of Aumale' and gave it to his chancellor to execute.[24] This is known because it was endorsed on the petition and many thousands of endorsed petitions survive recording royal decisions. Few give personal detail like this but they do record the king handing documents to the chancellor, the keeper of the privy seal, the Household chamberlain and occasionally to other officials with instructions to carry out his decision. Sometimes the queen or some other person is said to have furthered the petition. More abundant but impersonal evidence is provided by the practice begun in chancery, the king's main writing-office, in the 1290s of noting on the thousands of letters it issued each year and on its enrolled copies, the authority on which it acted.[25] These 'notes of warranty' are in the form of phrases such as 'Per ipsum regem' (By the king himself) or 'Per Consilium' (By the Council) (p. 47). They were recorded with a high degree of accuracy and they can be used to show who ordered letters year by year. It is also possible to deduce from well documented examples where other decisions, for example decisions to pay money, were taken. A clear picture can be built up of the king's work – and of the work of the Council and officials.

The best recorded and to modern eyes the most curious part of the king's work are the grants of grace. Thousands of written petitions were addressed to the king each year by people seeking pardons of particular crimes, for example of a killing, specifying the circumstances, the weapon and its value, or for grants – of advancement in the church, to a parish living, a prebend or a canonry, of minor offices, annuities, money, land, goods, timber, venison and many other things. Only the king himself could grant these things and it was the duty of a king to listen benevolently to them. John Stow praised Henry V because, like his father, he made a practice every day when no state was kept of spending an hour or more after dinner receiving petitions and hearing the complaints of any who came. At other times his Household officials took in petitions and those with access to the king clearly brought in and furthered others. Many petitions were of small moment but important people, even the queen and the royal children, petitioned or asked for grants, often of greater things, deaneries, extensive lands, custodies of heirs and heiresses and offices.

24 H.C. Maxwell-Lyte, *Historical Notes on the Use of the Great Seal of England*, (London, 1926), p. 148.
25 A.L. Brown, 'The authorization of letters under the great seal', *BIHR* 37 (1964), pp. 125–56 is the basis of this paragraph and the next.

A king had to be politic in dealing with these requests; he was expected to be generous but also not to waste his resources; he had to reward service and maintain good will without causing offence; he had to beware of favourites. He had to be hard-working, strong-minded, informed and sensitive to personalities and politics to be successful in a society where ambition and acquisitiveness, influence, favour, gossip and intrigue were rife. Each king had his own method of leading but a king who could not win respect and show himself capable and reasonably even-handed would find himself in trouble.

The other side of the king's work, the matters not of grace but of government, is less well documented because the issues often came before him verbally and not in writing, though the outcome of his decisions are generally to be found in the records. For example the decision to summon a parliament at a given place and time is recorded in the writs of summons and the roll of the parliament; the sending of an embassy in the commissions to the envoys, in their instructions, credences and other documents – if they survive – and in their advances of money and final accounts; and simpler matters such as the arrest or release of prisoners are recorded in the letters containing the orders. These matters and many others such as the appointment of officials, the garrisoning and provisioning of castles, the affairs of towns, dealings with noblemen, the investigation and suppression of disorder, down to many administrative orders to pay sums due, to order accounts or allow items in accounts, involved consideration by the king or the king and the Council or the Council alone, in practice probably often on the advice of an official. The work of the Council and of the great offices will be discussed in the following two chapters, and it is clear that government involved a close partnership of councillors, officials and the king. In normal circumstances however the king was undoubtedly the master. Notes of warranty show that important decisions and even many lesser ones came from the king; the Council made recommendations to him 'sil plest au roi'; and though there was clearly plain speaking between ministers and councillors and the king, the language of deference they used reflected his true status. The king himself did govern. This is best documented in the untypical period between 1437 and 1446 when two clerks, Henry Benet and Adam Moleyns, wrote informal notes of business done by the Council, the king and the Council and the king alone.[26] It is untypical because the king, Henry VI, relied much more than other kings on his advisers and the distinction between the work of the king and Council was blurred. But the notes show that even Henry VI was intimately involved in business and a normal king must have been much more burdened and decisive.

26 Printed in *Procs. & Ords.*, v and vi.

There was no typical royal year. Edward I was a very mobile king often on campaign, Edward III and Henry V were abroad for months and even years at a stretch, but in general kings of the fourteenth and fifteenth centuries were less peripatetic than their predecessors. Government was more extensive and bureaucratic and more centred at Westminster than in the past; kings expected a higher standard of living and they spent more time at their houses in and around London. They lived occasionally at the Tower, quite often at Westminster Palace, but much more at one or other of their houses within riding distance of what can now be called the 'capital', at Windsor Castle or the manor in its park, at Berkhamstead, Langley, Sheen, Eltham and a few others.[27] Each king had his favourite places. Edward III and Richard II particularly favoured Sheen; Richard II even had a wooden retreat built there but he destroyed the manor after Queen Anne died there in 1394; and Henry V rebuilt the house on a larger scale. 'House' is the correct word because the great age of castle-building ended with Edward I; royal castles on the Marches were maintained and in the late fourteenth century the defences of the south-east were improved and the new castle of Queenborough on the Isle of Sheppey was built; but many other castles were allowed to decay and so too were many royal manor-houses outside the London area. Kings preferred to remain in the south-east apart from hunting-trips to places such as Clarendon and Woodstock or pilgrimages to shrines such as Walsingham and Canterbury. When a king travelled far in the kingdom there was likely to be an immediate political or personal reason for doing so. When he did so he remained in control of government. If he was in England or Wales or Scotland he would take some of his seals and officers with him and a decision had to be made on the balance of advantage on each occasion. On several occasions during the Scottish campaigns of Edward I and Edward III government offices were transferred to York for years at a time. If he was in Ireland or France a member of the royal family was commissioned as keeper (*custos*) of the kingdom or king's lieutenant and empowered to carry on government with a Council. The keeper's authority was, however, severely limited and important decisions were reserved for the king who had always part of his administration with him. For example while Henry V was in France from 1417 until 1421 he had with him his signet, a second great seal and a second privy seal with clerks to write for them, and he retained a close, detailed control of affairs.

It was more difficult when the king was a child or incapable. Three kings succeeded as children but there were no regencies; nominally the

---

27 H.M. Colvin, *The History of the King's Works* (London, 1963), vols. i and ii are a fund of information about particular royal houses and castles and about royal life and tastes.

child-king ruled but a special Council governed. Edward III succeeded in 1327 at the age of 14 and was crowned; a group of bishops, earls and barons was appointed in parliament to assist him but in practice his mother and Roger Mortimer governed until Edward overthrew them in 1330 and began to rule himself. Richard II succeeded in 1377 at the age of 10 and was crowned; a Council of bishops, earls and barons was appointed annually in parliament until 1380 when the scheme was abandoned at the request of the Commons and Richard gradually assumed authority over the following years.[28] His authority was restricted by magnates in 1386 and 1388 and Richard declared himself of age (at 22) in 1389 and resumed government – but these were matters of politics not the minority. Henry VI succeeded in 1422 not quite ten months old but nominally he ruled. Great state events took place in his presence; in 1423 he was carried into parliament where the Commons' Speaker addressed him at length! Government was again conciliar but because his younger uncle, Humphrey, duke of Gloucester, claimed (with much justice) that Henry V had intended him to have a special authority in England while his elder brother, John, duke of Bedford, had authority in France, on this occasion arrangements were much more specific. Gloucester's claim was denied by the lords and a distinguished group of councillors was appointed by the king with the assent of the lords in parliament. A new title, 'protector, defender and chief councillor', was devised for Bedford, and in his absence for Gloucester, but a title which carried only slight personal powers though it did give pre-eminence at the Council. Gloucester continued to protest and in 1427 and 1428 a theory of minorities was propounded to answer him. In 1427 the Council declared that as the king could not govern personally, the execution of the king's authority for the rule and governance of the land 'belongeth unto the lordes spirituel and temporel of his land at suche tyme as thei be assembled in parlement or in greet counsail, and ellus hem nought beyng so assembled, unto the lordes chosen and named to be of his continuel Counsail . . .' and in 1428 the lords issued a further declaration that a king might not by will or otherwise provide for government after his death, that Gloucester had no right by birth to governance and that his title of protector did not confer this.[29] The protectorate ended when the king was crowned in 1429 but government by Council continued until 1437 when the king, barely 16 assumed royal authority.

28 The appointments were made in name by the king, first at a meeting after the coronation in July and then in the October parliament in 1377. *Select Documents*, pp. 113–16; *EHD*, iv. 122–3 and 448–9. See N.B. Lewis, 'The Continual Council', *EHR* 41 (1926), 246–51.
29 *Procs. & Ords.*, iii. 231–42 and *Rot. Parl.*, iv. 326–7; *Select Documents, 258–62; EHD*, iv. 463–5. See J.S. Roskell, 'The office and dignity of Protector of England', *EHR* 68 (1953), 193–233 and Patrick Strong and Felicity Strong, 'The last will and codicils of Henry V', *EHR* 96 (1981), 79–102.

The protectorate of 1422 was the model for minority protectorates in 1483 and 1547, for Richard, duke of York's protectorates of 1453 and 1455 when Henry VI had breakdowns and ultimately it supplied the name for Oliver Cromwell's protectorate. The problem of royal incapacity, for example senility in the case of Edward III in his last years, or 'simplicity' and depression in the case of Henry VI, was impossible to solve save in an *ad hoc* manner and inevitably it led to cliques and disaster. What is striking is how pragmatic the English could be. They had no custom about when a king came of age. The solution for most problems of government and royal incapacity in any form was a specially strengthened Council; later-medieval government was both thoroughly royal and thoroughly conciliar.

The Household*

Because the king himself directed government, the place where he lived, his Household, its offices and its members had a place in government. There was nothing necessarily sinister about this though the Household was often accused of extravagance and corruption – at times with justice. Every king had his circle of friends and an inadequate king, Edward III in his dotage for example or Henry VI, confided over much in men (and women) close to him and rewarded them too generously. Every king used his Household in administration – because it was at hand. All the Westminster offices and courts had developed within the Household and over time had grown out of it. For example, kings required letters to be written. In the late Anglo-Saxon period priests of the royal chapel in the Household wrote them and from this a writing office later called chancery developed, its letters authenticated by the king's (great) seal (p. 45). Chancery was still part of the Household in the twelfth century but by 1200 it was issuing so many letters, many of them on its own authority, and had become so bureaucratic and archive conscious, that it began to spend more time at Westminster and less with the king. By 1300 it had finally gone 'out of court'; it had ceased to be part of the Household. From John's reign at the latest a second seal, the private or privy seal, was in use to authenticate royal letters written by clerks of the

---

* There is an extensive literature about the Household. T.F. Tout printed a number of Household ordinances and documents in his *The Place of Edward II in English History* (Manchester, 1914 and 2nd ed., 1936) and in his monumental *Chapters in the Administrative History of Mediaeval England* 6 vols. (Manchester, 1920–33) which in practice is primarily about the Household departments. *The Household of Edward IV*, ed. A.R. Myers (Manchester, 1959) contains several 15th century ordinances and gives the best overall impression of the Household establishment. C. Given-Wilson, *The Royal Household and the King's Affinity* (London, 1986) considers the Household in terms of royal courtiers and retainers, a different and valuable approach.

Household; a century later a privy-seal office had developed; and in the fourteenth century it too went 'out of court'. A third royal seal, the secret or signet seal, then came into use in the Household and soon another writing office had formed. It remained within the Household, immediately available to the king throughout this period. The three writing offices had their 'demarcation' disputes and there often were justified allegations that the privy seal and signet were used for illicit purposes such as bringing pressure on judges to give favourable decisions, but all three were the king's offices, their staff served at his pleasure, they fulfilled different functions and in normal circumstances there was little conflict between them. The Household had its necessary place in writing letters, handling money and in other services as long as kings and queens had a personal rôle in government. This place was however rapidly diminishing because of the growing professionalism throughout government and partly also because kings became more sensitive to criticism of the Household, particularly in parliament.

The size of the late-medieval Household varied considerably, from perhaps 400 to 700 men and a few women at any one time, servants, clerks and officials, with considerable additional numbers of their servants and hangers-on. The majority worked 'below stairs' in a network of departments which provided everyday services such as food, drink, laundry and a stable on the grand scale that was customary in royal and noble houses until this present century. Corn for example was 'bought' by Household purveyors armed with royal commissions and baked into loaves of standard weights by serjeant and yeomen bakers and labourers in the bakery. The loaves were then purveyed to the pantry from which other serjeants and yeomen distributed them to the great Hall where most members of the Household ate according to fixed daily entitlements, or to the small hall and chambers in the king's own quarters where he, the most important members of his Household and his guests normally ate. There were similar organizations for the cellar, the buttery of ale, the pitcher-house, the chandlery, the wafery and other services. Each department had its establishment laid down in Household Ordinances and was required to keep written accounts and have them audited daily. Services had to be provided wherever the king was, and he moved a good deal, sometimes with a small entourage or part only of the Household but often with all or most of its members, their equipment and supplies in a procession of carts and pack-horses to re-establish the king's quarters in a castle, manor, religious house or even in the royal tents provided by the king's serjeants of pavillions and tents. Most of these 'domestic' servants, serjeants, yeomen, grooms, valets, pages, stablemen, the musicians, the physicians and surgeons, the priests of the royal chapel and others played little or no part in government. Some were on occasion called on to perform duties outside the Household, some were promoted to higher posts, all had a claim on the king's benevolence, but it was those who served 'above stairs' as clerks and officials of the king's Chamber and Wardrobe or who came into the royal presence who had the major part to play in the government of the kingdom and even in its politics.

The great officers of the Household were the Steward and the Chamberlain of the Household, deputies for the hereditary magnate Steward and Chamberlain of England. The Steward of the Household had over-all responsibility for its conduct and discipline and presided over its court, the court of the verge, whose authority extended beyond domestic matters. The Chamberlain of the Household's responsibility was the Chamber, the king's own apartments and officials. Both offices were held by notable knights and, increasingly, by lords and earls – an example of a general change in attitudes by which active office-holding became acceptable for laymen of high status. Both officers were often in the king's presence and clearly privy to most business. They were a prime channel in bringing matters to his attention and conveying his decisions. From the later fourteenth century they were reckoned with the chancellor, treasurer and keeper of the privy seal to be his five principal officers and ex-officio councillors but their importance was essentially in the inner circle at Court; they were not frequent attenders at the Council. The keeper, controller and cofferer of the Wardrobe were the senior Household administrators and in the early part of this period important men in everyday government. Names such as Wardrobe and Chamber ring oddly today, though they are no more odd than another domestic term, Cabinet, which we still use. The king's private part of the Household was the Chamber, the apartments, separate from the great Hall where most of the Household ate – they generally slept wherever there was space. Over centuries the Chamber had been growing more and more spacious and magnificent in both royal and baronial houses. In origin the Wardrobe was the chests or the space in the Chamber where the king's clothes and personal possessions were stored. By the thirteenth century Chamber and Wardrobe were also offices with clerks and servants who could and did turn their hands to a wide range of business. The Wardrobe was particularly experienced because its head, the keeper of the Wardrobe, was also the treasurer of the Household, responsible for receiving money for its expenses, for checking the accounts of its departments and for rendering its accounts in the exchequer. The controller kept a second set of accounts (the counter roll which gave him his title) as a check on the keeper and the officers of the Household, and it was he who had custody of the privy seal before it acquired its own keeper. The cofferer was responsible for holding coin and for the mechanics of its accounting. The Wardrobe also had clerks and workmen who manufactured and maintained its stores and two specialized sections came to have their own workshops and warehouses, the Privy Wardrobe in the Tower of London for military supplies and the Great Wardrobe from 1361 settled in premises in London near Baynard's Castle which handled civil supplies such as cloth, furs and spices (pp. 57–8). Edward I used the Wardrobe extensively to handle the finances of his military campaigns, because of course it was with him on campaign. The normal domestic expenses of his Household were then about £10,000 a year but in the 25 years of his reign for which accounts survive over £1.3 million passed through the Wardrobe.[30] Money came to it from the exchequer, and directly from collectors of taxes, from loans and from other sources. There was always a temptation to bypass the exchequer when money was short or slow to come forward and needs were pressing. Wardrobe staff were also active in the administration of campaigns, for example raising supplies and contracting troops, and the volume of letters under the privy seal in the custody of first the keeper and then the controller of the Wardrobe vastly increased. The Wardrobe was also active in diplomatic relations, writing letters, paying envoys and storing documents. After Edward I's death there was a reaction against his military and financial high-handedness and against the Wardrobe. There were demands that all royal funds should go to the exchequer in order to control expenditure and ensure that Wardrobe debts were paid in cash and not in parchment bills and tallies and that an independent clerk keep the privy seal. Restraint on the Household became a common demand of critics but it was supposed abuses that were the issue, not the Household itself, and it continued to be used for handling money, writing letters and administration – particularly during campaigns. Edward II used the Wardrobe in these ways and so did Edward III on a large scale during his campaigns. Both also used the Chamber to handle money and the third royal seal, the secret or signet seal, was at first held there. The Chamber always administered the 'privy purse' for personal royal expenses such as buying jewels and giving personal gifts and it could be given much more to do. Edward II and Edward III transferred the administration of some estates to it to help provide ready cash but enough land could not be provided and the scheme was abandoned in 1356. Edward III in the 1360s and 1370s and Richard II in the 1390s used it to hold the great windfalls of ransom, treaty and marriage money which they regarded as their own.

30 These figures come from Tout's table of Wardrobe receipts (*Chapters*, vi. 76–82). M. Prestwich, *War Politics and Finance under Edward I* (London, 1972) and *Edward I* (London, 1988) give a broader account of Edward's Household.

Henry V used the Wardrobe as a finance office on campaign and the York kings and Henry VII revived the use of the Chamber as a finance office. In these cases kings were using Wardrobe and Chamber staff to deal with matters of more than Household concern for practical reasons and rarely with any sinister intent. Too much has been made of this in the past. Late medieval government was not 'Household government' save in the sense that the king who directed government lived in his Household and its share in government diminished greatly from the early fourteenth century. As the succeeding chapters will show, government became increasingly Westminster dominated and professional.

There was however another aspect of the Household, one which was more important but is less documented and has been less studied, its military, social and political rôle. Armies were raised by contract and levy, but if the king was present their nucleus was his own men (p. 92). He had no standing army and there was no formal Household corps until Henry VII's Yeomen of the Guard, but there were always armed men in the Household and there were his own retainers. There were the serjeants-at-arms, up to 30 at a time, some of them on duty in the Household to maintain order and guard the king, but often on missions outside the Household, for example requisitioning ships, holding enquiries, obtaining loans and even delivering letters.[31] There were archers, often between 20 and 40 of them, acting as guards. Richard II recruited several hundred Cheshire archers serving on a rota basis but this was exceptional. All the lay servants and officials of the Household were expected to bear arms and fight when necessary, and on campaign they brought out others to serve with them. More important, the lords, knights, esquires and latterly the gentlemen of the Household provided a nucleus of men-at-arms, the cavalrymen and troop commanders who could be relied upon to bring out contingents of their own men. A major change took place in this group about the 1360s. The first three Edwards regularly retained with fees and robes about 50 and sometimes more than 100 bannerets and knights 'of the Household' as well as sizable numbers of esquires. Their duties were essentially military – as heavy cavalry, the élite of royal armies – not as residents in the Household. At Falkirk in 1298, for example, with their own contingents they formed one of the four battalions of the English army. This 'military Household' continued to be maintained and paid until about 1360. The immediate reason for its demise was no doubt the decline of royal campaigning in the decades following the Peace of Bretigny, but the Household was changing and armies were

---

31 See Given-Wilson, *Royal Household*. Mary C. Hill, *The King's Messengers 1199–1377* (London, 1961) discusses how royal and office letters were delivered.

now raised by different means. Both Richard II and Henry IV retained several hundred 'King's' (not 'Household') knights and esquires with fees, primarily to give support in the counties (p. 151). A number of them served on campaign and the Household always provided a contingent. On Henry IV's campaign in Scotland in 1400 for example the keeper and controller of the Wardrobe mustered 244 men-at-arms, the backbone of whom must have been Household men, and the retainers turned out in force.[32] In the Household itself from the mid fourteenth century there was a new group designated knights and esquires 'of the Chamber' with fees and robes – at first only a small number but rising to about a dozen by 1400. They provided the honourable service proper for a king. By the mid fifteenth century they were designated knights and esquires of the body and gentlemen of the Chamber and their number had risen. They had the king's confidence and considerable influence on affairs: they might be councillors or serve on missions in England and abroad; and they would fight for the king if the need arose.

The Household – the Court would now be a better term for it – was inevitably the political and social centre of the kingdom. The king took decisions there with the advice (and pressures) of his courtiers, his officials, his friends and the great men of the kingdom who seem to have come to Court a good deal. There is not a great deal of information about life there though there are many references to it and it was often the subject of gossip.[33] Kings were expected to show their authority by their magnificence – but without extravagance – and certainly the Court became more formal and more grand. There were more rooms and greater comfort; etiquette became stronger and books were written about it; clothes became more stylish and more regulated and people were more conscious of their status; though my impression is that the late-medieval Court was distinctly less formal than that of the sixteenth century. The greater nobility, the dukes and earls and the new marquisses and viscounts, seem to have come there with increasing frequency. Some lords and bishops did so too though many were stay-at-homes. From the fourteenth century, parliaments, Great Councils and Councils brought the great out more frequently and there were Court festivities at Christmas and the New Year, at

---

32 A.L. Brown, 'The English Campaign in Scotland, 1400' in *British Government and Administration. Studies presented to S.B. Chrimes*, ed. H. Hearder and H.R. Loyn (Cardiff, 1974), p. 47.

33 This is a subject yet to be properly studied. There are many references to purchases and some to visitors at Court in Household accounts; there are some lists of those present on particular occasions, for example when the retiring chancellor handed over the great seal and it was given out to his successor; the witness lists to royal charters gives a useful guide to the most important magnates who were about the Court; and there are many incidental references to particular Court occasions.

Easter and after 1348 there was often a Garter feast at Windsor on St George's day. There might be a campaign, a tournament or a hunting trip. These were occasions for the king to build personal relationships with the great landowners on whose good-will he had to rely so much. Every king had his own particular friends among the nobility, unwise kings such as Richard II created antagonism by favouring and being too generous to an over-exclusive group. Day by day the king relied a great deal on his officials, on the Steward and even more on the Chamberlain of the Household. The senior clerks in the Household were close to the king at the beginning of this period but over the fourteenth century they became officials rather than confidants and the knights, esquires and gentlemen of the Household became more influential. The great officers, the chancellor, treasurer and later the keeper of the privy seal divided their time between their offices, the Council and the Court; increasingly it must have been difficult to decide where it was most important to be. The image of the Court given in many miniature paintings is of the king seated under his cloth of estate with lords and officials standing round. This represents his formal presence and not everyday life which is known mainly from chance reports. For example, the record of the trial of Alice Perrers, Edward III's mistress, in 1377 mentions her asking the chamberlain to present a petition to the king, the lobbying that followed, the officials and retainers present with the king, and Alice herself in the king's bedchamber sitting at the head of the bed; financial accounts show Richard II 'getting away from it all' to his rustic lodge at Sheen; and an ambassador's report shows Henry IV receiving French envoys in state and retiring to discuss his responses with councillors; and there are minutes of Henry VI taking decisions with small groups of courtiers.[34] It was at Court that most important decisions were made, lobbying done, gossip exchanged, cliques formed and friendship and ill-will generated and where much of the politics of the kingdom took place. Sadly we know much, much less about these things than about the Household's domestic expenses.

34 *Rot. Parl.*, iii. 13; Colvin, *The King's Works*, ii. 998; *Oeuvres de Froissart*, ed. Kervyn de Lettenhove (Brussels, 1867–77), xvi. 366–77; *Procs. & Ords.*, v.

2

The King's Council*

The last chapter laid stress on the great personal role of the king in government, but no king could govern alone. Contemporary opinion indeed held strongly that he ought not do so. He needed advice – and increasingly he needed others to assist him bear the growing burden of decision-taking. Advice he obtained from parliaments and Great Councils which often met several times a year, from discussions and consultations in his Household day-by-day and from his Council. Assistance came primarily from the Council. Executive government became a close working relationship between a king who ruled and an organized Council which offered advice, drafted documents and briefs and relieved him by taking many decisions on its own initiative. Moreover, when the king could not himself govern or when it was felt that he was not governing well, the almost invariable solution was to strengthen the Council and give it more authority. There are many examples of this, particularly from the later fourteenth century onwards.

The early history of the Council is poorly documented. There are many references to it in the records of other institutions and there are some conciliar memoranda and agenda but it is rare to be told when and where a meeting was held, what was decided and by whom. Better record-keeping began only in the last quarter of the fourteenth century. This in itself is a sign of the increasing executive rôle of the Council though it was probably the personal initiative of a royal clerk, Master John Prophete, who began to write for the Council about

---

* The only comprehensive study of the Council is J.F. Baldwin, *The King's Council in the Middle Ages* (Oxford, 1913), a remarkable pioneering book, now only a source book. B. Wilkinson, *Studies in the Constitutional History of the Thirteenth and Fourteenth Centuries* (Manchester, 1937) includes an interpretative essay on the Council. There are several more recent articles on the 15th century Council. A.L. Brown, 'The Commons and the Council in the reign of Henry IV', *Hist. Studies*, ii. 1–30 (from *EHR*, 1964) and 'The King's Councillors in fifteenth-century England', *TRHS* 19 (1969), 95–118. J.L. Kirby, 'Councils and councillors of Henry IV, 1399–1413', *TRHS* 14 (1964), 35–65 and R. Virgoe, 'The composition of the King's Council, 1437–1461', *BIHR* 43 (1970), 134–60.

1389, which led to the practice of decisions being recorded in endorsements on petitions and draft documents and in memoranda which give the date, the place and the attendance. Prophete became the first 'Clerk of the Council' about 1392 and the office was almost continuous thereafter. Prophete wrote up information contained in loose documents to form a continuous journal of 34 Council meetings held between January and May 1392 which gives more hard information about the Council at work than ever before.[1] His informative recording was continued by his successors but no other journal survives and probably none was written until 1421 when the 'Book of the Council' was begun, again written up selectively from the loose documents on the files. This continued until 1435 and there are valuable but less formal minutes from 1436 until 1446. The 'normal' Council record was however a loose document with an endorsement and these survive for most years after 1389, unfortunately very unevenly as the result of a fire at Whitehall in 1619.

The Council as an institution seems to have originated in the early thirteenth century. In the twelfth century government had been so personal to the king that though he took counsel in his *curia regis*, the royal court, there was no separate Council and the word was little used. References to a Council and councillors become numerous only in the reign of Henry III. During his minority, though there was a justiciar and a rector, government was conciliar, and as an adult be always had a Council. Its membership was a political issue on a number of occasions and a Council of Fifteen was part of the scheme of government forced on him in 1258. References to the Council and councillors become frequent in Edward I's reign but it was an amorphous institution markedly different from the Council of a century later. There were clearly a large number of councillors. For example, when writs of summons to parliaments were regularly enrolled after 1295 bishops, abbots, earls and barons received individual writs of summons and so too did others summoned to treat of matters 'touching you and others of our Council' (p. 184). Forty such councillors described as 'justices of both benches, justices on eyre and justices assigned, deans sworn of the Council, barons of the exchequer and other clerks of the Council' were summoned to the August 1295 parliament. Numbers varied but over 30 were summoned to many parliaments until the 1320s. This agrees broadly with the statement in a

1 The major printed collection of council documents is the unfortunately-titled *Proceedings and Ordinances of the Privy Council*, ed. N.H. Nicolas, 7 vols. (1834–7). This prints only documents in the British Library which were 'removed' from the main collection in the Public Record Office. Prophete's journal is printed in Baldwin, pp. 489–504. The records are discussed in A.L. Brown, *The Early History of the Clerkship of the Council* (Glasgow, 1969).

curious tract written about 1321, the *Modus Tenendi Parliamentum* (p. 174), that the chancellor, treasurer, the chamberlains and
barons of the exchequer, the justices, all the king's clerks and knights
and serjeants-at-law who are of the king's Council must attend on the
second day of parliament.[2] The particularly full roll of the parliament
which met on 28 February 1305 contains many references to the Council. Three weeks before it met at Westminster Edward I wrote separate
letters from Cambridgeshire to the chancellor and treasurer in
London to have it proclaimed that petitions to the king and his Council in parliament should be handed in straightaway and that they with
others of his Council in London should answer as many of them as
possible before he arrived. Three weeks after parliament began, on 21
March, a proclamation ordered the archbishops, bishops and other
prelates, earls, barons, knights of the counties, townsmen and other
commoners to return home but 'the bishops, earls and barons, justices
and others of the Council of our lord the king' were told not to leave
without special permission. On 5 April a meeting was held at the house
of the archbishop of York where the king was staying, 'a general
parliament then in being there', to discuss the authority of a papal bull
granting Coldingham Priory to Scotland. Thirty-six 'councillors' are
named as present, the treasurer and two other bishops, three earls, 24
knights including 10 of the 94 men summoned to parliament as
barons, and eight (six justices and two barons of the exchequer) of the
33 who had been summoned to parliament as councillors, three 'discreet' Household men and three other clerks, and this is certainly not a
complete tally of the councillors in 1305. Maitland, who edited the
parliament roll, considered that he had identified 70 councillors in it,
and it is reasonable to conclude that Edward I had a large number of
councillors, bishops, earls, barons, officials, knights and clerks,
thought it is uncertain if all these men were formally appointed and
sworn of the Council.[3]

Council meetings clearly varied in character. A meeting such as that
of 5 April 1305 was exceptional, possible only during a parliament or
other specially summoned assembly, and appropriate for great rather
than ordinary issues. 'Ordinary' meetings known from references in
the records of the courts or the exchequer or in royal letters were much
less distinguished. Fewer magnates were present and the councillors
most often mentioned were the chancellor, the treasurer and the justices and – less frequently – barons of the exchequer and other royal
clerks. Most references however give a few names at best and often

2 N. Pronay and J. Taylor, *Parliamentary Texts of the Later Middle Ages* (Oxford, 1980),
  p. 70.
3 *Memoranda de Parliamento, 1305*, ed. F.W. Maitland (Rolls Series, 1893), pp. xxxvi–xlvii
  and cvi–cviii.

add 'and others of the Council'. Groups are recorded sitting with the justices in the courts of King's Bench and Commons Pleas and in the exchequer and these bodies referred difficult or important matters to the Council or to the king and the Council. At this period there was evidently a considerable community of interest and service among all the offices and courts, and the councillors were men of superior wisdom and experience in close touch with the king who were called upon to assist them. Parliaments, particularly until the 1290s, were primarily regular, reinforced sessions of the Council to deal with administrative and judicial business and the petitions which were presented in large quantities during parliaments were often addressed to the king *and the Council* (pp. 216–17). There are surprisingly few references to the Council ordering money to be paid or deciding matters concerning war or diplomacy or investigating cases of disorder, the sort of items which appear so often in the Council records of 1400. Few letters under the great seal are said to have been ordered by the Council or with the assent of the Council and they do not often concern important matters. Some war indentures were agreed by the king and the Council; drafting advice was sometimes given about diplomatic letters; and there is a memorandum of a mission by the Keeper of the Wardrobe from the king in Scotland to the chancellor and the lieutenant of the treasurer, delivered in the presence of the justices of both benches and others of the Council, ordering them to discuss how money and supplies could be found for the war.[4] No doubt much similar Council business went unrecorded or the records have been lost, but my impression is that a great deal of what would later be conciliar business was handled in the Household where the privy seal was still based and where the more senior officials were councillors. The councillors who remained at Westminster or wherever the courts and offices were sited seem to have been employed more on resolving difficult administrative and judicial problems and they do not seem to have met regularly. Letters from the king to the chancellor and the treasurer, mainly during the Scottish campaigns and after 1300, often order councillors to be assembled, sometimes specifying those who are suitable or should be called or are near or can assist. They suggest that formal meetings of the Council were often assembled on an *ad hoc* basis. Edward I seems to have had a large group of advisors, some likely to be with the king and the Household, some at Westminster or another centre with the great offices and courts. They turned to whatever business needed to be done, offering advice, investigating issues and complaints, sitting with officials of the courts and offices when important or difficult decisions had to be

4 Baldwin, *King's Council*, pp. 466–7.

taken, meeting in small numbers as the Council or in larger Council meetings with the king on occasions such as parliament.

The scattered nature of the sources undoubtedly makes the Council of Edward I seem more inchoate than it was, and the same is true of Edward II's Council for which there is more but equally diverse evidence. What is certain is that they contrast sharply with the more organized Council of the late fourteenth century when there were fewer but more distinguished councillors, when the Council met almost daily at Westminster without the king during a great part of each year and played a major rôle in executive government. When and why the change took place is still unclear. It was certainly part of a wider change in royal government as a whole rather than the result of a deliberate decision. The king's absence on campaigns and the burden war imposed must have had an influence. The great offices and courts became more and more professional and self-contained; Household officers took a lesser part in affairs outside the Household; government depended on continuous taxation and borrowing. A Council of greater status and authority was now needed to share decision-taking as well as giving advice and resolving technical problems. There are indications of the change taking place but little direct evidence. In the second decade of the century the privy seal ceased to be part of the Household and began to write letters on the instructions of the Council; most privy-seal letters were still ordered by the king but it was also the Council's secretariat and its clerks came to write and preserve the Council's records. In the 1330s the number of councillors summoned as such to parliament dropped to around ten, almost all of them justices or senior officials, and by mid-century only justices and a few other common or civil lawyers were summoned. In parliament they became lawyers on hand to give professional advice when called upon and clearly the same happened at the Council and probably about the same time. By the end of the century Council records provide hard evidence of this. Household officials and clerks (other than the Steward and Chamberlain of the Household), barons and chamberlains of the exchequer and clerks of chancery ceased to be councillors save on rare occasions. By 1350 the Council was probably much like that of 1392 with frequent meetings and a core of active councillors headed by the three great officers, chancellor, treasurer and keeper of the privy seal, a number of bishops – often bishops who had held one of the great offices, a few magnates and knights. The account survives of a knight, Sir Bartholemew Burgersh, for his wages of a pound a day on 82, 109, 249, 240 and 207 days at the Council in the years 1351 to 1355 and this suggests frequent meetings in the manner known from the end of the century.[5] In 1376 the Commons in parliament asked that

5 *Ibid.*, p. 89.

the Council be reinforced with equal numbers of bishops, earls and barons – nine in all – and regulations for the Council were announced. When Richard II succeeded as a child king in 1377 nine to twelve bishops, earls, barons, bannerets and knights were appointed annually over three years to be the Council with the chancellor, treasurer, keeper and possibly also the Steward and Chamberlain of the Household. Most councillors were paid wages, at first lump sums but from November 1378 for each day of attendance. Eight were paid, two bishops and a banneret for over 270 days attendance in a period of 14 months.[6] The parallels are all with the later not the earlier Council.

Other evidence of change is the building of a Council chamber. In the 1320s there are references to a chamber at Westminster near the exchequer where the Council meets and in the 1340s a new chamber, the Star Chamber, so called because of its gilded ceiling decorated with stars, was built there.[7] The terminology of the Council also becomes firmer about mid-century. The term 'Great Council' had long been used in an imprecise way for specially summoned assemblies akin to parliaments, but about 1350 it became a technical term for assemblies varying in size from 30 or 40 to several hundred men summoned by writs under the privy seal (pp. 174–5). On most occasions they were reinforced sessions of the Council, attended by councillors, some of the lords spiritual and temporal and a few others. They could not tax or approve a statute but they could discuss important matters with the king and their value is evident from the fact that after 1350 on average two or three Great Councils were summoned each year – distinctly more often than parliaments. The term 'Great Council' was sometimes applied to the reinforced Councils appointed at times of political crisis; it was also sometimes applied to the lords in parliament; but the normal meaning was these specially summoned reinforced sessions of the Council. The normal term for the Council itself was 'the Council', without qualification. Adjectives such as 'secret' or 'privy' were occasionally used, more often before 1350 than after. Some examples are puzzling but the sense seems to be meetings in the king's presence or groups of his special confidants. There is no solid evidence that there was ever more than one Council though it could meet in different circumstances, in particular as the Council at Westminster without the king and the Council at Court with the king. The 'Privy Council' was a creation of the 1530s not the Middle Ages. The term 'continual Council' was sometimes used in the fifteenth century but in the sense of the Council which met regularly throughout the year. A good statement of the position is contained in

6 N.B. Lewis, 'The Continual Council in the early years of Richard II, 1377–80', *EHR* 41 (1926), 246–51.
7 Baldwin, *King's Council*, pp. 354–6.

the declaration of the lords of the king's Council in 1427 that while the king was a child governance belonged to the lords assembled in parliament or Great Council or, when these were not in session, to the lords named and chosen to be of the continual Council.[8] The lords were less prominent at the Council than this may suggest but the hierarchy of institutions, parliament, Great Council and Council, is accurate.

The relatively abundant documentation after 1389 shows a businesslike Council, changing to a degree because of political circumstances such as royal minority, restraints imposed on the king and in particular the inability of Henry VI to rule as firmly as his predecessors, but with many common features over a long period. Most recorded meetings were held without the king and at Westminster, presumably in the Star Chamber; some were in London, at the Black Friars or in a house, for the convenience of councillors most of whom lived in the city or the suburbs and probably often for sessions held after the mid-day meal. Meetings could be held anywhere, at the royal residences near London or further afield, for example during parliaments, but Westminster with the great offices and courts at hand was the home of the Council. Meetings were held at all times of the year but there are references to Council terms and there was an attempt to confine less urgent and in particular judicial work to term-time. The Council sometimes met every day of the week save Sunday and several hundred meetings a year were clearly common. Proceedings must have followed some customary order but virtually nothing is known about this save during abnormal times such as Henry VI's minority. The chancellor is occasionally referred to as the 'president' of the Council but senior magnates may have stood on their dignity at times and the duke of Gloucester presumably presided when he was chief councillor during Henry VI's minority. One must imagine the councillors seated on the rich cushions provided for them, probably round a table, attended by their clerk and usher, parchments before them, day-by-day handling the detail of government, negotiating and frightening the recalcitrant and the law-breaker. There was also an ill-recorded aspect of the Council. There were always councillors at Court and on a number of occasions magnates were assigned to remain with the king to advise him; councillors and messengers often travelled between the Council and the Court with messages, letters and documents. Very occasionally when the king was in the country a letter refers to the Council 'with us' implying that there had been a meeting. Clearly councillors with the king often discussed business and gave advice and sometimes, perhaps often, met as the Council in his presence. The narrative of a French envoy to Henry IV, Jean de

8 *Procs. & Ords.*, iii. 233 – *Select Documents*, pp. 258–9.

Hangest, in October 1400 gives a rare glimpse of what the Council records do *not* tell. When Hangest reached London the king was on the way back from Wales and the earl of Worcester, an active councillor at that time, entertained him and arranged a meeting of the Council at the Black Friars to discuss his business. Worcester and the chancellor had several meetings with him and at length the king gave him three audiences at Windsor with councillors in attendance. Hangest had to withdraw several times while the king discussed tricky points with his Council, on the last occasion for two hours before he received an answer to his embassy.[9] Conversations, discussions and meeting of various degrees of informality must have been a common occurence but we know little about them. We also know little about the everyday lives of councillors but, like officials, they must have talked about business, gossiped, manipulated, been solicited for favour and enjoyed the pleasures of London. This was the 'oil' which enabled government to work smoothly.

The best way to obtain an impression of the working Council at Westminster is to read part of the printed Council journals, for example Prophete's journal of 1392. This begins with a meeting on Saturday, 20 January investigating the claim of the mayor and officials of London, who were present, to assent to and carry out any arrest of Londoners. The claim was apparently conceded and they undertook to produce a knight before the Council. The treasurer then reported that the king wished his confessor, the bishop of St Asaphs, to have a gift of some alien goods in recompense for his services and a pardon of £20 he owed in the exchequer at Chester. On the following Monday there was an investigation into loose talk by a royal clerk with a papal envoy about the making of the recent Statute of Provisors, leading to a grovelling apology and an oath not to repeat it. It was then agreed that the men of Cheshire be allowed to pay for their new charter in three instalments of 1,000 marks. On Tuesday letters were ordered summoning the earl of Devon before the Council under threat of forfeiture to answer unspecified matters and to bring one of his servants with him. This was the beginning of a famous case before the Council in which the earl admitted that his retainer had instigated a murder in the course of a feud in Devon and that the earl had perverted the course of justice. On Wednesday the mayor and sheriffs of London were again present for a discussion of the king's right to give 20 marks to two of his Household servants from the sale of a Thames lighter forfeited as a *deodand* because a man had fallen overboard from it and drowned. It was argued that a deodand should be given only as alms, and after the matter had been before the Council several

---

9 *Oeuvres de Froissart*, ed. Kervyn de Lettenhove (Brussels, 1867–77), xvi. 366–77.

times the king eventually restored the vessel to its captain 'Long John' as an act of charity. On Thursday evidence was taken about the death of a royal officer in Cornwall while seizing wreck for the king. On Friday these last two items were further considered, orders were given to release prisoners where there was a dispute about jurisdictions and there was a discussion about the need to send grain to Bordeaux with the chancellor advising caution and the decision reserved for the treasurer's comment. This is the record of one week's work at the Council and probably only a selection of mainly judicial or quasi-judicial items.[10] Other Council records give a slightly different emphasis. Financial items were often considered, occasionally major items such as reviews of income and expenditure and the approval of financial agreements, but more commonly individual items such as orders to pay money or allow disputed items in exchequer accounts – matters too important to be within the routine authority of the exchequer itself and too technical for the king to have time to handle. The chancery rolls contain letters ordered by the Council, not the grants of grace which the king conceded but, for example, commissions to enquire into complaints before the Council, say into piracies which were a frequent Council concern because the common-law courts did not hear them, and orders to arrest and release prisoners, appoint officials such as Justices of the Peace and muster troops or seize shipping. Letters giving effect to particularly important decisions such as the summons of parliament, the appointment of a warden of the Scottish March or an embassy were often ordered 'By the king and the Council', reflecting a decision taken after discussion. Diplomatic letters were often the result of discussion between king and Council but correspondence about the detail of negotiations was often between royal envoys and the Council.[11] The Council heard cases as a court (pp. 132–4). It is relatively easy to collect many references to Council work in any year but it is difficult to reconstruct the circumstances or the atmosphere of decisions. My impression is of a close but unequal daily relationship between king and Council. The king governed and he personally decided matters of grace and many other things but the Council and councillors individualy kept a discreet eye on these decisions and sometimes advised restraint or second-thoughts. It was a common theme in parliament that the Council ought to act as a

10 Baldwin, *King's Council*, 489–91. For the earl of Devon's case see J.F. Baldwin, *Select Cases before the King's Council, 1423–1482* (Selden Society, 35, 1918), pp. 77–81. It is a good example of the power of a magnate in his own 'country' and of the success, though only temporary success, of the Council in bringing him to answer.
11 A.L. Brown, 'The authorization of letters under the great seal', *BIHR* 37 (1964), 149–51. There is a collection of diplomatic correspondence, often with the Council, in *Le Cotton MS. Galba B.I.*, ed. E. Scott and L. Gilliodts van Severen (Brussels, 1896).

check on the king's benevolence and up to a point it always did so. Councillors always used the forms of deference, offering advice 'sil plest au roi', if it pleases the king, but behind the formalities there was clearly a deal of plain-speaking by men who knew one another well. Major political decisions were likely to be discussed by both king and Council. The Council was often told to ensure that decisions were carried into effect; royal letters to the Council often instruct it to do so. A considerable range of business was handled by the Council alone – with the general approval or knowledge of the king. Typical of this were the complicated and difficult issues of January 1392, financial detail and military preparations, the type of business which demanded experience of affairs – and time.

This is obviously a generalization but it is broadly true of the period from 1389 to 1440 and probably for half a century at least before 1389. Circumstances did change. For example while Henry V was in France everything was directed to furthering the war and less was done by a smaller body of councillors in England, probably meeting less often. A campaign in England might disrupt the routine of work. The minority of Henry VI meant that there was even more work for the Council because it was governing the country. But, allowing for these things, this was the character of the Council until Henry VI's incapacity disrupted the pattern.

Who then were the councillors? Prophete's journal records 24 men at the 34 meetings between January and May, 1392 – John of Gaunt, duke of Lancaster, three earls, three barons, nine bishops and eight gentlemen and clerks attended at least once. In addition judges and serjeants-at-law were present on two occasions. This is however only part of the story. The average attendance was only 6.4 and seven men contributed three-quarters of the attendances – the chancellor (Archbishop Arundel of York), the treasurer (Bishop Waltham of Salisbury), the bishops of Lichfield, Durham and Winchester, and two knights, Edward Dalynrigg and Richard Stury. This is a common pattern, a large number of councillors attend occasionally and a core of councillors attend frequently. The most noticeable feature of the seven in 1392 is their governmental experience. Skirlaw of Durham was a lawyer who had been a chancery clerk and keeper of the privy seal; Wykeham of Winchester had held several offices, the Privy Seal, the chancery twice and had been a councillor for over 25 years; they and Scrope of Lichfield had considerable experience of diplomacy and affairs. Dalynrigg and Stury were retainers and king's knights of long standing who had fought in the war, served in parliament and had much experience of Court and commissions. Dalynrigg's account for his wages at the Council between 8 January 1392 and 21 February 1393 survives – for 207 days attendance – which also indicates how often the Council met.[12] There is a contrast between these 34 meetings and meetings held between 12 and 16 February at which the king was present with eleven bishops, three dukes, seven earls, seven barons and a a small number of knights and clerks including Dalynrigg and Stury. These were meetings of a Great Council – though Prophete does not say so – and the business was high policy, for example negotiations with France and the Papacy, preparations for a military expedition and mutual promises of good faith by the king and the lords in response to the king's untimely suggestion that some of his friends condemned in parliament in 1388 might be allowed to return. This was an example of the king taking counsel with his lords and it is important to observe which lords were present – almost half the English bishops, all three royal dukes, more than half the earls, but under a fifth of the barons and none of the abbots and priors, a pattern similar to that of the lords at parliaments (p. 212).

The councillors of 1392 are not typical of every year, but they point to a common pattern. Dukes and earls were in general assiduous in coming to assemblies and to Court, serving as military commanders, ambassadors and commissioners. They regarded it as part of the duty and dignity of their rank to do so. Most lords of their rank were probably sworn of the Council but, except in special circumstances, only a few had the time or the inclination to spend long periods there. Many of the bishops owed their sees to service as royal administrators or lawyer diplomats and most such men gave some years of service at the Council, some such as Wykeham, Langley, Stafford and Kemp gave decades of service there. Most lords, barons, played little or no part at Court or Council. A minority did so and some held high office, particularly as treasurer of the Household or treasurer of England. It was this sort of man or the lord in the personal service of the king who was likely to be an active councillor. One step down the hierarchy the literate knight who was prepared to make a career in royal government was a common feature of the Council. Bartholomew Burghersh in the 1350s and Dalynrigg and Stury in 1392 have been mentioned; in the late 1390s John Bussy, Henry Green and John Russell were the most active of a group of knights and the first two were executed for it in 1399. Under Henry IV John Cheyne and John Doreward were the most active of a number of Lancastrian retainers at the Council and in government generally and among the Council knights of Henry VI's reign were John Tiptoft, Walter Hungerford, John Stourton, all of whom became peers. The layman who made a career in the king's service, the esquire or knight who might become a lord, is a feature of the period. Finally, a few royal clerks were councillors, not now office

12 Baldwin, *King's Council*, p. 133.

clerks but men such as Prophete himself who had the king's favour, became keeper of the privy-seal and had hopes, sadly unfulfilled, of a bishopric at the end of the day.

In normal circumstances, when the king was active and there was no political crisis, the Council was similar to that of 1392; there was a large circle of 30 or more councillors who attended occasionally and a smaller group of active councillors who attended frequently. On quite a number of occasions a Council was formally appointed – when Richard II and Henry VI were minors and after 'trouble' in parliament in 1376, 1385, 1386, 1401, 1404, 1406, and 1410 and probably on other occasions. Sometimes, for example in the early 1400s, the membership did not change much if at all because of these appointments and the significance lay in the promises of the councillors to ensure good government. On other, more tense occasions a limited number of councillors were chosen and they were always men of status. There was a widespread sentiment that the best Council was a substantial, lordly one; the ideal was equal numbers of bishops, earls and barons (or bannerets) reinforcing the officers. Lords were said to be the king's 'natural' councillors whereas knights and clerks were considered to lack the status to insist on 'good and abundant governance' which was what the lords and Commons sought. Every group in society was conscious of its status but the right of the lords to leadership was always recognized. It has been suggested that the lords deliberately sought and attained control or influence at the Council but I doubt this. They did not see government as a conflict with the king and few were assiduous councillors, at least for long. The striking example of this is 1422 when the king was an infant and the lords asserted, against the king's uncles, that government belonged to them during the inability of the king to govern. A Council consisting of the duke of Gloucester as chief councillor, five bishops, the duke of York, five earls and five lords or 'lordlings' was appointed, but in practice over the following three years the three great officers and the bishops, three of them ex-officers and two lawyers, provided 60 per cent of the recorded attendance. Gloucester attended assiduously and for three years so too did the earl of Warwick, the king's governor. Lord Cromwell and two knights, Walter Hungerford and John Tiptoft, whose claims to be lords were recognized in 1426, were also assiduous; all three served as treasurer and were active councillors for many years. There were good reasons why attendance was less aristocratic than the appointment suggests, war service, age and lack of interest which even the attraction of wages could not overcome. Even in the unusual circumstances of 1422 the Council in practice was a distinctly 'professional' body.

A change did take place in the 1430s and 1440s. The 'professional' or 'experienced' element continued to be strong but a larger number of lay lords began to attend in the 30s, probably because of the factional disputes at the Council. More important, after Henry VI declared himself of age in 1437, the Council changed because the king could not use it properly. The Westminster Council did meet but probably less often and more business was done by councillors and Council meetings at Court. Worse still, the king relied too much on Court and Council intimates, in particular the earl of Suffolk, and a number of these paid with their lives for this in 1450. It was the king's personal failure and the resultant political rivalries leading to civil war which caused the Council to change so much.[13]

The late-medieval Council was subject to constant change because of personalities and politics and because its rôle was to assist the king at the highest level of government and at times to take over government altogether. But government was not primarily a matter of great decisions of policy; much of it was concerned with the burdensome, day-by-day detail of administration and law and order. This was why the 'professional', experienced element in the Council was so strong. What is emerging from recent work is evidence of a long-term evolution – from the apparently amorphous Council of Edward I just beginning to be an executive board, to the more substantial and regular Council of 1350 which becomes the well documented Council of the end of the century with its clear character and importance in government. Professor Lander's study of the Yorkist Council has shown a similar Council when it used to be thought that the Council scarcely existed, and this in turn links with the Tudor Council in Star Chamber and the Privy Council.[14]

13 There is a full examination of this period in R.A. Griffiths, *The Reign of Henry VI* (London, 1979).
14 J.R. Lander, *Crown and Nobility 1450–1509* (London, 1976), pp. 171–219.

3

The Westminster Offices*

By 1272 England had a long history of ordered, literate royal government. Regular provision for writing the king's letters and handling his revenues had begun in late Anglo-Saxon times and by 1200 had developed into the highly organized offices of chancery and exchequer. During the late Middle Ages their workload and their records expanded further and two additional writing-offices, the Privy Seal and the Signet, were created. This was a true bureaucracy, bound to established procedures and proper warrants, keeping files, enrolling copies and served by career clerks. Westminster was their normal place of work and by the fourteenth century it was in all but name the administrative capital. Here again there is a long-term continuity because much of this bureaucracy and the accretions of succeeding centuries were swept away only in the late eighteenth and nineteenth centuries. The heads of these offices were men of power and influence. In Edward I's reign it was to the chancellor and the treasurer, not necessarily in that order, that the king wrote with instructions. In the course of the fourteenth century the keeper of the privy seal became the third great officer and, as we have seen, they were the most active members of the Council. The king's Secretary who kept the signet seal was a courtier rather than a councillor but in the sixteenth century he too became a great minister and eventually of greater political

---

* The vast records of the Westminster offices have been known and used by scholars for four centuries but it was only in the 1850s that they began to be collected into the Public Record Office and to be freely open for study, and it was only in the early 20th century that the offices began to be seriously studied. The pioneer was T.F. Tout whose *The Place of Edward II in English History* (Manchester, 1914, 2nd ed., 1936), the six-volume *Chapters in Mediaeval Administrative History* (Manchester, 1920–33) down to 1399 and many articles profoundly influenced the subject. In practice most of Tout's work was concerned with the offices of the royal Household and only incidentally with the Westminster offices, and this led to an imbalance and a theory of 'Household government' which has only recently been righted. S.B. Chrimes, *Introduction to the Administrative History of Mediaeval England* (Oxford, 1952, 2nd ed., 1959) is a useful survey much indebted to Tout. The *Guide to the Contents of the Public Record Office* (London, 1963) briefly explains as well as lists the office archives.

importance than the other three. There is unfortunately no source equivalent to the Tudor State Papers to reveal the 'inside' story of medieval government but it is clear that, in the manner of the times, the chancellor, the treasurer and the keeper were the peers of the Wolseys, the Cromwells, the Walsinghams and the less famous officials of the Tudors. Robert Burnell in the reign of Edward I, William Wykeham in the late fourteenth century, John Kemp in the fifteenth century and many other less outstanding officials exercised under the king great power and influence; they 'made' policy as well as executed it and they were with reason 'laboured' for their good-will and favour. The lesser officials and clerks in the offices were also cultivated for they could advise and act as agents for clients bewildered by the complexities of government. It was a promotion-conscious, money conscious, professional life that these men led in Westminster beside the temptations of big-city life in London.

The Writing Offices*

The first duty of the three writing offices, chancery, the Privy Seal and the Signet office, was to write royal letters issued under the great, the privy and the signet seal respectively. Sealing was a guarantee of the authenticity of letters in a society where reading and writing skills were limited. By the fifteenth century most men of substance and many lesser men could sign their names and signatures were being used for certain limited purposes but tradition still demanded a seal for formal purposes. Much of the work of the office clerks was literally writing but the more senior clerks had more demanding work. They drafted and checked the texts of letters which might have to stand up to legal scrutiny; some clerks were experts in fields such as diplomatic documentation and therefore in the conduct of diplomacy; and, particularly in the case of chancery, the most senior officers had authority to issue large numbers of letters on their own authority. To an extent chancery and the Privy Seal provided the services of a Foreign Office, a Home Office and a War Office. The Privy Seal, created to supplement chancery, was closer to the king and the Council and acted as a 'clearing-house' of the administration, giving effect to their decisions

* The best general introduction to the writing offices is P. Chaplais, *English Royal Documents: King John-Henry VI, 1199-1461* (Oxford, 1971) which includes photographs and transcriptions of documents. For Chancery see B. Wilkinson, *The Chancery under Edward III* (Manchester, 1929) and 'The Chancery', *Eng. Gov. at Work*, i. 162-205, and H.C. Maxwell-Lyte, *Historical Notes on the Use of the Great Seal of England* (London, 1926), a miscellany of information. Tout, *Chapters* has a great deal of information on the Privy Seal and the Signet Office, particularly in volume v, and this is supplemented by J.Otway-Ruthven's essay, *The King's Secretary and the Signet Office in the XV Century* (Cambridge, 1939).

by sending out written warrants, instructions to officials and less formal letters. The Signet, the youngest, remained always the king's own writing office, and wrote his more personal letters. It was strictly not a Westminster office at all because it always travelled with the king.

The origins of chancery go back to the writing-office of the late Anglo-Saxon kings. Immediately after the Norman Conquest and probably also immediately before, it was headed by an officer called the chancellor. By 1200 an organized office called chancery was in being, already keeping copies of the most important letters it issued on rolls, sheets of parchment sewn head to tail and then made into a roll for storage. By 1300 ten major rolls were in use, the letters assigned by type, subject matter or geographical area to the Charter, Close, Fine, Gascon, Liberate, Patent, Redisseisin, Scotch, Scutage and Treaty rolls, and voluminous files of loose documents were maintained.[1] Fortunately most of these rolls and many files have survived, in itself a tribute to the professionalism of the medieval office. The head of chancery was still the chancellor, the king's leading minister, a man often at Court, often at the Council which he probably frequently chaired, often the king's spokesman in parliament and before foreign envoys. He was normally a bishop or archbishop with considerable administrative experience in the lesser offices, though the first lay chancellor was appointed in 1341 and there were seven others before 1461. A chancellor had so many responsibilities that he must have delegated much of the departmental work to his staff which numbered well over 100 according to chancery Ordinances of the 1380s.[2] There were then 12 clerks of the first grade (the masters of chancery) each with three clerks under him save the Keeper of the Rolls who had six; 12 clerks of the second grade including the Keeper of the Hanaper, each with one clerk; and 24 cursitors who wrote the simple writs of common form. The same hierarchy existed early in the fourteenth century though the numbers were probably smaller. There were also the artisans and menials of the offices such as the *spigurnel* in charge of the sealing process, the *chafewax* who heated the wax for the seal, and the porters. Custom, like a restrictive practice, defined what each might do, who decided the form of each letter, drafted it, checked it and wrote it – in return of course for fees and favours. The Keeper or Master of the Rolls was the senior clerk, almost the chancellor's deputy, in charge of the enrolment of letters and the custody of the

1 Chancery rolls and files are described in the *Guide* to the Public Record Office. The Charter, Patent, Close and Fine rolls are published in calendar form in English by HMSO and are well worth sampling to obtain a flavour of late medieval government.
2 Printed in Wilkinson, *Chancery*, pp. 217–23.

rolls.[3] The Keeper of the Hanaper was in charge of the department where office fees and fines (to the king) were paid and letters issued – the term comes from the 'hamper' where letters were stored. The officers and the senior clerks were by and large men of great experience and capable of taking many of the day-to-day decisions, for example the prothonotary was an authority on diplomatic practice.[4]

The privy-seal and signet offices were small by comparison with chancery. King John was the first king to use a small or privy seal for official purposes, though earlier kings had personal seals. He did so because the chancellor and the great seal were no longer always at hand, and another seal was needed to authenticate less formal letters and send orders to the chancellor to issue formal letters under the great seal. After 1230 the privy seal was in the custody of the Keeper and later of the Controller of the Wardrobe, who were in a sense the king's private secretaries. It began to be used more extensively in the 1290s, because the king was so much on the move and because of the death of Chancellor Robert Burnell who had been so close to Edward I. It is a sign of its increased importance that the Ordinances of 1311 laid down that a 'suitable' clerk be appointed to keep the privy seal and that, like the other major officers, he should be appointed in parliament with the assent of the baronage. As a result Roger Northburgh became in early 1313 the first keeper of the privy seal who was not also a Household officer, and though it took many years before the last formal links with the Household were broken, the Privy Seal was no longer meaningfully a domestic office.[5] Northburgh was soon spending months away from Court and writing letters for the Council, and by mid-century the keeper was the third of the great officers of state after the chancellor and the treasurer, for example joining with them in writing (and receiving) letters from the king. He was almost invariably a cleric, often a man who would go on to a bishopric and higher office, though by one of those curious status customs, until John Wakering broke it in 1415, a keeper resigned office if he obtained the coveted bishopric. The office establishment was at first four clerks and this continued to be cited a century afterwards, but in practice by 1400

3 Several early Keepers of the Rolls were also wardens of the House of (Jewish) Converts established by Henry III in Chancery Lane. After 1371 the two offices were held together and the House became a storehouse for chancery rolls and documents. The Rolls Chapel continued to be used for this purpose and in 1851 the Public Record Office was built beside it and, appropriately, houses the rolls.

4 G.P. Cuttino, *English Diplomatic Administration 1259–1330* (Oxford, 1940).

5 A good example of the conservatism of medieval government is the fiction that the keeper's wages of £1 a day were paid only until arrangements were made for the continuous residence of himself and his clerks in the royal Household, a fiction last stated in 1409, at least three generations after it had ceased to have any meaning.

there were 10 or 12 privy-seal clerks, seniors and juniors. The Privy Seal was never as bureaucratic as chancery. It did not normally enrol copies of its letters but it did keep bulky files of documents strung on parchment strings. It is one of the major losses of medieval records that almost all these files, containing hundreds of thousands of documents, were destroyed by a fire at Whitehall in 1619.

A third seal began to be used for official purposes in the early fourteenth century at the time when the privy seal moved out of the Household and became less available to the king. It was at first called confusingly the 'secret' seal, a name also used for the privy seal. During Edward III's reign several secret seals and at times a ring seal were used but by the 1370s there was one seal called the signet and from 1377 its keeper was called the king's Secretary.[6] He was always a clerk and never a bishop. Nominally he had four clerks, in practice often more, and in time they too came to form a writing-office. Its duty was to write for the king himself and therefore during the minority of Henry VI there was no signet and no office. The Secretary's place was at Court and he did not have the public role of the chancellor and the keeper.

There was a clear customary division of work between the offices. Chancery wrote the most solemn letters, in particular those which were evidence of authority or title granted by the king. Appointments to office, for example as royal lieutenants, wardens of the marches, captains of castles, envoys sent to foreign sovereigns, the treasurer, judges, and down the scale to Justices of the Peace, commissioners of many kinds, tax collectors and buyers of provisions for the Household would be considered authentic only under the great seal. The same was true of major grants, for example of land, goods, money, privileges, annuities, pardons of crime and ecclesiastical benefices. Most of these letters were of such importance that they could be ordered only by the king himself or, in a restricted area, by the Council. From the 1290s the authority for their issue is known because this was noted on the letters and the enrolled copies in a phrase (a 'note of warranty') such as 'By the king himself', 'By the Council' or 'By a writ of privy seal' and it is possible to make judgements about the exercise of authority in government at any period.[7] In 1300 many letters of instructions from the king or Council, for example to the exchequer to pay or pardon money or to keepers of forests to deliver gifts of timber were sealed with the great seal and enrolled on the Close Roll but by 1400 such letters were sent under the privy seal. Summons to parliament

6 Tout, *Chapters*, v. 211.
7 A.L. Brown, 'The authorization of letters under the great seal', *BIHR* 37 (1964), 125-56 discusses the division of authority in 1404-5 in detail and generalizes about it. Wilkinson, *Chancery*, pp. 21-4 gives a necessarily more general assessment for 1341.

continued to be issued under the great seal but summons to Great Councils and to the Council came to be under the privy seal. Officials also ordered letters under the great seal. The exchequer had a seal for departmental business but the treasurer had to order the chancellor to issue some of his letters, for example giving custody of lands in the king's hands, and other officers such as the Chief Butler ordered great-seal letters commissioning their deputies. There were also *very* large numbers of letters issued on the sole authority of the chancellor or his officials – recognizable on the rolls because they have no note of warranty. Many were routine letters which required careful checking and drafting but not much initiative. For example thousands of writs were issued each year in connexion with actions in the courts and many hundreds to the treasurer and chamberlains of the exchequer or other royal officials to pay (*liberate*) wages or half-yearly instalments of annuities granted by royal letters-patent and to the treasurer and barons of the exchequer to allow (*allocate*) the payments made. There were often hundreds of general pardons a year issued as a matter of course under the terms of a general pardon proclaimed by the king; for example 616 were issued after the revolt of 1381 and more than 2,000 after Cade's rising in 1450. These were quite distinct from the pardons which the king himself granted for particular, named crimes. There were also many letters only slightly less standard and requiring some weighing of evidence, for example confirmations or recording of documents, pardons of outlawry, writs suspending proceedings in the exchequer or other offices on the basis of a statement on oath in chancery – for example where a document was lost or not delivered. Many writs in connexion with local inquests by jury into the transfer of land – for example when a tenant-in-chief died (*post mortem*) or when a licence to alienate land or the grant of a privilege had been requested (*ad quod damnum*) – were issued, the returns acted upon and then filed. There were also an increasing number of letters of much greater importance issued on the authority of the chancellor. For example many commissions to enquire into crimes, concealment of royal revenues, plundering of foreign merchants and the like, were little different from others ordered by the Council. Chancery had officials experienced in administration and increasingly in the law, a vast archive of material to refer to and in the chancellor the king's leading minister. It had become an administrative department not just a writing-office, a place where subjects and their attornies or agents came for letters, for example for the writs which were often necessary to make other parts of the warrant-conscious administration move, for their own personal agreements to be enrolled for security, for advice, for favour and for justice. This is the period when chancery became a court (pp. 132–4), the work which eventually became more important for it than letter-writing. The mid fourteenth century was probably a turning-point for the office. Since the early part of Edward I's reign the number of its letters – if we can use the number of sheets of parchment in the rolls as a rough guide – more than doubled. There was more writing because there was more government, more legal business, more taxation – no wonder the rebels of 1381 were said to be out to kill lawyers, indeed anyone who could read and write. The number of chancery letters levelled off after mid century though with considerable fluctuations, and they markedly declined in the reign of Henry VI. This does not mean that there was less government, at least not permanently, but rather that chancery's share of letter writing declined and the two small seals were use more extensively.

The role of the privy seal was quite different. It did not have the authority to authenticate solemn letters and the traditional hold of chancery over many areas of business could not be broken. The great seal is still used today for the most solemn documents, while the Lord Privy Seal receives only Queen Victoria's privy seal and never uses it. The privy seal however came to be used more and more to authenticate orders from the king and the Council and the office became the 'clearing-house' of central administration. The best known privy-seal letters are warrants, in particular those to the chancellor ordering the issue of letters under the great seal, most of them graces such as pardons or gifts conceded by the king.[8] These had originated from the need to convey royal orders to the chancellor in authentic form when he was not at Court. In the fifteenth century it was common, though not necessary, for a grant of grace made by the king to lead to a signet letter to the keeper of the privy seal ordering a privy-seal warrant to the chancellor ordering a letter under the great seal. Sometimes distance did make this round-about system necessary but it was also used to give the clerks an income. It was a restrictive practice, given statutory authority in 1536, which continued for centuries for the benefit of the clerks. Warrants to the exchequer ordering payments, accounts to be made and allowances given, were in 1300 mainly chancery business but by the later fourteenth century had become mainly that of the Privy Seal. For example when the king or the Council ordered a single payment, say for a military or Household purpose, a privy-seal writ would be issued; if it ordered a running credit, for example for the treasurer of Calais or a military commander, a writ 'current' would

---

8 Brown, 'Letters under the great seal', pp. 140. Many examples of privy-seal warrants are printed in E. Déprez, *Études de Diplomatique Anglaise* (Paris, 1908), the book which inspired Tout to begin his administrative studies. Examples of chancery warrants are printed in *Select Documents*, pp. 378–80.

convey the order and he would be paid money from time to time by agreement with the treasurer without further authorization.

Every royal official received orders under the privy seal. The Chief Butler and local officers were ordered to hand over royal gifts of wine, timber or venison, the Keeper of the Privy Wardrobe in the Tower to issue military supplies, collectors of customs to make payments or release goods, and on and on. Letters such as these often survive because they were produced as evidence in accounting in the exchequer. It is clear however that warrants were only part of a widespread correspondence under the privy seal. The office's surviving archives contain many examples of this but the best guide to it are privy-seal formularies, books of model letters used in the office. The best of these (MS. British Library 24,062), written in the early 1420s by the poet-clerk Thomas Hoccleve, contains over 900 model privy-seal letters, only 272 to chancery and exchequer. There are for example letters seeking loans – letters sometimes sent out in bundles with messengers instructed to induce religious houses or individuals to lend; letters to town officials to release prisoners, prevent disorders, enquire into complaints, prevent offensive smells and so on; to universities seeking advice or ordering the admission or ejection of students; and all manner of more personal letters summoning men to serve, excusing them, seeking support, encouraging widows to marry approved husbands and so on. Letter-writing was a commonplace in this society at least among the top ten or twenty thousand. The great seal had a virtual monopoly of the more formal letters issued on the direct orders of the king or the Council but the privy seal authenticated most of the others. By 1400 there must have been many thousands of these privy seals issued each year on all manner of subjects.[9]

The Privy Seal did not have a monopoly of less formal letters; some were issued from chancery but more and more came to be issued from the Signet office. Often the issue was a purely practical one – which writing-office was available. Every time the king left Westminster or London a decision had to be taken about which writing-offices would accompany him. The Signet would invariably go because its sole purpose was to serve the king. Chancery was least likely to move because so much of its work was done on its own initiative; sometimes a second great seal was brought into use and some of the clerks sent with the king. The Privy Seal often shuttled between the king and Westminster,

9 No large collection of these letters has been printed but the flavour of privy-seal and signet letters and private letters can be obtained from *Anglo-Norman Letters and Petitions*, ed. M. Dominica Legge (Anglo-Norman Text Society, 3, Oxford, 1941) and, in the case of diplomatic letters from *The Diplomatic Correspondence of Richard II*, ed. E. Perroy (Camden Third Series, 48, 1933). See also A.L. Brown, 'The privy seal clerks in the early fifteenth century' in *The Study of Medieval Records*, ed. D.A. Bullough and R.L. Storey (Oxford, 1971), pp. 260–81.

seeking to serve both the king and the Council for, as we have seen, it became very much the seal of the Council with one of its clerks serving as Clerk of the Council. The Signet however had a restricted use. Chancery would accept its letters only for a limited range of purposes and the exchequer would not normally accept them at all. There was a strong and lasting emotion, associated for example with Richard II's behaviour in the early 1380s, that the Signet could be used to express the king's own generosity and wilfulness unchecked by the good advice that the Council might give. The keeper of the privy seal certainly sometimes referred royal decisions to the Council and he probably was held to have a duty to do so if he was in doubt. It must be stressed however that in normal times this was part of the working relationship between the king and his councillors not a 'constitutional' issue. Where the Signet could and did expand its work was in the field of letters, 'letter missive' as they were called, rather than warrants. The signet seal was sometimes said to be more appropriate than the privy seal – because it was felt to represent more the king's personal will. On campaign it was sometimes the only seal available. The secretary and the seal were gaining in status in the same manner as the privy seal had done earlier. Henry V made greater use of the signet and so did Henry VI, but in 1461 the Privy Seal was still the 'clearing-house' and the signet still the personal seal.

The Signet office had no judicial or administrative authority, but the Privy Seal had a modest authority in several fields. For example the indentures retaining military commanders and captains of contingents resulting from decisions and bargains made by the king and the Council came almost invariably to be written in the Privy Seal and the copy sealed by the commander was filed there (p. 95). The keeper therefore had authority to issue supplementary warrants or bills to the exchequer to pay instalments of wages and to account with the commanders, and to the chancellor to issue protections (from actions in the courts) to men in the contingents at the request of the commanders. It was a modest but useful authority based on the evidence on file in the office; it oiled the painstaking machinery of administration. The Privy Seal by the second half of the fourteenth century had orderly files of diplomatic correspondence and this gave the keeper and the clerks a special knowledge and status in diplomatic matters. The keeper had authority to stay proceedings in the Court of the Constable and Marshal and he may have had authority delegated by the Council to further poor mens' causes which eventually led him to become president of the Tudor Court of Requests. These were however small islands of authority compared with the great areas of authority exercised by the chancellor and treasurer.

Writing-offices writing letters, many of them humdrum letters in standard forms, may not seem very important but this was the heart of late-medieval administration. Routine letters, writs to begin court actions or ordering payment of half-yearly wages and many more, were akin to today's forms which properly filled in and approved lead to administrative action. Other letters were not routine; letters of appointment as tax collectors and Justices of the Peace, orders to raise troops, instructions to officials, orders to hold enquiries into this and that disturbance, pardons for specified crimes, letters in all manner of circumstances covered the whole range of government because there was no Home Office, Foreign Office or other ministry. All business passed though the writing offices. Reading the Calendars of the Patent, Close and Fine rolls (in English!), gives the best insight into medieval government and society. For example the importance of patronage is plain in the many royal gifts of land, possessions, timber, offices, parish livings, prebends and many other things. Politics often centred on who received this benevolence. Each year the chancery rolls contain copies of thousands of letters and many more were never enrolled at all. Thousands were issued under the privy seal and signet, the great majority of them read but not preserved. This is particularly unfortunate because among them were many less formal letters of instruction from the king and the Council, to envoys on how to carry out their formal commissions, to a town about its municipal politics, appeals for support in an emergency, letters perverting the course of justice and so on. By the mid fourteenth century probably 30–40,000 letters were being issued each year by these three offices in the king's name, perhaps even more. Obviously the great majority had to be issued on the authority of officials, not by the king nor even the Council. Royal government, which over the centuries had been becoming more and more written government, can now be described justly as bureaucratic and professional government and increasingly government by officials under the king.

The Exchequer*

The third of the great Westminster departments was the exchequer, the principal royal treasury and accounting office. It had originated in the twelfth century though financial expertise had existed much earlier. The *Dialogus de Scaccario* (the *Dialogue Concerning the*

---

* The only history of the exchequer is still T. Madox, *The History and Antiquities of the Exchequer, 1066–1327* (London, 1711, 2nd ed., 1769). *The Pipe Roll for 1295, Surrey Membrane*, ed. M.H. Mills (Surrey Record Society, 7, 1924) has an excellent introduction. A Steel, *The Receipt of the Exchequer, 1377–1485* (Cambridge, 1954) contains a statistical analysis and commentary on the Receipt rolls and a valuable technical explanation of the receipt and issue procedure. The second volume of the *Eng. Gov. at Work* series entitled 'Fiscal Administration' does not deal directly with the exchequer.

Exchequer) of about 1179 gives a remarkable description of its work, its two parts, the Lower Exchequer of Receipt where money was received and issued and the Upper Exchequer where accounts were rendered and calculations made on a table covered with a chequered cloth which gave the exchequer its name.[10] This division and much of the procedure described in the *Dialogus* continued through the Middle Ages and long after – but the volume and complexity of the work increased greatly. Frequent taxation raised much more revenue to pay for more extensive and expensive government. The *Dialogus* is concerned almost exclusively with the accounts of the sheriffs but from the thirteenth century 'foreign' accounts such as those of the Household, military commanders and tax collectors multiplied. New series of records were begun, book-keeping became more complicated and reform was badly needed.

Three ordinances made by the king and Council in 1323, 1324 and 1326 apparently inspired by Walter Stapledon, bishop of Exeter and treasurer between 1320–21 and 1322–25, attempted to rationalize and simplify the documentation and procedure.[11] They tell of a multiplying quantity of records and warrants even since Edward I's reign and ordered reforms such as limiting the re-copying of 'foreign' from old accounts, defined the work of the two Remembrancers (p. 54) and demanded a speeding-up of accounting which was often years in arrears. Their success was limited and slow but they do show that contemporaries were aware of the weakness of the exchequer's monumental methods. These did change a little over the following century but not radically. It remained a cumbersome and parchment-bound office, though it must be remembered that every finance office must be cautious. The fundamental financial problem of the period was not the exchequer but almost continuous war which obliged kings to rely heavily on credit, borrowing and anticipating revenue. Creditors were often paid not in cash but in assignments, drafts on revenue collectors which might be difficult to cash. Royal debts and defaults were constantly the source of discontent. The exchequer did its slow, bureaucratic best at a time when royal finance was generally a hand-to-mouth affair.

The head of the office was the treasurer, almost always a cleric in the fourteenth century, almost always a layman in the fifteenth, at first often a knight, then a baron, then by mid century often an earl. This may on occasion have been a response to the criticism of royal finance from lay taxpayers, but it was much more the supreme example of laymen taking over the work of clerks as managers and

10 *Dialogus de Scaccario*, ed. C. Johnson (London, 1950).
11 They are printed and translated in the *Red Book of the Exchequer*, ed. H. Hall (Rolls Series, 1896), iii. 848–969.

administrators. By the close of this period laymen held most of the senior posts in the exchequer – for example the offices of the under-treasurer, the four or five barons of the exchequer who heard accounts and pleas in the Upper Exchequer and the two deputy-chamberlains in the Lower Exchequer. Below them were probably over 100 staff, designated officers, clerks, down to the ushers, door-keepers and messengers.

The best place to begin to describe the work of the office is the Great Rolls, called the Pipe Rolls because the individual sections or sheets of parchment were stored rolled into tubes or pipes before being sewn together at the head, exchequer fashion, into the Great Roll. They were the oldest exchequer record, the earliest to survive is for 1129–30, and they contain the accounts of sheriffs and bailiffs of liberties and franchises, county by county. A sheriff accounted annually for his shire farm, its increment and for annual rents – items that were more or less the same year after year, and also for variable items, in particular for fines and dues levied on behalf of chancery, exchequer and the royal courts and for lands specially committed into his custody. In this period the yield from the shires was small compared with that from taxation but great effort was expended on these accounts and they formed a model for other accounts (p. 63). The sheriff's account ran from Michaelmas (29 September) to Michaelmas. He was normally charged (warned of his duties) and sworn in the exchequer which had often had a hand in his appointment, watched over his work and invited complaints against him. He knew the traditional farms and rents he had to collect and twice a year the exchequer sent him a list of summons compiled from its own records, from the Originalia Rolls compiled in chancery and sent to the exchequer once a year, and from the Estreat Rolls, lists of fines and amercements imposed by royal justices, sent periodically to the exchequer. The exchequer often extracted items from these records into its own order lest any debts might be overlooked; copying, recopying and pursuing debts, even over generations, were features typical of the office. Two sets of Memoranda Rolls were written there each year, one by the King's Remembrancer, the other by the Treasurer's Remembrancer, hundreds of long sheets of parchment sewn together at the head to form a bundle the size and shape of a large cricket bag and divided into sections containing documents and evidence that might be useful. The sheriff was supposed to appear in the exchequer twice a year, eight days after Easter to make his proffer, his first payment, and then on the morrow of Michaelmas to make his final proffer and view, his preliminary account for the year. Normally about six months later he was summoned for his audit in the Upper Exchequer before the treas-urer, the barons of the exchequer and others, each side with its documents, rolls and tallies, meeting over days or months until each item was scrutinized and the final account made and entered on the Great Roll. In practice things often did not run as smoothly as this. At the close for example there were often items that could not be collected and had to be passed forward or the sheriff might have his property distrained for debt.

When the sheriff (or anyone else) paid in money at the Receipt of the exchequer he was given as a receipt a wooden stick (a tally) on which the sum was recorded by notches cut in the wood. According to a seventeenth-century description, the payer gave the money to one of the tellers in an upper room; the teller wrote a bill of receipt which was dropped through a pipe to the floor below where the tally cutter 'struck' a tally and the details were written on two of its faces; the junior deputy chamberlain struck with a mallet a cleaver held by his senior to split the tally lengthwise; the senior read out one part (the stock which the payer would receive) the junior checked the other (the counter foil which was filed in the exchequer) and clerks checked the written records.[12] Procedure was probably much the same in the early fifteenth century at the latest. Foils and bills were filed and four records of the payment were enrolled, on the Teller's Roll and in triplicate on Receipt Rolls – for security by the treasurer's clerk and the two deputy chamberlains. This cautious, formalized, bureaucratic procedure was characteristic of the exchequer – over many centuries. The use of tallies for example was abolished by statute only in 1783 and continued until 1826; it was clearly an unwise decision for centuries of tallies were then used to fire the boilers of old Westminster Palace and caused the fire which destroyed most of it in 1834!

The sheriff's accounts were the most ancient but the 'foreign' accounts were more important and are more interesting to the historian. They include the accounts of the Household which at times early in this period covered most of the king's expenditure, of collectors of direct and indirect taxes, military commanders and hundreds of small accounts of custodians of property temporarily in the king's hands. In the thirteenth century these were often enrolled at the end of the Great Rolls though some of the bulkier such as Household accounts were enrolled separately. The exchequer Ordinances of 1323 and 1324 took this a stage further by providing that Foreign Accounts should be heard and enrolled separately. This was done, though the separate set of annual rolls of Foreign Accounts begins only in 1368. What this meant at this time can be seen in a simple example such as the account

---

12 H. Jenkinson, in a note in *Proc. Soc. Antiquaries* 25 (1912–3), pp. 31–4. Jenkinson wrote two other important articles on tallies in *Archaeologia* 62 (1911) and 74 (1923–4).

of an envoy sent abroad to negotiate. He would generally be given an advance of money by authority of a privy-seal writ to the treasurer and the chamberlains of the exchequer, and the payment was entered on the Issue Roll – in triplicate with a note 'respondebit', – he must account for the money. The exchequer would in due course demand an account though normally the envoy would anticipate this by obtaining (normally by a petition to the king or the Council) a privy-seal warrant to the treasurer, barons and chamberlains ordering them to account with him, allow his expenses and pay what was due. The wording had to be precise to be effective. The account was made on oath before an exchequer auditor who set down the advance and against it the envoy's wages at the appropriate daily rate from the day of his departure until his return plus any other traditionally allowable expenses such as the Channel crossing. Unusual expenses would require a decision by the king or Council and another warrant. The account of a keeper of escheated or forfeited lands might be equally simple or it might involve a mass of detail about the profit of courts and the leases of land. A Household account was likely to be voluminous and include great detail, but the principles were the same. When the audit was approved the documents concerning the case and a detailed statement of the final account were filed and a more succinct statement of it enrolled.

The exchequer did not pay out money without written authorization, save for minor departmental expenses. Orders came in formal warrants under the great or privy seals, signet or informal instructions were not accepted. In 1272 most warrants were under the great seal but a century later, as in other areas of government, privy-seal warrants normally conveyed orders from the king or the Council. Almost all great-seal warrants ordered payment of instalments of annuities, the salaries of justices and other minor payments issued on the chancellor's own authority. Privy-seals, either warrants ordering single payments or warrants 'current' ordering a credit to major spending officials such as the treasurer of the Household or the treasurer of Calais, authorized the bulk of expenditure. Payments were recorded – in triplicate of course – on the Issue Rolls and the warrants were filed. Payments might be in cash but often they were in wood and paper – by assignment (p. 83).

This has been a description of only part of the work of the exchequer, mainly of its accounting methods and its records. Like finance offices at all times its strength lay in its detailed work and its cautious, over-documented approach. It did not make payments or concede other than traditional allowances on its own authority save in minor matters. It relied for this on the king and the Council and on chancery. It used its records and its expertise to ensure that the king received his dues, for example the seizure of every convicted felon's goods and the payment of a relief by the heir of every tenant-in-chief who had proved his age and sworn fealty. It pursued debts over generations and might badger the wrong man until ordered to stop. Its caution and dogged pursuits could be ridiculous but again these are the universal faults of bureaucracy today. It also did many other things. It had custody of important documents and treasures. It acted as a royal land agent, for example awarding the custody of lands in the king's hands at a rent fixed by one of its barons on the basis of a local inquest into its value and the evidence of its own records. In this case the treasurer had to order a commission from chancery but the exchequer had its own seal for its departmental letters. It was a busy, cautious office with a precise division of responsibility and an enormous archive. What it did not do was make financial policy. It rarely produced balance sheets or statistical information (p. 61). It could do so though its accounting methods were not designed for this purpose. Late-medieval administrators were not much interested in such things. They are yet another feature of modern times.

The Character of Administration

By 1272 chancery and exchequer were already large, long-established and record-bound departments, the backbone of royal administration, and this tends to obscure the changes that took place over the following two centuries. Government and therefore administration expanded considerably. The king had much more revenue and spent more extensively. He had more officials in and more dealings with the localities though he did not govern them closely (Chapter 7). At Westminster there were more letters to be issued and more accounting to be done. In the offices administration became more specialized and professional. Much that had previously been done from the Household was now done from Westminster and from the Council. The methods of administration became more formal and the men who worked in the offices can with some justice be dubbed bureaucrats and civil servants.

These changes can be seen not only in the major offices but also in smaller ones such as the offices which provided supplies and services for the Household and for the king's government generally, offices which were the distant ancestors of several government departments of today. Two offices, the Great Wardrobe and the Privy Wardrobe in the Tower, were Household offices which hived off and established themselves with storehouses and workshops in London.[13] The Great

---

13 Tout, *Chapters*, iv. 349–484.

Wardrobe had been part of the Wardrobe in the Household until the 1320s. It bought, manufactured and stored a great variety of items such as cloth, furs, furnishings, tents, medicines and spices and by the 1360s was settled in permanent premises at Baynard's Castle in the city, where it remained until the Great Fire of 1666. It had its own keeper and clerks and a number of tradesmen such as the king's tailor, pavillioner, armourer, sadler, jeweller and (banner) painter with their workmen. Much of their work was domestic, preparing clothes and beds and consumables for the Household and gifts from the king, but it extended further, for example to provide annual livery of clothes for the civil servants and retainers, tents for campaigns and clothing for soldiers. It was the royal stores or Ministry of Supply. The Privy Wardrobe in the Tower was a specialized offshoot of the Great Wardrobe settled in the Tower of London. It handled the bulkier war supplies such as armour, weapons, naval supplies and increasingly guns and gunpowder, and it also had its staff of tradesmen. The Clerk of Ships obtained some of his supplies there; his duty was to maintain and supply and sometimes to build the king's ships (p. 97). Kings built and maintained many buildings – at Westminster, the Tower, Windsor, and at castles, houses and colleges throughout the country.[14] The first three Edwards were great builders. Most projects were at first handled in an *ad hoc* way with their own master craftsmen and their own clerk and controller to handle the accounting. In the fourteenth century it became common to have a clerk of works administering a group of projects and from 1378 there was a Clerk of the King's Works responsible for all or almost all of the king's building works. He had deputies administering local projects but he was responsible for overall accounting and he had his office at Westminster. He was a civil servant not a builder, but about the same time a number of 'Patent Artisans' were appointed by letters-patent, officials such as the King's Master Carpenter, his Plumber and his Glazier. The office now had a structure of specialist officials with annual wages and robes – and it survived until the late eighteenth century. Close by the office, on the west side of Westminster Hall, was its builders' yard with stone and timber and storehouses for iron, glass and other materials. Significantly also, whereas much of Edward I's building work had been financed through the Wardrobe, by the second half of the fourteenth century the financing and accounting of this and of the other offices had become an exchequer matter.

In the course of the late Middle Ages, indeed by the mid fourteenth century, Westminster and London became the administrative capital

14 H.M. Colvin, *The History of the King's Works*, i–ii: *The Middle Ages* (London, 1963). The offices are discussed in vol. i. 161–227.

of the kingdom where the king's Council and the courts and offices outside the Household were almost invariably to be found. They formed what may justifiably be described as a bureaucracy with their hierarchies of officials, their demarcation of duties, their demands for proper authorizations and their voluminous records in the form of rolls and files. The men who worked there may equally justifiably be described as 'civil servants' – though the term came into use from the East India Company only in the nineteenth century. For a century before 1272 there had been some clerks who made a career of service in royal administration; in the fourteenth century the 'civil service' became a professional career for many clerks; and in the fifteenth century, remarkably quickly, it became a career for laymen as well as for clerics.[15] Most office clerks began their careers at the bottom of the office ladder, some as 'apprentices' to established clerks, and increasingly they spent their whole working life there, though few reached the most senior posts. They were often taken into the office because of family or birth-place connexions with senior clerks or ministers or the patronage of the king himself. They came in literate, perhaps with some training in writing documents and they then learned the skills of the office though it was rare for an office-trained clerk to become head of a major office. Some were men of even more education and experience, a few university men, who advanced immediately to senior posts and higher rewards.

The junior clerks were largely routine scribes but most clerks acquired professional skills by experience or training. They knew how to frame documents of all kinds with a precision which would stand up to professional scrutiny. Their work required a knowledge of Latin and French and increasingly of written English. They might compile books of model letters, make collections of fine phrases, even understand the *cursus* – how to compose modulated Latin prose. They learned how to handle the routine administration of their offices although decision-making was tightly defined. To the outsider the king's offices and courts were an expensive jungle, slow and tortuous, with fees and rewards to be paid at each stage. Clerks often sold their services as advisers and agents, writing petitions, obtaining the necessary documents, collecting annuities, and guiding their clients. This was important to them because most were not paid regular wages. Most received only annual liveries of clothes, occasional gifts of money for special services and grants of forfeited goods, minor offices or church benefices and pensions from the king. Their outlook became understandably mercenary, always on the look-out for clients

15 See in particular R.L. Storey, 'Gentlemen-bureaucrats' in *Profession, Vocation, and Culture in Later Medieval England*, ed. C.H. Clough (Liverpool, 1982), pp. 90–129.

and opportunities for gain. In the fourteenth century most clerks looked on the Church as a source of income, not as a vocation or career, and few took major or even minor orders. This culminated in the early fifteenth century in a rapid growth in the number of lay clerks. The exchequer was the prime example, probably because administration and management work had become a layman's career throughout the country, even chancery had to abandon its regulations requiring senior clerks to be clerics and laymen were soon to be found in almost every department. This was perhaps part of a certain disillusionment with the Church but more the result of a change in the attitude of laymen to service, career and administration.

There are some fifteenth century literary sources which give a cynical insight into government at Westminster and the fast life of London.[16] The theme of the poem 'London Lickpenny', perhaps by John Lydgate, is 'for lack of money, I could not speed' – without money there was no remedy to be obtained in the Westminster offices and nothing to be had from the merchants, hucksters and cooks that abounded in Westminster and London. Even the writer's hood was stolen and offered for sale in Cornhill. Thomas Hoccleve was a clerk in the privy-seal office for about 40 years who wrote some 13,000 lines of verse, the most interesting about himself. He tells about the hard life of a clerk, bent over the parchment and straining his eyes, and worrying about his future and his retirement. He was a pious man but, after waiting in vain for a benefice which would give him financial security, he married, had a breakdown and came back to work until shortly before he died. He tells about the pleasures of London, the taverns and cooks, the pretty girls, his civil-service dining club, the pleasure of taking a boat to work rather than walking. His theme also is often money; there is no ill that money cannot cure; if only his annuity was paid on time and he was not cheated by clients in the office. These are stories of disappointment. Other stories are of successful clerks who were good business men or rose to rich benefices, even to a deanery. It was a professional world of skilled men who understood the traditional, technical work of their offices and of government as a whole, who hired out their professional services, who schemed for rewards and promotion and gossiped about them, and who lived in a high-cost, commercial city full of temptations. It is a familiar story.

16 'London Lickpenny' is printed in *Historical Poems of the XIVth and XVth Centuries*, ed. R.H. Robbins (New York, 1959), pp. 130–4. Thomas Hoccleve's verses are printed in the *Early English Text Society – The Regement of Princes*, ed. F.J. Furnivall (72, 1897) and *The Minor Poems*, ed. F.J. Furnivall and I. Gollancz (61 and 73, 1892 and 1925). See also A.L. Brown, 'The privy seal clerks' for Hoccleve's career.

4

Royal Finance and Taxation*

Kings of the late Middle Ages were heavily dependent on revenue from taxation to carry on government. They could call on a large amount of unpaid service in the localities, many civil servants did not receive salaries, and gentlemen might perform tasks without wages in expectation of reward in other ways, but the king's Household, the defence of the borders, and, above all, foreign war demanded large sums of money, which could be raised only by taxation. And taxation required the assent of those who paid it, by the mid fourteenth century assent in parliament or convocation. Precise figures of revenue and expenditure are difficult to determine. There are voluminous financial records but they were not designed to give statistical information of the kind we expect today. Nothing that can be described strictly as a national balance sheet survives and probably none was prepared, but estimates of varying degrees of completeness and accuracy were produced from time to time. The most comprehensive is the statement ordered in 1433 by Ralph, Lord Cromwell, the new treasurer, to demonstrate the gravity of the financial situation, and there are others, less complete, from 1284, 1324, 1362–3, 1415–6 and 1421.[1] There had to be some

* There is no one, reliable source book of financial information. J.H. Ramsay used record material for the tables in his *A History of the Revenues of the Kings of England, 1066–1399* (Oxford, 1925) and for the financial summaries in his *Lancaster and York* (Oxford, 1892) but he did not fully understand the sources and his figures cannot be trusted. G.L. Harriss, *King, Parliament and Public Finance in Medieval England to 1369* (Oxford, 1975) is an excellent analytical study and there are scholarly works on particular topics, in particular B.P. Wolffe, *The Royal Demesne in English History* (London, 1971) dealing with the crown estate; J.F. Willard, *Parliamentary Taxes on Personal Property, 1290–1334* (Cambridge, Mass., 1934); and A. Steel, *The Receipt of the Exchequer, 1377–1485* (Cambridge, 1954).

1 The 1433 figures are in *Rot. Parl.*, iv. 432–9 – *Select Documents*, pp. 270–4; *EHD*, iv. 516–22 and are discussed in J.L. Kirby, 'The issues of the Lancastrian exchequer and Lord Cromwell's estimates of 1433', *BIHR* 24 (1951), 121–51. The others are in M.H. Mills, 'Exchequer agenda and estimates of revenue, Easter term, 1284', *EHR* 40 (1925), 229–34; T.F. Tout and D.M. Broome, 'A national balance sheet for 1362–3' *EHR* 39 (1924), 404–19-*Select Documents*, pp. 86–8; *EHD*, iv. 512–14; Harriss, *King, Parliament and Public Finance*, pp. 523–30 for 1324, 1342–43 and 1362–63; and *Procs. & Ords.*, ii. 172–80 and 312–15 for 1415–16 and 1421. Statements and estimates were probably made in other years and there are references to annual figures in 1338 and 1437 – *Select Documents*, pp. 47 and 275, but annual accounts were not prepared.

financial planning for example for a campaign, but kings tended to muddle through, relying heavily on credit and from time to time facing a financial crisis.

Revenue and Expenditure

Lord Cromwell's estimates of 1433 are a good starting-point to discuss the revenue. They give gross figures and then net figures after deduction of fees, annuities, repairs, and other costs paid locally. They were prepared with care, though they were intended to emphasize the bleakness of the situation facing Cromwell. Grouping his detailed figures and taking them to round pounds, his estimate of revenue was

		Gross £	Net £
1	Shire and other farms, fines, lands in the king's hands	13,711	6,873
2	Duchy of Cornwall and County of		
	Chester	3,553	162
	North and South Wales	2,238	1,061
	Ireland	2,340	(19 deficit)
	Duchy of Lancaster	4,953	2,408
	Aquitaine	808	77
	Calais	2,866	(9,065 deficit)
3	Hanaper, Mint and Exchanges	2,214	305
4	Other Revenues	612	262
	Total	33,295	11,148
5	Customs and Subsidies – average over three years	31,520	27,221
	Total	64,815	38,369

The outstanding features of these figures are, first, the small yield from traditional sources such as the shires and the courts – they were not sufficient to meet even the relatively low estimate of £13,000 for the costs of the boy king's Household – and, second, the importance of indirect taxation (the customs and subsidies). Direct taxes, normally the tenth and fifteenth which at this time produced on each levy about £34,000 from laypeople and £10,000–17,000 from the clergy, are not included because they were granted only for particular needs and were never regular taxes. Estimates from other years are different in detail but the broad pattern of revenue was the same throughout the late Middle Ages.

Expenditure was more variable but Cromwell's estimates give an indication of its scale. He estimated £13,678 for the Household and royal works, a much lower figure than normal; £8,047 for wages and rewards to senior officials, judges, and councillors, a figure inflated by the unusual salaries paid to councillors, £7,556 for annuities paid at the exchequer; £22,820 for the administration and defence of Ireland, the Scottish March, Gascony and Calais, more if war broke out with Scotland; £2,626 for embassies; £2,149 for other items. The total was £56,878 with nothing provided for continuing the war in France. A more normal Household or more building would have increased the total. Active defence of the Scottish and Calais Marches would have inflated it and a campaign would have required special taxation. Cromwell estimated that there was a debt of £164,814 in 1433 and this had increased to an estimated £372,000 by 1450, primarily because of the war in France.

This is the broad picture. We need to look more closely at revenue and in particular at taxation, the most productive source. The first item of revenue in the summary of Cromwell's estimates is made up of many small sums from a variety of sources. First the fixed shire farms (which had been reduced in 1284 from a nominal £10,000 to a little over £2,000 to take account of lands granted away by Edward I and his predecessors), increments and small rents rendered by the sheriffs. They included items such as payments made by the tenants of certain lands and the fines and amercements in the shire courts and in hundred courts not in private hands; the 'summonses of the Pipe and the Green Wax' – fines, amercements, and reliefs arising from proceedings in chancery, exchequer and the courts which the sheriffs were instructed to collect; and the income from lands temporarily in the king's hands, for example during minority or by forfeiture, or town farms which might be accounted for by sheriffs, escheators, bailiffs or keepers. The individual amounts were often small and collecting them and accounting for them meant a great deal of labour for local officials and for the exchequer. Part of the money received was spent locally in carrying out royal orders, for example to pay alms, maintain buildings, provide defences or weapons and pay annuities, and the cash yield in the exchequer probably never reached five figures in this period. Miss Mills estimated the entire gross shire revenues to be no more than £13–14,000 in 1284, while Strayer and Morris's figures for the first decade of Edward III's reign and the estimates of 1362–63 are several thousand pounds lower.[2]

2 Mills, 'Exchequer Agenda', p. 231; *Eng. Gov. at Work*, ii. 4–5 and 73–100.

The income from royal lands may seem surprisingly low but, apart from a few castles, manors, and hunting lodges, late-medieval kings did not possess large amounts of land. Land did come into their hands but they used it to endow their queens, provide for their families and reward service and support. Wolffe's conclusion was that 'the significance of the royal lands in the workings of English government . . . lay primarily in supporting the king's family. Next in importance they provided a cement of patronage, which, if prudently used, helped to bind together the political structure of the kingdom in loyal service to the head of state. Last of all, they made some intermittent, fluctuating and normally rather insignificant contributions to the current expenses of government.[3] The most striking example of this policy was setting up a patrimony for the king's eldest son by Henry III, Edward I, and Edward III which still makes him Earl of Chester, Prince of Wales and Duke of Cornwall. In 1433 the king was unmarried and the revenues from these lands came to him but if there had been a son of sufficient age this would have reduced the king's revenues. Edward II's queen, Isabella, and subsequent queens received substantial endowments made up to a considerable extent of the same lands. The king's younger sons, magnate supporters and loyal gentlemen also required to be endowed and rewarded in due measure. Contemporaries expected the king to be generous though they protested at royal extravagance and in the fifteenth century often proposed the resumption of grants. There was no opportunity for the king to build up a large estate in land. Death did however bring him a flow of land for custody during the minority of heirs or the vacancy of bishoprics and abbeys. In 1433 for example 2,000 marks of income under this first heading came from the farm of the lands of the Duke of Norfolk during his minority. War produced another source when lands belonging to alien religious houses were seized. These items produced a fluctuating but significant income, though always a small one by comparison with the proceeds of taxation.

The second heading of income in Cromwell's estimates could vary considerably. The incomes from Wales, Cornwall and Chester would often be the endowment of the heir to the throne; in time of rebellion, as under Henry IV, Wales might be a charge rather than a profit. Ireland, which had yielded a profit in the thirteenth century, was a steady drain on the king's revenue thereafter and the king's lieutenant had to be subvented.[4] The duchy of Lancaster had come into the king's hands in 1399 when the duke became king. Its revenues were kept separate from those of the kingdom and, though heavily

---

3 Wolffe, *Royal Demesne*, p. 65.
4 A.J. Otway-Ruthven, *A History of Medieval Ireland* (London, 1968), p. 147.

burdened with annuities and other charges, they did produce a surplus in the order of £6,000 a year during Henry V's reign. In 1433 however they were in large part reserved to carry out the provisions of Henry V's will and the amount available to the king was only £2,408.[5]

The third source of revenue was the profits of chancery, the mints and exchange, and the sums the courts themselves collected. Chancery produced the largest profits, normally between £1,000 and £2,000 after deducting costs, the others at most a few hundred pounds. And when charges, in particular annuities, had been deducted the net yield to the exchequer, as in 1433, might be only £200–£300[6].

These three 'regular' headings of income were small compared with the king's needs or his income from taxation and it is taxation which must be the major theme of this chapter because it was in this period that kings first persuaded their subjects to pay large sums, more or less continuously, towards the cost of government. Taxation itself was not new. Danegelds, scutages, tallages, aids and others taxes had been important sources of revenue in the past but from Edward I's reign taxation on a much larger scale became normal and its form changed. Henry III in 56 years received 10 scutages, 14 tallages and 4 taxes assessed on laymen's movable property. Edward I in 35 years received 4 scutages, 1 tallage, 9 taxes on laymen's movables and relatively large sums in customs duties. Moreover it has been estimated that while all Henry III's scutages produced about £15,000, Edward I's taxes on laymen's movables produced well over £500,000.[7] Here is a turning point in the history of the revenue and taxation, and of the history of consent to taxation.

The Customs and Subsidies*

In 1433 the largest item of regular income was the customs and subsidies, and this had been the case since the latter part of Edward I's reign. Customs were the 'ancient' duties on exports granted in 1275

5 R. Somerville, *History of the Duchy of Lancaster* (London, 1953), pp. 199–202.
6 N. Pronay, 'The hanaper under the Lancastrian Kings', *Proc. Leeds Philosophical and Literary Society* (Literary and Historical Section) 12 (1966–8), 73–86.
7 F.M. Powicke, *The Thirteenth Century* (Oxford, 1953), pp. 35–6. J.F. Willard, 'The taxes upon movables in the Reign of Edward I', *EHR* 28 (1913), 517–21.
* N.C.B. Gras, *The Early English Customs System* (Cambridge, Mass., 1918) is a documented but now old-fashioned study; *Finance and Trade under Edward III*, ed. G. Unwin (Manchester, 1918) and B. Wilkinson, *Studies in the Constitutional History of the Thirteenth and Fourteenth Centuries* (Manchester, 1937) are still useful; R.L. Baker, *The English Customs Service, 1307–1343*, American Phil. Soc. Trans., 51, (Philadelphia, 1961) is valuable; E. Power, *The Wool Trade in English Medieval History* (Oxford, 1941) is a deservedly famous survey; T.H. Lloyd, *The English Wool Trade in the Middle Ages* (Cambridge, 1977) is another valuable book which discusses the politics of the trade; and E.B. Fryde has written a number of important articles on the trade and on royal financial manipulation of it.

and 1303 and levied continuously thereafter without need for renewal. Subsidies were additional duties granted for short periods, though in practice from the mid fourteenth century they were continuous. The immediate history of the customs goes back to 1266 when Prince Edward was appointed by his father protector of first foreign and then native merchants and reached an agreement with them to levy duties on exports. These continued to be levied when Edward became king, but in 1275 they were replaced by new duties of half a mark on each sack (364 lb) of wool and each 300 (later 240) wool fells (skins with wool attached) and a mark on each last (200 hides) of leather, paid by all merchants, native or foreign. They were granted by the magnates and commons in the April parliament of 1275 at the request of the merchants, and behind this probably lies an agreement with the merchants to pay the duties in return for the re-opening of the export trade to Flanders. By far the largest yield came from wool, England's most valuable export. The income of course varied with the volume of the trade; it averaged over £11,000 between 1275 and 1291 and was even higher in the last two years of the reign.[8] Wool exports reached a peak in the mid fourteenth century, then declined, and the tax became obsolete in the sixteenth century when wool exports became minimal.[9] At first the 1275 custom was the 'new' custom but it acquired its traditional name, the 'great' and 'old' customs, the *magna et antiqua custuma*, in 1303 when Edward I negotiated another agreement, this time with foreign merchants. They agreed to pay an extra 50 per cent on the 1275 duties, new duties on wine, cloth and wax, and three pence in the pound sterling on all other exports and imports in return for a charter, the *Carta Mercatoria*, which gave them freedom to trade, regulated their status and rights in England and exempted them from some local taxes.[10] English merchants were summoned to an assembly at York and invited to make a similar agreement but refused for they had nothing comparable to gain. The new duty, called the *nova* or *parva custuma*, was levied continuously, save between the Ordinances of 1311 and Edward II's recovery of power in 1322, through the late Middle Ages and long after. A third duty was amalgamated with these in 1347 when a Great Council imposed a duty on exported cloth on the ground that the king should not lose because wool exports had fallen and cloth exports had risen. There were three rates, 14, 21 and 28 pence for natives, 21, 31 and 42 pence for foreigners on each 'cloth of assize', approximately 24 yards long and 1.5–2 yards wide, depending on whether the cloth was 'in grain' (wholly dyed with grain, that is

---

8 Lloyd, *Wool Trade*, pp. 62–3 and 99.
9 Export figures for wool and cloth from the customs' accounts are tabulated in E.M. Carus-Wilson and O. Coleman, *England's Export Trade, 1275–1547* (Oxford, 1963).
10 The text is in Gras, *English Customs*, pp. 259–64.

scarlet dye), 'in half grain' (dyed partly with grain) or 'without grain' (using only a cheaper dye). Trade in cloth grew rapidly in the second half of the century and came to be much more valuable than wool, but the tax yield fell because the cloth rates were relatively light – perhaps 4–4.5 cloths contained the wool in one sack.[11] In the estimates of 1433 these duties were described as the wool custom and the *parva custuma*, and their gross annual yield averaged over three years was £6,942 in a gross annual yield from all customs and subsidies of £31,520.

Much the larger share of the duties in 1433 came from extensions of the customs, from the subsidy on wool and from tunnage and poundage on wine and all other commodities. The history of the subsidies, particularly that on wool, is complicated and is inextricably bound up with the efforts by Edward I after 1294 and by Edward III after 1336, both beginning ambitious continental campaigns, to exploit the wool trade for financial and diplomatic reasons. Wool was seized and sold, the trade manipulated, and new duties imposed. Edward I in 1294 ordered the seizure (prisage) of all wool, skins and hides with the intention of selling them abroad, repaying the producers and cutting out the merchants, but he was quickly persuaded to abandon this in favour of a duty of three marks on each sack of wool granted by the merchants. This duty, called abusively the *maltolt* or 'unjust exaction', produced about £110,000 in three years, but baronial opposition in 1297 forced Edward to lift it and promise never to levy it again without the assent of the community. He was never able to propose its resumption, and Edward II was in no stronger position. In 1317 the merchants agreed and the magnates accepted a duty on wool, skins and leather, half a mark from natives, ten shillings from aliens, for one year *as a loan* and in 1322 a subsidy of half a mark on wool and skins and a mark on hides from natives and double from aliens was granted for one year apparently by an assembly of merchants. Compared with these, Edward III's taxes on wool were enormous. They began modestly with a forced loan in the form of a duty in 1327, and a plan to make exporters pay a second time the customs on wool, skins and leather exported between Michaelmas, 1331 and 1332, postponed for a year because of opposition, and finally changed to a subsidy of 10s. on wool and skins, and 20s. on hides granted by merchants for a year from May, 1333, which produced over £14,000. With the beginning of the French war in 1337 Edward began to think of much larger sums. By the end of 1340 he had spent about £400,000 in the Netherlands in payments to his allies and in war expenses and the subsidy on wool, which was effectively continuous from 1336, was part of schemes

---

11 Harriss, *King, Parliament and Public Finance*, pp. 457–9 discusses the imposition of the custom; Carus-Wilson and Coleman, *Export Trade*, define it and tabulate the exports; and E.M. Carus-Wilson, *Medieval Merchant Venturers* (London, 1954) writes about the trade.

designed to raise these enormous sums[12]. Ready cash was obtained by loans from Italian financiers and a group of English merchants who were repaid mainly by exploiting wool, by seizing the crop, controlling the trade and from subsidies. Until the early 1350s the trade was manipulated in a remarkable and unique way. For example, in 1337 a 'contract' was made with some English merchants giving them authority to acquire 30,000 sacks of wool for the king's use from wool producers, half on six months', half on a year's credit. Producers were safeguarded by fixing minimum prices, and the wool was to be sold in the Netherlands which had been starved of it for a year, and the profit shared with the king. The merchants agreed to lend the king £200,000 in instalments. The contract however turned sour. Producers were unwilling to surrender their wool; there was smuggling; both the king and the merchants were greedy; and only some 10,000 sacks reached the Netherlands where the king's agents, after haggling with the merchants over the loans, (legally) seized it, mismanaged the sale and issued promissory notes which were only slowly honoured and often discounted. A series of unusual levies followed; and through the 1340s there were a number of agreements with companies of English merchants to advance money in return for trading advantages, agreements which led to a number of long-remembered bankruptcies. This is only a small part of an astonishing story of royal persistence and financial naivety, but what is also striking is the ability of the king's administration to handle the various schemes.

It was against this background that the subsidy became a regular tax and the largest regular source of royal income. The principle was simple, increase the rates of duty on wool, skins and leather and collect the increase by the traditional method, and from 1336 this was done continuously. For some 20 years there was contention about the burden of these subsidies and who bore it and about who should grant them. From 1355 it was accepted that they must be granted in parliament and in effect parliament granted them continuously, though normally for a few years at a time (pp. 226–8). In 1398, 1415 and 1453 they were granted for the king's life and they were collected from the beginning of each reign, receiving retrospective authorization from parliament. They had become in effect a normal part of the king's revenue, no longer associated with war expenditure and therefore included in Cromwell's estimates. The rates varied but normally were about £2 on each sack of wool and £4 on each last of leather, with differential rates for natives and foreigners. A second subsidy, tunnage and poundage, also became a regular tax by the end of the

12 E.B. Fryde, 'The financial resources of Edward III in the Netherlands, 1337–40', *Revue Belge de Philologie et d'Histoire* 45 (1967), 1142. The story is told also by Lloyd, *Wool Trade*, and by E.B. Fryde in a number of articles.

fourteenth century.[13] It began with a number of intermittent levies, the first in 1345, on exports and imports to provide protection for English shipping; once the merchants themselves were to hire troops, but normally the money was granted to enable the king to provide 'warships'. The first true tunnage and poundage was granted by the Council in 1347, 2s. on each tun (252 gallons) of wine, 6d. in the pound value of other goods, and 2s. on each sack of wool; more normally at this time it was granted by the merchants on wine and all other goods save wool, skins and leather. In 1372 the burgess members of parliament met with the lords after the county knights had been sent home, and granted a duty of 2s. on the tun and 6d. in the pound for one year to provide protection at sea; in 1373 the lords and all the Commons renewed the duty when they made their grant of direct taxation and the wool subsidy; and thereafter it was always granted in the same manner as other taxes. The connection with naval defence was maintained for a time and the duty was not continuous until the 90s, but it then became another regular tax, voted in parliament, at rates which varied slightly from period to period. In the estimates of 1433 its gross yield was £6,707 in the total gross yield from customs and subsidies of £31,520.

The detailed story of the subsidies is a confusing one which is still not completely clarified, but it is the development as a whole which is significant. Edward III had succeeded in persuading his subjects away from their earlier stand against any *maltolt* to granting regular subsidies which raised sums far in excess of any other source of revenue. The issue became not whether subsidies should be granted, but at what rate. The average yield from all customs and subsidies in the last 20 years of his reign with the subsidy on wool at 43s. 4d. was in the order of £70,000 a year. The rates fluctuated thereafter, sometimes a little lower, often a little higher, with an extra levy on foreign merchants, but the yields dropped to slightly under £50,000 a year in the reigns of Richard II and Henry IV and V, and to a little over £30,000 in the reign of Henry VI, partly because of disruption of trade, partly because the export of wool declined drastically. Cloth exports increased considerably but the subsidy on these was low and did not compensate for the loss of wool revenue.

Customs and subsidies required officers to levy them, not over a short period as in the case of direct taxes, but continuously and it is a testimony to the governability of England and its literacy that machinery was quickly set up in 1275 to do this, and was expanded to handle

13 Harriss, *King, Parliament and Public Finance*, pp. 459–65.

the later taxes.[14] Basically, in each of the 10 to 15 major ports there were two or more collectors, a controller, searchers, a tronager, clerks, porters, boatmen and others responsible for the port and the surrounding coast and minor harbours; later there were normally three sets of collectors and controllers handling the old and new customs, the cloth custom, the subsidies and tunnage and poundage. The collectors were usually substantial local merchants appointed by the king, though sometimes chosen locally. They were responsible for assessing and collecting the duties, issuing letters under the cocket seal (a two-faced seal of which they and the controller each held a half) testifying that a cargo had been assessed, keeping detailed written records and accounting for their receipts in the exchequer. They were paid little or nothing by the king – probably much of their work was done by their clerks who were paid – but there were no doubt hidden advantages and profits to be had from the office. The controller was responsible for checking on the collectors by writing a second, counter roll of assessments. Under Edward I the office was normally in the hands of foreign bankers who were being repaid their loans from the customs, and it was not until the 1330s that it was regularly filled. It was then a salaried post held by a local man of less substance than the collectors or by a royal clerk or servant for whom it was an 'office of profit' performed by deputy. The searchers boarded ships and searched for contraband and perhaps also for precious metal or papal bulls coming in illicitly; the tronager weighed goods on the tron or beam; both were salaried royal appointments. In the major ports there was therefore a regular customs staff, sometimes with a permanent customs house. The system worked reasonably well though there was smuggling, evasion and corruption and fees and favours were probably expected at every turn in typical medieval and early modern fashion. But bearing in mind how much the system depended on local, unpaid support, it is surprising that so much was collected, so regularly.

Direct Taxation*

By far the commonest form of direct taxation was the levy on movable property. In England this type of tax goes back to the Saladin tithe of

14 M.H. Mills, 'The collectors of customs' in *Eng. Gov. at Work*, ii. 168–200 gives a clear guide to the work of the officials and Baker, *English Customs Service* traces the history of the customs' administration to 1343. See also A. Steel, 'Collectors of customs of Newcastle on Tyne in the reign of Richard II' in *Studies Presented to Sir Hilary Jenkinson*, ed. J. Conway Davies (London, 1957), pp. 390–413 and O. Coleman, 'The collectors of customs in London under Richard II' in *Studies in London History*, ed. A.E.J. Hollaender and W. Kellaway (London, 1969), pp. 181–94.

* There are general discussions of direct taxation in S.K. Mitchell, *Studies in Taxation under John and Henry III* (New Haven, 1914) and *Taxation in Medieval England*, ed. S. Painter (New Haven, 1951), and in Harriss, *King, Parliament, and Public Finance*. This section relies heavily on Willard, *Parliamentary Taxes*, a detailed but exciting book. Willard tabulated the yields of taxes on movables, county by county, under the three Edwards in articles in *EHR* 28–30 (1913–5). M.W. Beresford, *Lay Subsidies and Poll Taxes* (Canterbury, 1963) is a useful, brief, account of the records of the taxes.

Henry II's reign, and every subsequent king obtained grants of this type. Richard I had one, John two and Henry III four. Edward I had nine – in 1275, 1283, 1290, 1294, 1295, 1296, 1297, 1301 and 1306 and the succession of grants in the 1290s marked a turning point. Taxes on movables became frequent though never regular thereafter, and always granted to meet some specified need. Until 1334 they were genuine levies on the assessed value of movable property. All laymen, male and female, free and unfree, save at one extreme the king and his immediate family and at the other the poorest, those who owned less than a stated minimum of movable property, normally about ten shillings, should have paid, and so should clerics on their temporalities, the property which was not taxed when the clergy granted similar taxes in convocation. Lepers and a few groups such as the inhabitants of the Cinque Ports who were held to render naval service were also excused. These are necessarily generalizations for in this early period the regulations varied from levy to levy. The administration is impressive. When a levy was granted the exchequer and perhaps the Council appointed commissioners to assess and collect it in each county or part of a county. They were usually natives of the county, laymen, often knights or gentlemen, assisted and supervised by royal clerks. They were sworn, given their instructions, and they then appointed or had chosen local men from each hundred or vill and town to act as sub-taxers. The latter then went from house to house assessing the value of the movable property and entering the details, often listing the goods assessed, in duplicate on rolls from which briefer county rolls were prepared, also in duplicate. The levy was different in towns and counties. For a start it was often, and came to be always at different rates, a higher for towns and lands of the ancient demesne, and a lower for the remainder of the counties – a tenth and a fifteenth came to be traditional. This may have been due to the greater prosperity of the towns but it is more likely that the towns and the ancient demesne which had both been open to tallage at the king's will were more at the king's mercy.[15] The assessment was also different. Land and buildings were everywhere excluded, and in rural areas it was 'the larger domestic animals (horses, cows and draft animals), grain, and some peas and beans' which were usually assessed.[16] Household goods and tools, and food stored for the house-

15 The choice of towns to pay the higher rate was left to the taxers and their list was slightly different from that of towns sending members of parliament. J.F. Willard, 'Taxation boroughs and parliamentary boroughs, 1294–1336' in *Historical Essays in Honour of James Tait*, ed. J.G. Edwards, V.H. Galbraith and E.F. Jacob (Manchester, 1933), pp. 417–35. Ancient demesne was land which had been held by the king in the past but had been granted away. Henry II and his successors exploited this to tax it by tallage. Wolffe, *Royal Demesne*, pp. 24–6.

16 Willard, *Parliamentary Taxes*, p. 75.

hold's own use were ignored. Military equipment and at first sight surprisingly the jewels, clothes and plate of the gentry were also excused. The principle behind this, Willard suggests, was the same as in the amercement clauses of Magna Carta; a man's status and livelihood, his plough, his weapons and his status objects must be protected. The assessment in the towns is more of a puzzle; household goods and articles of personal use apart from the bed and clothes of the man and his wife were taxed; tools of trade were not normally taxed but merchandise sometimes was; probably a merchant's wealth was merely roughly and favourably assessed.

By any standard of equity this cannot have produced a fair assessment of wealth; the less well to do paid proportionately much more than the rich. Land and income were not being effectively taxed. Landowners of course could claim that they were burdened by service in other ways, and that the burden on the poor was tempered. The overwhelming proportion of women clearly paid nothing; normally only the wealthy and widows had property to assess, and many men, probably the great majority also escaped. There are no trustworthy figures for the total population upon which to make an accurate judgement, but there are pointers, for example lists of those who contributed to local taxes may contain many more names than those on the king's assessment rolls. In Leicester for example, local tallage rolls in the early fourteenth century often have 300–400 names while the king's subsidy rolls contain only from 73 to 190. In 1332 the roll of the tenth has 73 but the roll of the tenth in 1336 which was levied as a lump sum on the town and not by individual assessment has 445 names.[17] The 372 or so who escaped in 1332 may have been poor, but some probably escaped because the assessors often used conventional valuations which meant deliberate under-assessment. It may well have often been only those with a modest degree of comfort who paid regularly. In the counties, where a cow might be valued at four or five shillings and an ox a little more, the man with over ten shillings of property would not be poor by contemporary standards. But the fundamental inequity of the tax remained.

This tax down to 1332 is another example of how governable England had become. It involved hundreds of men in the localities investigating and valuing the property of their fellows, writing this down in duplicate and finally collecting and handing over the money that they had collected. Presiding over the whole operation from 1290 was the exchequer and the Council, the exchequer showing its customary doggedness and attention to paperwork. The detail of the levies

17 *Ibid.*, p. 177. J.R. Maddicott, *The English Peasantry and the Demands of the Crown, 1294-1341*, Past and Present Supplement i (1975) discusses the burdens of taxation and purveyance.

also gives an insight into contemporary *mores*. For a start, as they became more frequent, people compensated by paying less. This is particularly striking in the 1290s. The fifteenth of 1290 produced over £116,000 but in 1301 the same rate produced a little under £50,000 and the heavier ninth of 1297, the year of a political crisis which Edward mishandled, only £34,419. From 1334 the tenth and fifteenth produced a composition of some £38,000. Medieval people had their own standards. The king's taxes were not normally robbed by highwaymen, but the assessment and collection was riddled with entertainments, bribes and corruption. Many people who might have been assessed seem to have escaped and many benefited from conventional valuations and under-assessment; this is perhaps on a par with juries refusing to convict of capital crimes (p. 138). There is also evidence that the sub-taxers benefited by being under-assessed by chief taxers, probably as a form of reward for their unpaid service. The villagers of Cuxham in Oxfordshire learned to entertain the assessors well and pay a courtesy to the chief assessor; their assessment fell by almost four-fifths between 1294 and 1295 and there are other examples of the same sort of thing.[18] There are also a good many examples and complaints of corruption, of local collectors filching money and making false returns. The government realized this and a number of investigations were made into corruption, extortion and under-assessment, and in 1334 a new and simpler method of assessment was introduced following complaints about corruption in the levy of 1332. An abbot or prior or other senior churchman from the county was appointed with a royal clerk to negotiate with the commonalty of each town, hundred and vill, whatever unit was traditional, on how much their area should pay, as long as the sum was not less than the assessment of 1332. The local community itself had then to decide how the money was to be raised. If no agreement could be reached the taxers were to assess the amount. The yield was £37,430 – it should have been £38,000 but three northern counties were exempted this year – and thereafter whenever a lay subsidy was granted until 1623 the rate was a fifteenth and a tenth – though a half levy or more than one might be granted, and the yield and the division of the burden was that of 1334. No new assessment was necessary and in each locality traditional ways of raising the money grew up, for example assessing the holders of particular properties with fixed sums. The tax was now relatively simple for the exchequer and local men, now yeomen rather than gentlemen, to collect. The total yield however declined because exemptions were granted and because attempts were made to assist impoverished areas.

18 P.D.A. Harvey, *A Medieval Oxfordshire Village: Cuxham, 1240–1400* (London, 1965), pp. 105–8.

In the 1350s fines for breaches of the Statute of Labourers and later fines on fugitives and felons were applied to ease the burden on villages hit by the Black Death, and from 1433 a rebate of £4,000 (increased to £6,000 in 1445) was granted to be shared by impoverished towns and villages. The yield was then about £30,000.[19]

There is some evidence, for example that from Leicester already cited, that the lump sum demanded from a town or village was distributed by local people among more, and therefore poorer people. In Kent the numbers contributing rose inexplicably from 11,016 in 1334 to about 17,000 in 1338.[20] Even so, the tenth and fifteenth was unpopular among the relatively wealthy who served as members of parliament, though this was probably basically dislike of any taxation, particularly the kind they had recently paid, rather than dislike of the weight or inequality of the tax. No tax on movables was granted between 1357 and 1372 and subsidies on trade, which had so recently been much criticized, were granted instead. Then in the 70s a number of new forms of tax were tried to make direct taxation more palatable.

The first was the parish tax granted in parliament in March 1371. The intention was to raise £50,000 by a flat levy of 22s. 3d. on each parish with the impossible proviso that richer parishes should assist poorer.[21] Within a month it was discovered that the number of parishes had been grossly overestimated and the bishops were asked to supply true figures. On the basis of these a Great Council in June, to which some who had attended the parliament were summoned by name, increased the levy to 116s. from each parish. Commissioners were appointed in each county to assess with the help of six or four from each parish, what each parishioner should pay on the basis of the value of his land and goods. Within a year more than £49,000 had been collected, more than the tenth and fifteenth but more troublesome to collect, and, because parishes varied in size and wealth, no more equitable. It was never repeated.

In 1377 another type of direct tax, a poll-tax or head tax, was tried, and variants were granted in 1379 and 1380. The first, granted in parliament in February 1377, was at a flat rate of a groat (4d.) from every man and woman over 14 save genuine beggars. Commissioners in each county and in major towns conducted what amounted to a census through village constables, town officials, and good men of each locality, preparing lists of the inhabitants, and collecting the tax.

19 Beresford, *Lay Subsidies*, pp. 10–11.
20 C.W. Chalkin and H.A. Hanley, 'The Kent lay subsidy of 1334/5' in *Documents illustrative of Medieval Kentish Society* (Kent Arch. Society, Records Branch, 18, 1964), p. 58.
21 *Rot. Parl.*, ii. 303–4 – *Select Documents*, pp. 90–1. The heavy taxation of the decade before 1381 is documented and discussed in E.B. Fryde's introduction to C. Oman, *The Great Revolt of 1381* (new ed., London, 1969) and some of the documents relating to it are printed in translation in R.B. Dobson, *The Peasants' Revolt of 1381* (London, 1970).

It was readily done; 1,355,201 people were enrolled and should have paid £22,586.13s.8d., much less than a tenth and a fifteenth, and most was quickly collected. In May 1379 a second and much more elaborate poll-tax designed to relate the burden to status and wealth was granted in parliament. All men and women over 16 save beggars were to be assessed; the minimum payment was again a groat but married couples were to pay no more unless they belonged to grades which were taxed more heavily. These ranged for example from dukes (who were assessed at ten marks), through earls and widowed countesses (£4), barons and widowed baronesses (£2), knights (£1), judges (£5) – a heavy sum comparatively as were the levies on all lawyers, the mayor of London (£4), serjeants and franklins (40–80d.), down to pleaders (6d.). It seems a comparatively equitable tax but the total assessment was only £19,304. The third poll-tax granted in parliament in November, 1380 was much heavier and much less equitable. It was designed to raise 100,000 marks – though only £44,843 was assessed, and was basically the 1377 tax at triple the rate. Everyone over the age of 15 save beggars was to pay three groats (12d.) but in each township the rich were to help the poor save that no one was to pay more than £1 and no married couple less than one groat. Two-thirds was to be levied by the following 27 January and the remainder by June. It was in every way more burdensome than a tenth and fifteenth and the possibilities of sharing the burden within a township must have varied considerably. In general it gave an advantage to the richer who had granted it at the expense of the poorer. The striking result was that many fewer heads were counted than in 1377, a third less, even when commissioners were appointed to check the first return, and the yield by June, 1381 was about the same as that of a tenth and fifteenth, about 83 per cent of the assessment, which in turn was a third less than envisaged. This poll-tax was the immediate cause of the great revolt which broke out in the south-east in June 1381, and it ended the period of experiment with new direct taxes. The men of property who sat in parliament had failed to shift some of their comparatively light burden to the shoulders of others.

In addition to these major, high-yielding taxes there was a miscellany of lesser taxes, some of which deserve to be mentioned briefly. The commonest taxes in Henry III's reign had been scutage and tallage, and these continued into the early fourteenth century but they had lost their meaning and value. Scutage had traditionally been paid by tenants-in-chief by military service after a campaign to which they had not sent men or paid a fine, but by the reign of Edward I feudal military service meant much less, the quotas had been cut to a fraction of what they had once been, and armies were now composed predominantly of paid men. Henry III's last scutage had been in 1257 and with Edward I's reign a new and puzzling phase in its history began.[22] It was demanded some time after the campaigns of 1277, 1282, 1300, 1303, 1310 and 1327 for which feudal service had been summoned, and at the rate of two marks or two pounds from each knight's fee on the *old* assessment, perhaps 6,500 fees. The exchequer tried to ignore claims that service had been performed or a fine paid, and to make scutage a general tax on the knight's fee, pursuing the policy doggedly for 60 years, at first through the sheriffs and after 1314 through county collectors with orders to hold inquisitions to obtain information about fees, many of which were now subdivided. Tenants-in-chief did not object to the old assessment when they were collecting scutage from their tenants, but they were able to resist the new policy and scutage could be collected readily only when fees were in the king's hands or service had not been performed. It is puzzling why an unpopular policy which required so much effort and yielded such trivial sums, £400 in one case, was pursued until the beginning of Edward III's reign.

The king also possessed the feudal right to an aid to ransom his body, knight his eldest son, and marry his eldest daughter – without consent.[23] The first was never required, but the second and third were exercised in 1302, 1346 and 1401, years when any income was welcome. The yields were only £6,832, £9,003 and less than £2,000 respectively. Feudal taxation was now an unpopular anachronism.

Tallage was a levy by prerogative right on the ancient demesne and the towns and required no consent.[24] It was levied only in 1304 and 1312, on both occasions probably because no tax would have been granted. The former produced £2,862, the latter was resisted by London and was apparently abandoned. Edward III ordered a tallage to be taken in 1332, but withdrew it when parliament granted a tenth and a fifteenth and, though it remained a threatening memory, it was never taken again. The tax on movables had outdated it.

There were also a few more general taxes intended to overcome the defects of the tenth and fifteenth. In March 1340 the lords and commons granted a unique tax; the ninth sheaf, fleece and lamb for two years – in practice collected in cash; a ninth of the movable goods of citizens and burgesses; and a fifteenth from others who did not live in a settled community. This was granted only in return for promises by Edward III embodied in statutes but the yield was only £38,274, almost

22 H.M. Chew, 'Scutage under Edward I' and 'Scutage in the fourteenth century', *EHR* 37 (1922), 321–36 and 38 (1923), 19–41.
23 M. Prestwich, *War, Politics and Finance under Edward I* (London, 1972), p. 184; Harriss, *King, Parliament, and Public Finance*, p. 415; J.H. Ramsay, *Lancaster and York* (Oxford, 1892), i, 152.
24 On tallage see Mitchell, *Taxation*.

the same as a tenth and fifteenth. It had been granted with reluctance and collected with difficulty, and it was not repeated. Direct taxes on the lands and incomes of the wealthier members of society were granted in parliament in several fifteenth-century parliaments, each levy different in detail.[25] The richer landowners who contributed proportionately little to the tax on movables were accepting that their main source of wealth should be taxed but the assessments were not realistic and the yields only from £1,000 and £9,000. An equitable reassessment of the tax burden was not being seriously contemplated.

Clerical Taxation*

The history of direct taxation of the clergy follows a pattern similar to that of the laity. The clergy had paid taxes to the pope and the king before 1272 but the reign of Edward I, and in particular the 1290s, was the first period of heavy, sustained clerical taxation, and it provoked a confrontation between the king and the Church in 1297 as dramatic as that in the same year with the lay magnates. The outcome was the same. The clergy were reluctant to grant taxes in the early fourteenth century, yet by the early years of Edward III's reign clerical taxation became common and the machinery of consent became established in a form which lasted in essence until the late seventeenth century when separate taxation of the clergy ceased. Clerical taxation raised special problems because the clergy regarded themselves as a separate order, owing obedience to both the king and the pope, and not subject to the decisions of laymen on matters spiritual – including taxes on their 'spiritualities', the property or income related to their spiritual duties. This offered great scope for debate and resistance and though the king won his battle to tax the clergy frequently, the taxes came to be granted, not in parliament as the king would have wished, but in

25 On the ninth of 1340 see Harriss, *King, Parliament and Public Finance*. On the 15th-century income taxes see *Calendar of Fine Rolls, 1399–1405*, pp. 251–64 – *Select Documents*, pp. 213–14, H.L. Gray, 'Incomes from land in England in 1436', *EHR* 49 (1934), 607–39 and T.B. Pugh and C.D. Ross, 'The English baronage and the income tax of 1436', *BIHR* 26 (1953), 1–28.

* The history of clerical taxation has to be pursued in a number of studies. H.S. Deighton, 'Clerical taxation by consent, 1279–1301', *EHR* 68 (1953), 161–92; J.H. Denton, *Robert Winchelsey and the Crown 1294–1313* (Cambridge, 1980); W.E. Lunt, 'Clerical tenths levied in England by papal authority during the reign of Edward II' in *Anniversary Essays in Mediaeval History* (to C.H. Haskins), ed. C.H. Taylor and J.L. LaMonte (Boston, Mass., 1929), pp. 157–82; M.V. Clarke, *Medieval Representation and Consent* (London, 1936), pp. 15–32; and A.K. McHardy, 'Clerical taxation in fifteenth-century England: The clergy as agents of the crown' in *The Church and Patronage in the Fifteenth Century*, ed. R.B. Dobson (Gloucester, 1984), pp. 168–92. More generally see W.E. Lunt, *Financial Relations of the Papacy with England to 1327* and *Financial Relations of the Papacy with England 1327–1534* (Cambridge, Mass., 1939 and 1962).

church councils called convocations of the two provinces of Canterbury and York, and levied by clerical collectors appointed by the bishops. Ironically, where the king won, the pope lost. Both Edward I and II took considerable advantage of the pope's right to tax the English clergy by receiving or sharing taxes he imposed, but by the end of Edward III's reign lay attitudes to the Papacy had changed. It was no longer acceptable to the king or the laity that the pope should tax without royal permission; by and large direct papal taxation ceased; and the Papacy had to rely for income from England on payments such as 'services' and annates on benefices provided by the pope.

In the first half of Edward I's reign the clergy contributed direct taxes more often than the laity, taxes either granted by the pope or granted in provincial church councils in the form of tenths on clerical income. It was in the mid 1290s, when Edward was desperate for money for the war in France and Scotland, that the great confrontation with the Church took place. It began with the seizures of wool belonging to both clergy and laity and of the proceeds of earlier papal taxation held by the Church. Then in 1294 Edward browbeat the clergy in a national church council into granting him half their income for one year, levied on the basis of the valuation made in 1291 for Pope Nicholas IV. The levy amounted to about £105,000 and more than 75 per cent was paid within a year. In 1295 Edward summoned his so-called 'model' parliament at Westminster in November and for the first time the lower clergy were represented. Bishops were ordered by the *premunientes* clause in their own personal writs of summons to have the dean of their cathedral chapter and the archdeacons of their diocese attend in person along with one proctor on behalf of the chapter and two of the clergy of the diocese (pp. 205–6). In parliament the laity granted an eleventh and a seventh, the clergy reluctantly granted a tenth. The lower clergy were again represented in the next parliament, at Bury St Edmunds in November 1296, and a chronicler records that they met in four groups – archbishops and bishops or their proctors; abbots, priors and other regular clergy; deans and archdeacons; and the proctors of the lower clergy, an arrangement also known in church councils of that period.[26] The clergy were asked for taxation but it was already known that Pope Boniface VIII had issued a bull *Clericis laicos* forbidding any lay taxation of the Church without papal consent under pain of excommunication, and a grant was postponed without any decision being reached. A clerical council in January 1297 heard the bull read out and a grant was refused. The king's response was to outlaw the clergy and seize their goods. He offered to restore his protection to individuals on payment of a fine of

26 Bartholomew Cotton, *Historia Anglicana*, ed. H.R. Luard (Rolls Series, 1859), pp. 314–15.

the equivalent of a fifth of their income and many submitted. A reconciliation of sorts was made with Archbishop Winchelsey in July 1297 because the political situation demanded it and because the pope was beginning to modify his position to permit a king to seek financial aid from his clergy if he believed his realm to be in danger. Edward continued to demand taxation but Canterbury and York church councils in August did not recognize a danger and he simply ordered the collection of a fifth. In November the threat from the Scots led to a change of mind and the two church councils granted a tenth and a fifth to the king in his necessity – to be levied by clerical not lay collectors and with some modifications to ease the burden on poorer clergy. The crisis was over but this was the last clerical tax Edward I obtained from the English Church. He did receive several tenths in and after 1301 but these were collected by order of the pope without any form of consent. The extent of the clergy's financial contribution is shown by Professor Prestwich's estimate that over his whole reign Edward probably received some £540,000 from direct lay taxes and some £340,000 from the clergy; in the years 1294 to 1297 alone some £150,000 and £130,000 respectively. When all their contributions are taken into account, including their share of direct lay taxation, the clergy probably paid even more than this, possibly even as much as the laity.[27]

The legacy of these disputes lasted until the 1330s. Edward II had to rely heavily on papal grants of clerical tenths though he did obtain two grants in parliaments and two in church councils; and in the first decade of Edward III's reign the old clerical fears and assertions were still being expressed. Both kings would have preferred to obtain their grants of clerical taxation in parliament and representatives of the lower clergy were summoned to most of Edward II's parliaments and to every parliament from 1334. Ironically, it was in the 1330s that the attempt to tax the clergy in parliament was abandoned and the lower clergy soon ceased to attend parliament in significant numbers (p. 206). Clerical taxes were now granted in the two provincial councils, called convocations, often summoned at or about the times that parliament met. The normal tax was the tenth levied on the valuation of spiritualities prepared for Pope Nicholas IV in 1291. At first this was worth about £21,000 but, as with lay taxes, the assessment was reduced and by the fifteenth century the yield was somewhat between £10,000 and £17,000 – the precise figure is uncertain. A working distinction between spiritualities and temporalities was devised. Spiritualities, sprirtual income, meant effectively 'the whole of the income appertaining to parish churches'. Temporalities were 'the

---

27 Prestwich, *War, Politics and Finance*, p. 191. Denton, *Winchelsey*, pp. 297–301 gives a higher estimate.

baronies, manors and lay tenements belonging for the most part to prelates and religious institutions' and were taxed as part of the lay taxes on movables granted in parliament and so too was clerical property acquired after the valuation of 1291.[28] This division raised problems and the exchequer had to hear evidence and decide under which levy a particular property or income was to be taxed, but collection was always in the hands of clerics appointed by the bishop of each diocese. The usual voluminous written records were generated and accounts were rendered in the exchequer.

From the early years of Edward III's reign direct taxation of the clergy became as common as direct taxation of the laity, indeed the convocation of Canterbury, for example in Henry VI's reign, became more amenable than parliament. The normal tax was the tenth based on the 1291 assessment but the clergy shared the burden of the poll taxes of 1377–81 and in the fifteenth century granted several poll taxes and other forms of tax. They were apparently more concerned than the laity to spread the burden more fairly. Probably clerical tenths raised about half the amount raised by lay tenths and fifteenths. When the Commons in 1380 insisted on the clergy paying a third of the poll-tax burden, their judgement was well-founded.[29]

Loans and Credit Finance*

So far this has been a discussion of revenue and taxation in terms of cash yields, but to think of late-medieval finance in these terms alone is quite misleading. Taxes came in slowly, money was often required at short notice or in large amounts for a campaign, and every king relied in large measure on loans and credit. Royal finance was a hand-to-mouth business. The first three Edwards relied heavily on loans from Italian firms of financiers who were repaid by allocating them revenues from customs and subsidies or direct taxes or by schemes involving the export of wool. Edward I's debts to the Riccardi of Lucca amounted to some £392,000 in the period 1272–94; they largely financed his Welsh wars; and the 'old' custom of 1275 was continuously pledged to them in repayment. When the French war

---

28 Denton, *Winchelsey*, p. 57. The income from spiritualities was about double that of temporalities. There is a table of the diocesan valuations of 1291 in W. Stubbs, *The Constitutional History of England* (4th ed., Oxford, 1896) ii. 580.

29 *Rot. Parl.*, iii. 90.

* There is a very informed survey of loans by E.B. Fryde 'The Royal Credit System' in *The Cambridge Economic History of Europe*, ed. M.M. Postan *et al.* (Cambridge, 1963), iii. 451–72. K.B. McFarlane, 'Loans to the Lancastrian kings: the problem of inducement', *Cambridge Hist. J.* 9 (1947), 51–68 argued that most loans were made for profit but this has been seriously qualified by G.L. Harriss, 'Aids, loans and benevolences', *Hist. J.* 6 (1963), 1–19 and 'Cardinal Beaufort, patriot or usurer?', *TRHS* 20 (1970), 129–48. A. Steel, *The Receipt of the Exchequer, 1377–1485* (Cambridge, 1954) totals the loans recorded on the Receipt rolls term by term and identifies groups and the principal individual lenders.

broke out, the French king confiscated their assets and the firm was bankrupted, but in 1298 the Frescobaldi of Florence took over their rôle. Over a period of sixteen years they lent Edward I and Edward II some £150,000 until the Ordainers expelled them and their firm also collapsed.[30] Edward III borrowed heavily from the Bardi and Peruzzi of Florence from the beginning of his reign until the 1340s when both firms collapsed, owed about £180,000 by the king.[31] Foreign merchants continued to lend money but the time of the great companies was over. They had lent for profit and had gained privileges and protection for their other financial business in England, but the risks in dealing with kings with ambitions so much greater than their income were too heavy. For a time in the late 1330s and 1340s syndicates of English merchants almost matched the Italians. William de la Pole of Hull, the outstanding broker of the period, contracted to raise £100,000; he was knighted and his son became an earl; Walter Chiriton and Thomas Swanland by contrast were bankrupted. From this time, though large-scale borrowing continued, it was mainly from Englishmen and mostly in modest sums. The city of London as a corporation often raised money, sometimes by making a levy on the wards in the same way that a fifteenth was raised; between 1431 and 1449, for example, almost £19,000 was lent. The company of the Staple at Calais, mainly Londoners and wool merchants, raised even larger sums in the fifteenth century for their fortunes were tied up with defending Calais; for example they raised £43,000 between 1454 and 1456 alone.[32] Other towns and individual merchants also lent. The most infamous was Richard Lyons who with another Londoner, John Pyall, was accused – justly – in the Good Parliament of 1376 of lending 20,000 marks to the king and being repaid £20,000 when two other London merchants were prepared to lend 15,000 marks without interest.[33] Dick Whittington – Sir Richard Whittington – lent in all £13,784 to Henry IV and his London contemporary, John Hende lent more.[34] Merchants were considered most able to lend substantial amounts but many others did so also. The prince of lenders was Henry, Cardinal Beaufort, who lent at least £212,000 between 1404 and 1446, and at one time was owed over £26,000. Sir Richard Knolles, a hero in the war against France, lent almost £7,000 to Richard II; and John Norbury,

30 Prestwich, *War, Politics and Finance*, pp. 206–7 and 210–12.

31 Fryde, 'Royal Credit System', p. 460.

32 E.J. Davis and M.I. Peake, 'Loans from the city of London to Henry VI, 1431–1449', *BIHR* 4 (1927), 165–72; W.I. Haward, 'The relations between the Lancastrian government and the merchants of the Staple from 1449 to 1461' in *Studies in English Trade in the Fifteenth Century*, ed. E. Power and M.M. Postan (London, 1933), pp. 293–320.

33 G.A. Holmes, *The Good Parliament* (Oxford, 1975), discusses the accusations of 1376 and the loans of this period.

34 C.M. Barron, 'Richard Whittington: the man behind the myth' in *Studies in London History*, pp. 197–248. Over 34 years he lent almost £35,000 to kings.

esquire, a retainer and treasurer of Henry IV, repeatedly lent him large sums. Treasurers often came to the rescue. Lord Cromwell lent over £8,000 between 1432 and 1442, and councillors and officials, even the clerks in the offices of central government, lent money to provide ready cash in emergencies.[35] Organized drives to obtain loans from religious houses, bishops, magnates and gentry go back to the thirteenth century, and were common in the later fourteenth century and particularly in the fifteenth century. Commissions were issued to local men of substance, sometimes to royal clerks or serjeants who toured an area, explaining the king's need and inducing people to lend money on promise of repayment at a given date out of future tax revenue. Devices such as sending down royal letters with the name of the addressee or the sum asked left blank to be filled in at local discretion were employed. These were not forced loans or forced gifts or benevolences as they were called in the late fifteenth century. There was pressure to lend, even summons before the Council on occasion, but there are many examples of refusals and some drives were dismal failures. For example, in 1400 serjeants were twice sent round religious houses seeking gifts or loans to be set against the next clerical tenth, but more letters of excuse or delay than of promises survive, and the yield was less than £2,500.[36]

The advantages of these loans to the king are obvious, but why did lenders lend? In some cases the answer is simply profit; they charged interest or received gifts or advantages in return. The Bardi for example received a gift of £11,000 following loans of £42,000 between 1328 and 1331, a 'gift' of 26 per cent. Usury was forbidden by the church, but it was widely practised. The Anonimalle Chronicle reports that John of Gaunt told the Speaker of the Commons in 1376 that it was sometimes necessary to pay 50 per cent interest to obtain a loan; Sir John Fortescue wrote with his experience of the reign of Henry VI in mind that an impoverished king had to pay 20 or 25 per cent interest to obtain loans; and on a number of occasions kings admitted they paid interest.[37] The extent of this is however problematical for in only a few cases is the interest openly declared in the exchequer records. It has been suggested that the record of a loan and repayment of, say, £1,000 probably often conceals that the true loan was £600 or £800, but Dr Harriss makes a distinction between the financial transaction, the loan at interest, normally called a *chevisance*, and the loan proper. Cardinal Beaufort's immense loans for example do not seem to have been at

---

35 Harriss, 'Cardinal Beaufort'; Steel, *Receipt of the Exchequer* mentions and classifies many of the loans.

36 J.L. Kirby, *Henry IV of England* (London, 1970), pp. 96–7.

37 Fryde, 'Royal Credit System', *The Anonimalle Chronicle, 1333 to 1381*, ed. V.H. Galbraith (Manchester, 1927), p. 86 – *Select Documents*, p. 99; Fortescue, *The Governance of England*, ed. C. Plummer (Oxford, 1885), p. 118.

interest; his motive probably was to 'buy' status and influence. A councillor or official might be helping out, a merchant might gain commercial advantage, and the many small loans from, say, monasteries or country gentlemen were anticipated taxation, advanced in part out of a sense that subjects had a duty to aid the king in his need with their bodies or their goods. Probably the larger loans in general carried interest or at least profit, while the many smaller and in total less important loans in general did not.

Another pillar of later medieval finance was credit. Government was riddled with it. Supplies for the Household were often bought not for cash but for promises in the form of wardrobe debentures to be redeemed later, military commanders often complained that they were heavily in arrears with pay for their troops, and the system of assignment employed in the exchequer where creditors were often paid not in cash but in drafts against, say, a customs collector in the port or the collectors of direct taxes was another form of the same thing. In times of financial stringency these drafts might be uncashable and require to be renewed several times over, and there are complaints, for example in the parliament of 1376, of royal debts being bought at heavy discounts. Steel's tables from the Receipt rolls of cash and nominal receipts and of dishonoured tallies show the extent of credit between 1377 and 1485. In the reign of Henry VI for example cash receipts were more often than not under 20 per cent and quite often under 10 per cent and dishonoured tallies were at times very common.

Closely related to taxes on property and credit finance was the royal right of purveyance, of taking food and drink, timber, military supplies, carriage, and other things for the king's use, properly on immediate payment of the agreed or the market price, but often on credit.[38] The 'normal' form of purveyance which went on day-by-day was for the king's own Household and those of his immediate family. Household officers regularly asked chancery to issue commissions to purveyors or buyers, and complaints about them are numerous, about their failure to pay for goods and their extortions. A great deal of legislation from Westminster I (3 Edward 1), through the *Articuli super cartas* 1300, to the important statute of 1362 (36 Edw. III, st. I, c.2.) which replaced the term 'purveyor' with that of 'buyer' and laid down sensible rules for their work, tried to prevent abuse. Purveyance for the Household or local purveyance to supply a castle was one thing, but large-scale purveyance for military expeditions was a major grievance. If a sheriff was ordered to provide a substantial amount of grain from his county and bailiffs seized this in small quantities from

38 Harriss, *King, Parliament, and Public Finance* and C.J. Given-Wilson, 'Purveyance for the royal Household, 1361–1413', *BIHR* 56 (1983), 145–63 and *The Royal Household and the King's Affinity* (London, 1986), pp. 41–8.

all and sundry, often on credit, and with a deal of petty extortion, this was a grievance and almost a tax or a loan. The campaigning years of Edward I and Edward III were understandably the times of greatest complaint. Edward I ordered large seizures from 1294 and the protests went on into Edward II's reign. In his Confirmation of the Charters in 1297 Edward I had to promise that he would not take 'aids, mises, and prises save by the common assent of all the realm and for the common profit of the same realm, saving the ancient aids and prises due and accustomed'.[39] 'Prises' were these large-scale seizures which were equated with taxation; the ancient prises were the purveyances for the Household. Edward I was careful to obtain approval for prises thereafter but not by formal grants in parliament. The Ordinances of 1311 condemned prises other than the ancient and accustomed prises, but the campaigns of Edward III revived the issue. There were many complaints and the depth of feeling is shown in a commons complaint about prises in 1339 that 'no free man ought to be assessed nor taxed without common assent of parliament.[40] Edward never conceded this but with the peace of 1360 the extreme complaints died away. Demands were less frequent and burdensome and greater use was made of normal commercial methods of supply. In the late fourteenth and fifteenth centuries there were many complaints in parliament about purveyance for the Household and demands for restraints on its expenditure. Household expenditure was certainly high then but the basic problem was probably that when the king was short of money, household creditors were likely to suffer heavily.

These continuing complaints about the king's failure to pay promptly for supplies are an indication of the almost continuous struggle that the king and the Council waged to find the cash or credit to pay for government. The king's domestic costs and in particular his war costs had escalated, normally ahead of even the heavy, regular and frequent taxation which was such an unprecedented feature of this period. It is striking that while heavy taxation could be readily collected and administered and while the exchequer could supply detailed financial information on request, budgeting was apparently so casual at most times. Annual balance sheets are a relatively modern preoccupation. A major consequence of the increased costs and increased taxes was the evolution of the unusual form of parliament which developed in England, a parliament representing the whole nation and able to criticize the financial failings of government.

---

39 *Select Charters*, p. 491; *EHD*, iii. 486.
40 *Rotuli Parliamentorum Anglie Hactenus Inediti*, ed. H.G. Richardson and G.O. Sayles (Camden Series,, 51, 1935), p. 269.

5
Royal Armies*

The most demanding and the most costly activity of late-medieval government was the conduct of war, defending the marches, particularly after the mid fourteenth century from the fortresses of Berwick and Calais, holding Wales and Ireland, defending the coasts and the seas and mounting overseas campaigns. It was a time of almost constant warfare, much more so than for almost a century before or a century after. Much of Edward I's energy was given to war and the war he began in Scotland continued intermittently throughout the fourteenth century. From the 1330s until the 1450s there were frequent expeditions and sometimes periods of sustained campaigning in France. In part because there was so much fighting, so much of it outside the kingdom, in part because of social change, the organization and conduct or war changed considerably, and once again a major change can be seen in the late thirteenth century. Feudal military service died out, paid service became universal, the men recruited in a variety of ways which reflect the new society. A new tactic evolved with the cavalry fighting mainly on foot alongside the infantry, now mainly archers. Late medieval war is a rich and major theme, but this chapter is concerned primarily with organization – how men were recruited, ordered, and supplied, on land and on sea, and necessarily in general terms, with no discussion of particular campaigns.

Feudal military service was obsolete by 1340, but it was important

* There is an extensive but mainly specialized literature on war. M. Powicke, *Military Obligation in Medieval England* (Oxford, 1962) is a good account of how men were raised. J.E. Morris, *The Welsh Wars of Edward I* (Oxford, 1901) is a classic, now supplemented by the lively study of M. Prestwich, *War, Politics and Finance under Edward I* (London, 1972). A.E. Prince, 'The army and navy' in *Eng. Gov. at Work*, i. 332–93 deals with the early years of Edward III. K. Fowler, *The Age of Plantagenet and Valois* (London, 1967) is an illustrated account of the Hundred Years War with a good bibliography and H.J. Hewitt, *The Organization of War under Edward III* (Manchester, 1966) is a practical guide to all aspects of war. C.W.C. Oman, *The Art of War in the Middle Ages* (Oxford, 1885, rev. ed. by J.H. Beeler, Ithaca, New York, 1953) is still useful on tactics.

to the first two Edwards and its ethos continued to give a particular character to the duty the greater landowners felt to fight for the king. Since the Norman Conquest many tenants-in-chief had held land in return for producing a fixed quota of mounted knights for 40 days a year without payment. The total service they owed the king was about 5,000 knights, but for various reasons, for example because many tenants owed the service of a fraction of a knight, because the quality of some knights was low, and because 40 days was militarily restrictive, the full quota never served and armies included both popular levies and paid troops. In the later twelfth century it became common to summon only fractions of the feudal host, the better prepared serving while the others supported them financially, and in the thirteenth century the quotas were drastically reduced. A major reason for this was the change in the character and equipment of the knight. He had originally been a relatively lightly armed cavalryman who might be a landless household retainer or a tenant with little land. In the twelfth century his armour became heavier and more expensive with more chain-mail and later still pieces of plate armour. His horse had to be stronger and more protected ('barded'), and a good war horse (*dextrarius*) could cost up to £80. The ceremony of knighthood became more elaborate and expensive and the knight had to be a man of middling wealth to support the status, the norm in the thirteenth century was land worth £20 a year. He now stood at the head of the lesser nobility or country gentry in the social hierarchy (p. 149). It is not therefore surprising that the quotas of knight service were reduced, though in a piecemeal and irregular way. The greater tenants-in-chief benefited most; the earls of Gloucester and Norfolk for example, holding 455 and 279 knight's fees respectively, had their quotas reduced to ten and six knights.[1] The lesser tenants-in-chief benefited less, probably because the king wished to retain their personal obligation to serve. The total service due to the king was reduced to about 500 knights, and the greatest amount known to have been performed during Edward I's reign was on the Welsh campaign of 1277 when 228 knights and 294 less heavily armed troopers, each counting for the service of half a knight, represented 375 knight's fees and made up about half the cavalry force.[2] Feudal military service was however still valuable. It was the traditional mark of status of the highest form of tenure. It was a guarantee – if it was not abused – that the greater landowners would feel obliged to turn out and bring retinues which were often larger than their feudal dues.

1 Morris, *Welsh Wars*, p. 60. I.J. Sanders, *Feudal Military Service in England* (Oxford, 1956).
2 Morris, *Welsh Wars*, p. 127.

Retinues were sometimes paid, sometimes not, sometimes paid part of the time, for obligation, honour and employment were all involved. In 1300 the greater tenants-in-chief, in particular the earls who were the mainstay of recruiting, still regarded it as personally dishonourable to serve for wages on a normal campaign in Britain, though it is a sign of changing times that even earls might accept wages for service overseas or on a campaign outside the summer campaigning season. For example five earls and a major baron contracted to serve for pay with 500 cavalry in Scotland during the winter of 1297–98.[3] Feudal service had also lesser advantages; it allowed the king to levy scutage and fines for absence, and, more important, it allowed tenants-in-chief to levy scutage on their tenants, on the old not the reduced assessments!

Edward I demanded feudal service six times, five for campaigns in Wales or Scotland, once, abortively, for a Gascon expedition in 1294. Sometimes all who owed service were summoned, the greater tenants-in-chief by individual letters, the lesser by a general summons through the sheriffs, sometimes only named tenants were summoned. The 1294 expedition raised an issue that had been contentious since the reign of Richard I; where, if at all, was military service owed overseas. Edward summoned the host to serve in Gascony but cancelled it, probably though not certainly because of opposition, and sent instead a paid expedition under the earls of Lancaster and Lincoln.[4] The issue was again raised in 1297 when Edward proposed expeditions to Flanders and Gascony, the former led by himself, the latter by the Constable and Marshal, and the summons of feudal service, but there was so much opposition both to service abroad and service without the king that the plan was abandoned. The king did go to Flanders, but with a relatively weak army, most of the cavalry provided by Household retainers and all the men at wages.[5] The charter which Edward was forced to concede to end the crisis did not mention military service, but it was now clearly impossible to enforce feudal service overseas.

Edward II also demanded feudal military service, more often indeed than his father, and probably because many of his magnates were at odds with him and unwilling to fight voluntarily. The last full and meaningful feudal summons was in 1327 for Edward III's first Scottish campaign, but it is proof of how decayed the service had become. Some tenants paid fines for failing to serve, some scutage was paid, a few tenants did serve, but at least some of the leading magnates

---

3 H. Gough, *Scotland in 1298* (Paisley, 1888), pp. 64–5.
4 Prestwich, *War, Politics and Finance*, pp. 75–6.
5 N.B. Lewis, 'The English forces in Flanders, August-November 1297' in *Studies in Medieval History presented to F.M. Powicke*, ed. R.W. Hunt, W.A. Pantin and R.W. Southern (Oxford, 1948), pp. 310–18.

brought large contingents at the king's wages.[6] Edward III never summoned the host again; he did issue a few partial summons in the 1330s, but it is not certain that any tenant served without wages; and he turned deliberately to other methods. Payment was now the rule and he was able to bring out his tenants without recourse to a feudal summons. There was one later summons, the quite exceptional general feudal summons for Richard II's first campaign in Scotland in 1385, but the motive may have been an antique sense of propriety or merely an attempt to encourage a large turn-out; it was not intended to and it did not raise a feudal army.[7]

Obviously the six feudal summons during the reign of Edward I could not have provided him with the armies he needed, and indeed feudal service had never been the only way of raising troops. All men had a duty to help defend the realm, mercenaries could be hired, contracts made with foreign rulers to provide contingents, and knights and esquires retained in the Household. All these methods were used by Edward I alongside feudal service, and they continued to be used. The major problem posed by the decay of feudal service was how the greater landowners, lords and gentry, could be mobilized for they were the heavy cavalrymen and, as the leaders of local society, the best recruiting agents of the lesser men. It may seem surprising that there was a problem at all in a military-minded society where men of status were taught as children to ride and fight, carried weapons, bore coats of arms, and were often buried under military effigies. The values of the upper ranks of society were certainly chivalrous and military, but it was a somewhat artificial chivalry, and enthusiasm for war had to be cultivated by the king. Among the gentry in particular there were many men who were not bellicose, and the same was true of the lesser people in the community. The dukes and earls were conscious of their military and political obligations – as the earls had been of their feudal duties. They were the 'natural' leaders of 'battles' in armies led by the king himself or the commanders of independent expeditions which were common during the French war, and almost all who could brought companies to serve with Edward III and Henry V in France or with Richard II and Henry IV in Scotland. In 1385 for example John of Gaunt and all the adult earls with the possible exception of Thomas Holland, earl of Kent, brought companies which

---

6 N.B. Lewis, 'The summons of the English feudal levy, 5 April 1327', in *Essays in Medieval History presented to Bertie Wilkinson*, ed. T.A. Sandquist and M.R. Powicke (Toronto, 1969), pp. 236–49; Prince, 'Army and Navy', pp. 348–51.

7 N.B. Lewis, 'The last medieval summons of the English feudal service, 13 June 1385', *EHR* 73 (1958), 1–26, criticized by J.J.N. Palmer, 'The last summons of the feudal army in England (1385)', *EHR* 83 (1968), 771–5 and countered by Lewis (with a comment by Palmer), 'The feudal summons of 1385', *EHR* 100 (1985), 729–46.

made up almost two-thirds of Richard II's army in Scotland, and there was a similar response for Henry IV's campaign in Scotland in 1400.[8] But even earls could refuse to serve if they did not have confidence in the king, as Edward II found to his cost. Barons, lords of parliament, felt the same obligation, but less strongly. In 1415 for example almost all the dukes and earls but only about half the lords accompanied Henry V to France and the same had been true in Scotland in 1385 and 1400. Knights and esquires were even more reluctant to fight and special measures were taken to induce them to do so. Moreover, serving with the king himself was one thing, serving under a commander or on a long campaign was quite different. Even Henry V had difficulty in recruiting by the end of his short reign and there was very limited interest in serving in France during Henry VI's reign. The political consequences of a situation where kings had to win the confidence and acceptance of an increasing number of their greater subjects to fight – and now to vote the taxes which were necessary to pay those who fought – were enormous. As always, in all aspects of government, the fundamental factor was the personal ability of the king to give leadership.

The first and simplest alternative to feudal service as a means of bringing out the great men and their followers was to summon numbers of them, not to perform feudal service but to serve personally on the basis of their faith and allegiance, not their homage, and to bring as many men as they could. The wording varied from the more peremptory to the more polite, the numbers summoned might be greater or less according to the need, and it might be addressed mainly to one part of the country, for example to the North for a Scottish campaign. Edward I used this method much more often than feudal service; normally he was prepared to pay wages and occasionally the letters said so; and it seems to have been an effective enough way of bringing out the great.[9] A summons of this kind at first applied extra pressure on the magnates, and this is why Edward I used it more in his last years and why Edward II used it more frequently than his father. The next stage was for the king to make agreements about the number of men to be brought, then to formalize the agreements into written contracts, and finally to make the contracts in the form of indentures. Setting it down like this makes the development much too logical and deliberate; in practice it was piecemeal and unplanned, and the details are far from clear. There is no evidence that Edward I ever made contracts for normal compaigning though it is quite likely that he

---

8 Lewis, 'The last medieval summons', p. 24 and A.L. Brown, 'The English campaign in Scotland, 1400' in *British Government and Administration: Studies presented to S.B. Chrimes*, ed. H. Hearder and H.R. Loyn (Cardiff, 1974), p. 46.
9 Powicke, *Military Obligation*, pp. 100–2.

reached informal agreements on occasion so that he could gauge the size of his armies, and he certainly made written contracts for garrisoning castles and commands in Scotland and for special service such as that of the earls in Scotland in the winter of 1297–98. Wages were more common and agreements perhaps more formal in Edward II's reign, but it is only in the 1330s that there is much clear evidence. Edward III began by relying mainly on personal though not feudal summons, but agreements and then contracts became common as the reign progressed. In 1337 parliament approved the policy of maintaining a garrison in Scotland, the king appointed the earl of Warwick to command it, and negotiations took place in the north of England between royal officers and local men about bringing contingents. Lords and gentry agreed verbally to bring in all 580 men-at-arms, and these with 400 light horsemen and 4,000 archers levied from midland and northern counties were to form the garrison – and broadly this is what was done.[10] In 1338 a different method was used for raising an army in Scotland, 50 or so magnates and gentry were ordered to bring specified contingents of men-at-arms.[11] From this time it was the French war that was of major importance, and it was probably a combination of factors, the character of the war with its raiding expeditions (*chevauchées*), the need for greater planning and certainty about numbers going overseas, the success and profitability of the war, and Edward III's good relations with his magnates which led to voluntary contracts, later embodied in indentures, becoming the normal method of raising armies during the remainder of the period.

An indenture was a common type of document, the equivalent of the modern carbon copy, and used for a wide variety of purposes. The military indenture was the written record of an agreement to provide specified numbers of troops, the text written twice on a single sheet of parchment, the copies separated by an indented (tooth-like) cut, one copy sealed by the king (normally with his privy seal) remaining with the captain, the other sealed by the captain remaining on file in the privy-seal office.[12] It was probably only in Edward III's reign, and probably in the middle of the reign, that indentures became common for companies on campaigns. It is necessary to be cautious because the lack of surviving indentures is not evidence that they were not made,

10 N.B. Lewis, 'The recruitment and organization of a contract army, May to November, 1337', *BIHR* 37 (1964), 1–19. In practice some promised contingents, particularly the smaller ones, did not serve, but a sizable army was raised.

11 *Rotuli Scotiae*, ed. D. Macpherson (Record Commission, 1814–19), i. 527–9.

12 The surviving indentures in the Public Record Office are itemized in *List and Index of Warrants for Issues, 1399–1485* (Public Record Office, Lists and Indexes, Supplementary Series, IX, 2, 1964), pp. 426–52. See also A.E. Prince, 'The indenture system under Edward III' in *Historical Essays in Honour of James Tait*, ed. J.G. Edwards, V.H. Galbraith and E.F. Jacob (Manchester, 1933), pp. 283–97.

and search among the Household and exchequer accounts might disclose earlier references to them. But if indentures were at first unusual, contracts were common. For example a number of earls and magnates received assignments of money in August, 1341 to pay their own and their men's wages because they had contracted to lead companies on an expedition to Brittany; they had contracted but there is no mention of indentures.[13] These became common over the next generation and by the 1370s their contents had become standardized in the form that continues through the period. The captain is retained to serve for a period, a year or half a year perhaps, from the date and place given for the muster (gathering for inspection) of his men; the numbers are laid down – so many men-at-arms (the numbers of bannerets, knights and esquires perhaps specified) and so many archers. Wages are laid down in detail or perhaps merely said to be as 'usual', and so too are the reward (regard) paid for each quarter over and above the wages, and the times and conditions attached to the payment of each instalment. The king normally promises to pay for the transport of the men and the horses overseas. And finally the profits of war are regulated; important prisoners must be handed over to the king, though compensation will be given; and the king will take one-third of the captain's other profits and a third of the third of his men's profits which have been paid to him.[14] The clauses become almost standard, significantly more standard in the later years of Edward III's reign and equally standard indentures were devised for the custody of, say, a castle or a march. Indentures were made with dukes, earls, lords, knights, esquires, even with royal surgeons.

Contracting to hire soldiers and in particular cavalrymen helped to solve a problem that became acute in the thirteenth century, how to bring out the gentry to fight.[15] A knight was by then expected to be heavily armed and mounted and therefore necessarily a moderately wealthy man. The accepted qualification was £20 of land a year, after 1292 normally £40. It has been estimated that in the late thirteenth century there may have been 3,000 landowners so qualified but only some 1,500 were knights and only half were 'warrior' knights. Men were avoiding knighthood because of the expense involved and the military and civil obligations it brought. From the reign of Henry III therefore attempts were made to oblige such men to become knights by distraining (fining) them. The primary reason for this was apparently

13 *Calendar of Patent Rolls, 1340–1343*, pp. 259 *et seq.* Pace Prince (p. 287) these refer to contracts not indentures.
14 D. Hay, 'The division of the spoils of war in fourteenth-century England', *TRHS* 4 (1954), 91–109. An indenture of 1415 is printed in *Select Documents*, pp. 381–3.
15 Powicke, *Military Obligation*, pp. 103ff. C. Given-Wilson, *The English Nobility in the Late Middle Ages* (London, 1987), pp. 14–16.

military and there was a coincidence in the issue of distraints and military campaigns. The policy continued into the fourteenth century but with diminishing confidence and it did not produce a significant rise in the number of knights. Edward I also occasionally used direct military summons of qualified landowners; for example in 1297 he summoned those with £20 of land to serve in Flanders; he met strong resistance but 100 or more probably did serve. In 1306 he offered to provide the equipment necessary for the ceremony of knighting to all qualified men who would accept it and almost 300 gentlemen were knighted at Whitsuntide. Social customs had changed, and though some landowners were military-minded their general sense of obligation to campaign had diminished. It required a successful warrior king such as Edward III or Henry V or an immediate lord or a great captain such as Sir John Chandos – and a good prospect of profit – to induce men to serve abroad enthusiastically. There was now a country gentry of knights, esquires and 'gentlemen' who bore and carried arms, but who as a whole were more familiar with the affairs of their county than the battlefield, and yet retained a sense of military obligation into modern times. The 'gentleman's' code survived into the nineteenth century and 'esquire' was a courtesy title into the twentieth century. Another response to the problem of recruiting cavalrymen was to recruit bannerets, knights and esquires with annual fees and robes to serve as Household retainers – though not to live permanently in the Household. This was done on a substantial scale through the thirteenth and fourteenth centuries down to about 1360.[16] Most were men of substance in the counties with war experience in the king's service, their sons early in their careers, sometimes foreigners such as Arnald Gaveston, father of Edward II's favourite Piers Gaveston, and they were an important part of royal armies. For example on the Flanders Campaign of 1297, admittedly not a typical campaign because so many magnates boycotted it, 475 of the 670 men-at-arms who set out with the king were Household retainers with their contingents. Sir John Berwick brought four knights and 28 esquires, Sir John Drokensford, Keeper of the Wardrobe, three and 29, Sir Robert Fitzpain five and 20, and so on.[17] In the latter part of the fourteenth century the emphasis changed. Richard II, Henry IV and, on a more selective basis, Henry V retained county men as king's knights and esquires with fees to serve in peace and war for life, primarily for their support in the counties though with the expectation that they would come out with their men when danger threatened (pp. 27–8). Indeed

16 C. Given-Wilson, *The Royal Household and the King's Affinity* (London, 1986), pp. 204–6. For Edward I's Household knights see M. Prestwich, *Edward I* (London, 1988) pp. 147–55 etc.
17 Lewis, 'English Forces in Flanders', p. 317.

it became common to summon all those in receipt of grants from the king to turn out under threat of losing their grants. The élite of armies, the cavalry, now served for a variety of reasons, from a sense of 'class', family and personal duty, out of loyalty to their county lords, as retainers of their lord the king, hot blood and adventure, and for the spoils of war, its opportunities for advancement and of course for the king's wages. There was also another dimension. The lords and the gentry served or were represented in parliament. They did not determine high policy such as war and peace but they were much more privy to it and, because wars could now be financed only out of taxation, even the gentry had a strong negative voice.

Cavalry were the élite of armies but infantry often considerably outnumbered them in late-medieval armies. Edward I employed infantry in particularly large numbers until the very last years of his reign. In 1296 he ordered the exchequer to provide for the payment of the army at Newcastle, including, he said, 60,000 infantry. They did not materialize, but 10,000–20,000 infantry were assembled at times, 25,700 for the Falkirk campaign of 1298.[18] Armies in France in the fourteenth century were smaller; the largest was about 32,000 men in 1347 at the seige of Calais but few exceeded 10,000 men, and the same is true in the fifteenth century.[19] In Edward I's time the infantry were mainly foot-sloggers, many of them archers but from the 1330s they were often mounted archers who of course fought on foot. Infantry were recruited in a variety of ways but basic to recruitment was the obligation on all men between 15 or 16 and 60 to be armed and trained according to their status, ready to preserve the peace and defend the realm. This ancient obligation on those below the rank of knight and esquire was re-stated in 1285 in the Statute of Winchester (13 Edw. I) and remained virtually unchanged throughout the period.[20] Its primary intention was not to provide an army but to preserve the peace and the provision about arms comes after matters such as ensuring the accusation of criminals and the watch on town gates. It laid down that 'every man between 15 and 60 shall be assessed and sworn to arms according to the quantity of their lands and chattels', that is

> from £15 of land or goods worth 40m., a hauberk (coat of mail), an iron helmet, a sword, a knife, and a horse;
> from £10 of land or 20m. of goods, a hauberk, an iron helmet, a sword, and a knife;
> from £5 of land, a doublet, an iron helmet, a sword and a knife;
> from £2–£5 of land, a sword, a bow and arrows, and a knife;

18 Prestwich, *War Politics and Finance*, p. 94–5.
19 A.E. Prince, 'The strength of English armies in the reign of Edward III', EHR 46 (1931), 353–71.
20 *Select Charters*, p. 466; *EHD*, iii. 460–2.

from less than £2 of land, cutlasses, halberds (spears), knives, and other
lesser weapons;
all others to have bows and arrows if they lived outside the forest, bows
and bolts if inside it.

Constables in each hundred or franchise were to 'view' these arms
twice a year, and the justices on eyre and later the Justices of the Peace
were required to oversee their work.

The first duty on all men was to defend their community and
county, help maintain order and pursue criminals, but they formed a
pool from which some could be conscripted or persuaded to serve
outside it, for example when there was a threat of invasion, on campaigns in Wales or Scotland or even overseas. Edward I was the first
king to 'array' them systematically.[21] During his Welsh wars he sent
commissioners to array a given number of infantry within a number of
counties. They were to select the best men, have them equipped and
either send them to an assembly point or hold them in readiness. The
selection could be made at a general muster or more commonly by
sharing out the required numbers among the hundreds and townships.
The men would be organized in groups of 20 (*vintenaries*) under a
leader, five groups forming a century led by a mounted commander,
their centenar; sometimes there were even county 'batallions' of 1,000
men. The cost of preparing the men, feeding, arming where necessary
and at least in some counties providing them with a common uniform,
fell on the county. Service within the county was unpaid; service
outside or occasionally from the assembly point was considered to be
the king's responsibility. Edward II tried various methods of arraying
and obliging the local communities to pay more of the costs but in the
first half of Edward III's reign the Commons in parliament obtained a
series of statutes against 'abuses' of the system such as excessive
demands for men or equipment, levies of money and unpaid service
outside the county. The system worked well enough and was used
throughout the period. Some men were willing to serve, others paid a
fine or employed a substitute to avoid it. There are stories of bribery
and trickery, for example of the man who took money from every
member of a troop of arrayed men to serve in his place, and then
disappeared! The larger towns were subject to the equivalent of array;
they were often asked to provide specified contingents of men at their
own expense.

Personal obligation, contract service by indenture and array were
the most common but not the only methods of raising armies. For
example Gascon or allied troops might be hired or criminals offered
pardons in return for service. The particular needs of each campaign

21 Powicke, *Military Obligation*, pp. 118–33.

and political circumstances demanded different combinations of methods. A threat of invasion or a raid on the English coast would lead to county arrays in a number of counties and letters to the nobility and gentry to resist it, and there were established arrangements including warning beacons on the southern coasts to meet invaders. Service in Scotland and Wales offered limited opportunity for booty and ransoms and more pressure and compulsion was needed to raise armies to serve there for any length of time; men from the North and from the Marcher counties and from Wales itself would be prominent. Service in France during the long war was generally attractive, particularly under a successful captain and when the war was going well for plunder was likely on a *chevauchée* and for a time during the war of conquest in the fifteenth century there were opportunities for offices and lands in France. Armies there were generally smaller and most men served by contract, the captains raising them from their own retainers, their estates and from volunteers, the numbers topped up where necessary with arrayed men, criminals and in other ways. Men from some areas were particularly valued, for example men from Cheshire, Welsh archers, and sappers from the Forest of Dean. The Duchy was understandably good recruiting ground for the Lancastrian kings. Royal armies were not gathered easily and smoothly; delays and mix-ups were common; direction and attention to detail had to come from the king himself or the commander – Henry V was exemplary in this; but there were well-tried methods in every aspect of war. For example, when indentures became common for garrisons and campaigns the privy-seal office became a war secretariat. It prepared the indentures following agreements made normally by the Council; it filed the part sealed by the captain and routinely supplied him with the necessary documents subsidiary to it, such as warrants to the exchequer to pay him the war wages of his company and to account and orders to chancery to issue protections to his men giving them freedom from legal actions during the period of their service. Military supplies were needed to supplement the soldiers' own weapons and the Privy Wardrobe in the Tower of London was an arsenal and munitions factory. It bought or made items such as bows and arrows, armour, cannon and gunpowder and issued them as directed (pp. 57–8). Guns of varying sizes were a subsidiary but increasingly important weapon from the fourteenth century and the Privy Wardrobe had a clerk in charge of them from the 1360s and by the early fifteenth century there was a clerk and office of the ordnance. The king's tents and horses were also provided by specialized officers and their staffs. Supplies of food, drink and carriage were of vital importance. Soldiers in receipt of wages were supposed to find their own food, but in practice it was necessary for the king to provide it on a large scale at his own expense. He had the right to 'purvey', that is requisition for payment, for his Household at all times and the same method was applied to war supplies. Sheriffs, the maids-of-all-work in the counties, serjeants-at-arms, clerks and commissioned purveyors were ordered to buy and seize supplies and have them transported where they were needed. The purvey was done with some efficiency because officials were accustomed to it, the problem with all kinds of purveyance was that the owners complained with justice that they were not offered full or fair payment for what was seized, often had to wait for payment over long periods and sometimes were not paid at all. Edward I had to make promises in 1297 and 1301 not to abuse purveyance but it was a major and grumbling source of complaint throughout the period (pp. 83–4).

Transport of men and supplies by sea and fighting ships were essential for an island kingdom – to support campaigns within Britain, maintain armies across the Channel, prevent raids on the English coast and combat piracy. Sea forces were however still essentially ancilliary to land forces; the age of deep-sea actions with naval guns had not yet arrived; most actions at sea were fought in shallow waters between soldiers serving on ships.[22] The naval battle at Sluys in 1340, for example, one of Edward III's great victories, fought to eliminate a threat of invasion and clear the Channel for his campaign in France, took the form of an assault by English soldiers serving on a fleet of largely impressed merchants ships against a similar French fleet at anchor and massed together as on a battlefield. English fleets were assembled in *ad hoc* ways similar to those for armies. There was no regular royal navy until the sixteenth century though there were always royal ships, most of them for transport purposes and the personal possessions of the king. The three warrior kings who campaigned across the Channel, Edward I, Edward III and Henry V, created significant royal fleets by building, capture or hire, but these were not maintained by their successors. Henry V has been credited with founding the Royal Navy, and though this is not true, he did see the advantage to his plan to conquer, not merely campaign in France of having a fleet immediately available in the Channel. He built up a fleet of 30 ships including the impractical *Grace Dieu* of 1,400 tons which dwarfed most contemporary ships of 200 tons or less. He even

---

22 There is no good, recent history of the navy but N.H. Nicolas, *A History of the Royal Navy* 2 vols. (London, 1847) and M. Oppenheim, *A History of the Administration of the Royal Navy* (London, 1896) are still useful. A.E. Prince, 'The army and navy' in *Eng. Gov. at Work*, i. 376–93, C.F. Richmond, 'The war at sea' in *The Hundred Years War*, ed. K. Fowler (London, 1971), pp. 96–121 and the articles he cites by J.W. Sherborne and himself are all valuable. *The Navy of the Lancastrian Kings*, ed. S. Rose (Navy Records Society, V. 123, 1982) is an edition of a Clerk of Ships accounts with an introduction on the provision of ships.

maintained a naval base and a royal dockyard at Southampton to service his ships. Henry's fleet was however dispersed soon after his death – on his own instructions to pay his debts – and *ad hoc* arrangements returned. These relied on bringing merchant ships into royal service. There were ancient obligations on coastal towns to provide ships for the king, the greatest the duty of the Cinque Ports to provide 57 ships and their crews at their own expense for 15 days each year. These were demanded on occasion, but like other ancient services, they came to be reduced or commuted to agreed, paid service. The normal method of obtaining ships came to be to commission a clerk or serjeant-at-arms to impress the required number of merchant ships of a given tonnage from all the ports on a stretch of coast. The ships could then be readily adapted for transport service, for example by fitting hurdles to contain the horses, or converted to warships by building castle-like structures fore and aft from which men-at arms and archers recruited by array or indenture could fight at close quarters. The ship masters and crews were paid wages but until 1380 the ships themselves were requisitioned without payment as part of the king's prerogative to purvey and payment was not regular even after this. There was inevitably resentment among the owners and merchants for normal trade was disrupted and long delays were common in assembling fleets and in setting sail on expedition. The command of naval forces was given to specially appointed admirals, either soldiers or merchant captains, commissioned like other commanders to raise and command troops, often to two admirals, one for the waters and ports north of the Thames, the other for the (south) west. At least from the early part of Edward III's reign there was a permanent storehouse and workship for naval supplies, a subsidiary of the Privy Wardrobe in the Tower of London under the keeper or clerk of the king's ships (p. 58). He stored and manufactured naval supplies such as cordage and timber; he had his own docks near London Bridge and down river; and he could repair and even have ships built when necessary.

By the standards of the last 300 years the organization and supply of military and naval forces in this period appear amateurish, but in their own time they were effective and even sophisticated. The composition, arms and tactics of armies changed a great deal, military and naval ordinances were well understood, and, in embryo, offices such as the Ordnance and the Navy were formed. Most striking of all, in relation to the size of the population, are the large sea and land forces that were deployed. Edward I had armies of about or more than 30,000 men on several campaigns in Wales and Scotland; Edward II, poorly supported by the magnates, had about 17,000 at Bannockburn; Edward III had about 32,000 at the siege of Calais in 1347, more than in any other English army before the seventeenth century. The field armies in France during the Hundred Years War were necessarily smaller; Edward III led about 15,000 men on the campaign which included Crécy and Henry V about 10,000 on his first French campaign before Agincourt; and these do not include the thousands of sailors and soldiers on the ships which transported and supported them. And virtually every one of these soldiers and sailors was paid wages. The rates were almost entirely standard throughout the period, 6s.8d.–13s.4d. a day for an earl, 4s. for a baron or banneret, 2s. for a knight, 1s. for an esquire or other man-at-arms, 6d. for a mounted archer, 2d. or 3d. for a foot-soldier or sailor. The costs of campaigns were immense by comparison with earlier warfare. It has been estimated that Edward I's second Welsh war of 1282–83 cost in all about £150,000 and 'the overall cost of the war with France in alliances and in direct military intervention probably amounted to the impressive figure of £615,000,[23] Edward III's war expenditure in his early continental campaigns was on an even greater scale (pp. 67–8). The soldiers on Henry V's more modest first French campaign were due over £9,000 a month in wages and to this must be added the wages of those on board ship and the supporting tradesmen and domestics and all the military supplies. Garrisons too were costly; Calais cost about £17,000 a year in Henry IV's reign; Berwick and the East March was held for £3,000 a year in peace, £12,000 a year in war in the later fourteenth century; even the small garrison of Oye on the Calais March cost about £900 a year in wages alone at the same period. Full and precise costs are impossible to establish but war on any scale had come to be costly, far beyond the king's normal income and sustainable only by taxation. The indirect effect on the English economy and society of this huge investment in war, even when the 'profits' of war are taken into account, must have been very considerable.

The political effects of war are easier to identify. It is no coincidence that this is the first period of heavy, sustained taxation of the laity and the clergy and that this began with Edward I's wars. Taxation however could be taken only by common assent. By the late thirteenth century in the case of the laity this meant the assent of more than the tenants-in-chief, by the mid fourteenth century it had come to be the assent of parliament, and by the late fourteenth century the Commons were acknowledged to have the right to grant taxation while the lords merely assented to it (pp. 229–31). The raising of armies and ships also came to be the responsibility of the men who sat or were represented in parliament. The nobility bore the greatest responsibility and brought the largest retinues but within them were lesser men's contingents;

23 Prestwich, *War, Politics and Finance*, pp. 170–5.

many gentry brought out their own contingents or served as commissioners to array their county forces; merchants were the losers by impressed shipping and loss of control of the sea. Kings of course had never been able to raise armies without the support of their greater subjects but support was now to an extent institutionalized. The great 'crisis' of Edward I's reign in 1297 arose from his demands for war service and war taxation and although he was able to shoulder his way through discontent, his son, Edward II, was obliged to promise in the Ordinances of 1311 that he would not make war nor leave the kingdom 'without the common assent of his baronage, and that in parliament'. This provision was repealed in 1322 but it was normal practice for kings to discuss campaigns with their lords in parliament or in Great Council. The initiative came from the king; it was certainly so under the three great warrior kings but even they had to win over their lords – and each ran into trouble when their war ambitions outran this support. The Commons had a different rôle. They were, they claimed, petitioners and demanders. They certainly often complained about the effectiveness of defence measures, for example, on the Marches, on the South Coast or at sea, about the cost, about the abuses of array, and, most often of all about purveyance. But they granted the taxes which paid for wars and on some occasions they gave positive opinions on how best the realm could be defended, for example about how the seas could best be guarded, and occasionally about proposed campaigns. They were however chary of giving advice which the king could construe as committing them to pay for campaigns and they tended to retreat into assertions that they were too ignorant or simple to advise on such great matters and asked the king to consult the lords. War and the cost of war were the substance of much of the business of parliament.

6

The Legal System*

The legal system, of all the subjects in this book, was the one that ordinary Englishmen must have known best because it came frequently into their towns and townships. It gave them some protection for life, limb and property but they probably saw it more as yet another burden; hostility to lawyers and the law was a feature of the great revolt of 1381. One reason for this was that the law had expanded considerably over the previous century. This may seem surprising because it had changed so much in the century or so before 1272 when the king's courts had gained considerably at the expense of the communal and private courts; central royal courts of Common Pleas, King's Bench and exchequer had come into existence; royal justices often visited the counties; and a new law, the common law, the law common to all England, had come into existence. Henry de Bracton's great legal treatise on 'The Laws and Customs of England' (*De Legibus et Consuetudinibus Anglie*) written in the 1250s describes this unique law with its writs, forms of action and juries. Pollock and Maitland brought their classic study of English law to a close in 1272 because in their opinion 'most of the main outlines of our medieval law had been drawn for good and all'.[1] This is true, but in the late Middle Ages this new royal legal system matured and developed considerably. At Westminster the common-law courts became more professional, indeed they became too inflexible, and other royal courts developed in chancery and at the Council, courts which later became

---

* There are many histories of the law. F. Pollock and F.W. Maitland, *The History of English Law Before the Time of Edward I*, 2 vols. (1985, re-issue by S.C.F. Milsom, Cambridge, 1968) is still a magnificent classic. W.S. Holdsworth, *A History of English Law* (London, 1903–72) is a monumental 16 volume work, full of material and the first volume on 'The Judicial System' was re-issued with an introductory essay by S.B. Chrimes in 1956. T.F.T. Plucknett, *A Concise History of the Common Law* (5th ed., London, 1956), S.F.C. Milsom, *Historical Foundations of the Common Law* (London 1969), A. Harding, *The Law Courts of Medieval England* (London, 1973) and J. Bellamy, *Crime and Public Order in England in the later Middle Ages* (London, 1973) are all useful books with the different emphases their titles suggest.

1 Pollock and Maitland, *English Law*, i. 174.

their rivals. In the counties a major change took place; the general eyre died out but professional justices and lawyers came regularly to hold the assizes, deliver gaols and enquire into and punish disorders; most important of all, local landowners and lawyers were appointed Justices of the Peace to keep the peace, receive indictments, try criminals and enforce the law. The older communal and private courts continued to lose business to the partnership of local gentlemen and professional justices and lawyers. The content of the law itself did not remain static; its principles became refined and new actions were formulated. The legal system of which Sir Thomas Littleton and Sir John Fortescue wrote in the fifteenth century was considerably more sophisticated and professional than that of Bracton.

It is impossible to discuss every aspect of this system for in addition to the royal courts with their voluminous surviving records, literally thousands of rolls and millions of writs on file, there were many other courts. Durham, Chester and later Lancaster had their own courts and judges though they applied the same common law; there were the county and hundred courts; and there were borough courts, church courts, forest courts, military courts and many others. This chapter must be selective, dealing first with the most important local courts and then and principally with the royal courts which dominated the system. The content of the law receives little space for this would require another book and a lawyer to write it. English law was more elaborate than the law in any other kingdom in Europe at that time – Fortescue and no doubt other English lawyers thought it superior to any other. It was more professional and arguably more humane. But was it effective and was it fair? This is traditionally a lawless period and the struggles of the Paston family to obtain 'justice' against powerful opponents and partial judges have been known for two centuries. Was there much that was rotten behind the fine façade? This is the fundamental question that must be faced in the last section of the chapter.

Forms and Procedures

It is necessary to begin briefly with some of the terms and procedures used in the courts. For us the legal system is a matter of public authority; the courts are the queen's courts; and crime is a public wrong to be prosecuted by the crown. In early times this was not so. An assault or a robbery was a matter for the parties concerned; if a man's goods were stolen he might pursue the thief, recover them or accuse him. The king was involved only where his own peace was broken, for example when the deed was done in his house. From Anglo-Saxon times however the king's interest gradually became extended to cover other places and circumstances and, most important of all, to the most grave wrongs such as killing. By Edward I's reign there was a distinction between the major offences, treason, which was a case apart, or felony, and the lesser offences which were called 'trespasses' (*transgressiones*) and in the sixteenth century 'misdemeanours'. Felonies – the word has the sense of the wickedest, most base crimes – included homicide, arson, rape, robbery, greater thefts (grand larcenies, that is of goods worth a shilling or more, as distinct from petty larcenies), and harbouring. Felonies together with treason were 'pleas of the crown' to be determined only by the king's justices as Magna Carta (cl. 24 of 1215) had laid down. The punishment for the traitor or felon was death and forfeiture of land and goods to the king; if the lands were not held of the king he had them for a year and a day to 'waste' before they returned to the lord. Traitors and felons were brought to trial in several ways. 'Appeal' or private accusation by the injured party or his kinsman leading to trial by battle between the parties was still available, but it was becoming much less common and battle was almost always avoided. A form of appeal was that made by an accused or convicted felon when he turned 'approver' and accused his associates in crime to try to save his own skin, and battle was then waged between them. The most common way was however public accusation, indictment by a jury, a 'grand' or presenting jury of neighbours, placed on oath by a royal officer to answer questions about felonies in their locality, though behind this must often have lain the complaint of an individual. Sheriffs, coroners, Justices of the Peace and visiting royal justices sought out accusations in a systematic way. The accused might of course have been caught in the act or arrested after a chase by men of the neighbourhood who had done their duty and raised the hue and cry; if so he had little defence. He might have been arrested by an official on suspicion, but this was a power rarely given. What is strikingly absent is indictment as we know it by the crown, for the crown did not have the means to find criminals save through the action of its subjects. In 1200 the guilt or innocence of the accused might be determined by ordeal, but in 1215 the Lateran Council had forbidden the clergy to take part in this appeal to God, and in England trial by 'petty' jury had gradually taken its place. To modern eyes the trial may seem barbarous; the accused was normally allowed neither counsel nor witnesses and could only deny the accusations as best he could and rely on his reputation and the good will of his neighbours. He apparently did not trust in vain because a high proportion of felons were acquitted (pp. 137–8). The jury, normally of twelve men from the immediate neighbourhood who were expected to know or be able to find out the truth about an incident, was a feature of royal courts in both civil and criminal trials. Chief Justice Fortescue writing in the mid fifteenth century compared it favourably with the methods of proof in other countries;[2] it was an obstacle to arbitrary authority, it probably did encourage reasonableness and it certainly was popular. In the period two important changes were made in the law relating to it. In 1352 (25 Edw. III, st. 5, c.3) the accused was given the right to object to a juror on a petty jury on the ground that he had been a member of the grand jury which had indicted him, and in 1414 (2 Hen. V, st. 2, c.3) a property qualification of lands or tenements to the annual value of 40 shillings was introduced for jurors determining cases of homicide, real (i.e. land) actions and personal actions where the debt or damages amounted to 40 marks.

The less serious offences such as assault, wounding, damage to property and a range of others down to breaches of the assizes fixing the price of bread and beer, were trespasses not felonies and did not necessarily come before the king's courts at all. The king did not have the resources to deal with all the petty villains and there was no tradition that he should try to do so. A trespass could, to use modern terminology, be either a criminal or a civil matter. It depended on how the defendant was brought to trial. If he was indicted by a grand jury it was a 'criminal' trespass; if this was before the sheriff it would be decided summarily; if before visiting justices or before the JPs, and the latter became the common method in the fourteenth century, the issue would be decided by jury. The punishment would not be death and forfeiture, but amercement (i.e. fine), imprisonment or corporal punishment such as the stocks. Mutilation, common in the twelfth century, was now rare, but imprisonment, though of course known before, became much more common about 1300. Trespasses could also be brought to court by the injured party as a 'civil' action to obtain damages – before a private court or before the king's justices. Most of the lesser wrongs and injuries were decided locally, but in the second half of the thirteenth century there was a flood of such cases before royal justices. Plaintiffs brought complaints verbally or in written 'bills' before visiting justices and kings encouraged the justices to hear such complaints against officials. Procedure by bill was a major development which came to affect every court and which arguably meant 'the beginning of a second stream in English law'.[3] Plaintiffs could also buy a writ to begin an action before the central courts. These trespass actions had both a criminal and a civil flavour about them. The plaintiff brought them to obtain damages but he

2 Sir John Fortescue, *De Laudibus Legum Anglie*, ed. S.B. Chrimes (Cambridge, 1942), pp. 57–65.

3 A. Harding, 'Plaints and bills in the history of English law, mainly in the period 1250–1350' in *Legal History Studies 1972*, ed. D. Jenkins (Cardiff, 1975), pp. 65–86 is a good guide to this important development.

alleged that the act had been done against the king's peace and with force of arms and so involved the king. This brought the case to a royal court and gave the advantage of speed and force; he could obtain writs from the justices to the sheriff to summon the defendant, take pledges for his appearance, arrest him, even outlaw him for non-appearance. From the king's point of view the development was no doubt attractive because it brought in fees and amercements but it severely strained his courts. The popularity of the action is shown by the provision in the Statute of Gloucester in 1278 (6 Edw. I, c.8) that the sheriff should hear pleas of trespass as in the past and that to obtain a writ to have the action heard before the king's justices the plaintiff must swear that the value of the goods was at least 40 shillings. The effect of this was to limit actions in the county court to cases involving less than 40 shillings. The criminal element gradually dropped out of the action in the fourteenth century; the issue became avowedly merely a private wrong; and the range and number of cases of trespass multiplied. Maitland wrote that the time came when 'the older forms having been neglected, an action for damages. . . . seemed to be almost the only remedy offered by the common law'.[4]

The procedure in the courts of Common Pleas and King's Bench had been formalized in relation to those older civil actions, the 'real' actions about the ownership of land and its tenure which were of fundamental importance in a society so land-conscious as that of the twelfth century. The king's courts did not have a monopoly of such cases; a lord was entitled to do justice to his tenants in disputes about their holdings, but by 1300 few took the trouble to do so. In the twelfth century a rule had been laid down that no action about freehold land could be begun without a royal writ, an 'original' (originating) writ bought in chancery, either a writ to the lord of a court to do right or a writ ordering the defendant to answer in the king's court if he would not surrender the land. The same rule was applied to all other actions such as trespass or debt in the central courts. Once the original writ had been bought proceedings could be desperately slow, dragging on from term to term because the case had degenerated into a struggle to get the defendant into court. This was the 'mesne' (middle) process; the defendant would be summoned, perhaps a number of times, but he might delay by offering *essoins* (excuses). In 'real' actions the land itself could be seized and if the defendant continued to ignore the courts, judgement could be given against him. In 'personal' actions such as trespass, debt and demands for an account to be rendered, a more complicated process was necessary which varied slightly according to the type of case. The defendant might be

4 Pollock and Maitland, *English Law*, ii. 525.

'attached', that is pledges for his attendance might be taken; next his property might be 'distrained'; and finally he himself might be arrested or outlawed. Each stage required a 'judicial' writ bought from the court itself ordering the sheriff to execute it, and the defendant would decide where the balance of advantage lay for him, to answer or not. Litigation was likely to be lengthy and expensive, but many embarked on it, and a highly trained profession offering ever more sophisticated processes grew up to serve them.

If and when the defendant appeared, the next stage was the pleading. The case was presented, 'pleaded', in formal language by lawyers, the defendant trying to defeat some part of the plaintiff's plea or raising some point of law; at first witnesses were not examined and evidence was not presented in the way that seems obvious to us. Pleading was intended, hopefully, to clarify the issue of fact that would be put to the jury and the jury was supposed to be a body of neighbours, even men of the same street or profession, who knew the truth of the matter or could find it out for themselves. Indeed the jury normally gave its verdict in the locality without coming to Westminster at all. During this period however lawyers were exploring ways of adding to the information jurors possessed and the way was opening to a new type of proceeding where counsel presented evidence. Chief Justice Fortescue in the 1460s indeed gives a very modern sounding description of witnesses being heard, even being kept apart so that they could not influence one another.[5] A major reason for this was that in this period the range of issues on which litigation might begin in the royal courts was enormously extended, in particular by the extending action of trespass. Even 'real' actions multiplied to take account of new situations, particularly those relating to the new types of landholding such as the entail. The details do not concern us but it is important to stress the great growth that was taking place in the content of the common law in the late Middle Ages. The law was far from static.

One final point deserves to be made before turning to the institutions of the law. The criminal in the late Middle Ages had several avenues of escape which are not open to the modern criminal. He might not answer the accusation or escape from custody and hide away. Many did so successfully and it was difficult to catch them for society was now much more mobile and there was no national force to pursue them. The fugitive traitor or felon would probably be outlawed. He was exacted (called to appear) at five separate meetings of the county court, and if he did not do so he was outlawed. The king received his goods and chattels, his lord any land he held, but this was

---

5 Fortescue, *De Laudibus*, p. 61. J.B. Thayer, *A Preliminary Treatise on Evidence at the Common Law* (Boston, Mass., 1896) has a useful collection of references.

no deterrent if he had few possessions to lose. Some of the terror also went out of the process because after 1329 the outlawed traitor or felon could not be killed at will, though if he was caught he had short shrift before the courts.[6] Another avenue open to the accused or the convicted or the outlaw was to buy a royal pardon, either a particular pardon for his own specified crime or a general pardon in standard terms covering a whole range of crimes, and hundreds did so in every year from the mid fourteenth century. A man might take sanctuary, either permanent sanctuary in one of a few places such as St Martin le Grand in London which had this privilege, or in any parish church which gave sanctuary for 40 days. During the 40 days he could confess his crime before a coroner and abjure the realm for ever or make a run for it or surrender or wait to be starved out. Finally, if he was brought to court and convicted, he might then claim 'benefit of clergy', that is, claim he was in holy orders. If he could prove this, normally by showing that he could read a few lines, he would be handed over to the bishop for the (lighter) punishment of the Church.

The Communal Courts*

The smallest unit in the county to have a public court was the subdivision called the hundred or, in the Scandinavian-settled areas of the north and east, the wapentake. Both were pre-Conquest divisions varying widely from one or two townships to as much as 30 square miles, with an average of between ten and twenty townships.[7] An ordinance of 1234 provided that the hundred court should meet every three weeks, and many did so, some still in the open air in 1300. In theory all freemen should have attended its meetings but in practice the obligation had become attached to certain pieces of land which owed 'suit of court', and the same had happened with the county court. Normal meetings of the hundred court probably consisted of some 40 or 50 people, some of the 'suitors' (perhaps taking turns to attend), those who had business there, constables and officials of local landowners under the presidency of the hundred bailiff. He was

6 Holdsworth, *History of English Law*, iii. 605.
* The local courts have been little studied after 1307. W.A. Morris made important studies of the local courts but mainly before 1300 – *The Early English County Court* (Berkeley, 1926), *The Medieval English Sheriff to 1300* (Manchester, 1927) and 'The Sheriff' in *Eng. Gov. at Work*, ii. 41–108. R.C. Palmer, *The County Courts of Medieval England 1150–1350* (Princeton, 1982) is a significant supplement. H.M. Cam, *The Hundred and the Hundred Rolls* (London, 1930) is invaluable for the late 13th century and she wrote many other pieces including 'Shire Officials, Coroners, Constables and Bailiffs' in *Eng. Gov. at Work*, iii. 143–83, *Rolls from the Office of the Sheriff of Beds, and Bucks., 1332–1334*, ed. G.H. Fowler (Beds. Hist. Record Society, Quarto Memoirs, 3, 1929) has a very clear introduction. R.F. Hunnisett, *The Medieval Coroner* (Cambridge, 1961) is authoritative.
7 Cam, *Hundred and Hundred Rolls* prints a list of the hundreds in 1274.

probably a local man holding a little land; he was counted a royal officer but was appointed by the sheriff of the county and rendered a farm for the office which he recovered from his duties and hoped to make an additional profit for himself. The hundred court dealt summarily with minor criminal and civil cases, batteries and brawls that did not amount to felonies, maiming of beasts, cases of trespass and debt as long as the sums involved were less than 40s., breaches of contract, slander, and offences against the assizes of bread, ale and measures. By Edward I's reign more than half the hundreds in England (358 out of 628) had been granted away by the king, and in these cases it was the lord's bailiff, normally the steward of his lands, who held the hundred court and the lord received the profits.[8]

Twice a year, at Easter and Michaelmas, there were specially full meetings of the hundred court presided over by the sheriff on his 'tourn' or tour of the county or by the lord's steward. Each township should send its reeve and four men, each tithing its tithing man, and sufficient freemen should be present to make up a jury of twelve men from the hundred, for this was the occasion to enquire into major crimes and the arrangements for checking crime. These meetings were also known as 'views of frankpledge' from the frankpledge or tithing system, by which men over 12 years old (save those whose wealth or status guaranteed that they would stand to trial if they were accused or at least had goods to seize if they defaulted) were joined in groups of ten or twelve neighbours under a chief-pledge or tithing-man, and were responsible for producing any member of their tithing who had committed a crime. The sheriff was supposed to enquire into the working of the system at the Michaelmas tourn and ensure that the tithings were full and that all men were members, but by 1300 this mutual responsibility was in decay and by 1400 it was almost dead. Society had developed beyond such a system and in 1285 the Statute of Winchester (13 Edw. I, c.2) made the men of each hundred, including any franchise, responsible for robberies where no suspect was accused. The tithing-man continued to be important because he joined with the reeve and four men from each township to report on crimes committed in the hundred since the previous tourn and sometimes arrested suspected criminals. At the tourn the sheriff presented the men of the township with a list of articles or questions, and their answers formed the basis of indictments by the jury of twelve freemen of the hundred.[9] At least this was the theory though in practice the two stages were probably not as distinct as this. Felonies could not be tried by sheriffs or other local officials and the accused would be held for

---

8 *Ibid.*, pp. 260–85 lists all the hundreds in private hands in 1274.

9 F.J.C. Hearnshaw, *Leet Jurisdiction in England* (Southampton Record Soc., 1908) contains a collection of these articles.

trial by the king's justices but lesser offences such as failings in the frankpledge system, obstructing highways, diverting watercourses, failing to raise the hue and cry after an escaping criminal or raising it wrongfully, assaults, breaches of the assizes of bread and beer, cloths and measures and breaches of local customs would be decided there and then by the sheriff and punished by pillory, stocks or amercement. The tourn was an important occasion in the life of the locality. Ideally it was a broad inquisition into police measures, crime and mis-behaviour including that of officials in the previous six months, a miniature eyre in fact.

The hundred court was the court of the neighbourhood, but the county court has been described as 'the cornerstone of the English legal system'.[10] It sat for one day on a fixed day of the week which varied from county to county, normally once every four weeks but once every six weeks in Northumberland, Lancashire, Yorkshire and the county and town of Lincoln. There had earlier been a distinction between ordinary meetings and larger, general meetings twice a year, but this was apparently meaningless by 1300. The sheriff presided and the members or 'suitors' of the county were now a group of perhaps several hundred men who had the duty by custom of attending because of the tenure of their lands. They were the judges and they probably took it in turn to attend. In practice a meeting would consist of the sheriff, the coroners, some of the bailiffs, those involved in suits, lords' stewards, sufficient of the suitors to do the business and some of the sheriff's clerks and officers. Bracton in the 1250s makes the revealing comment that the justices on eyre should 'call before them four or six or more of the greater men of the county, who are called the "buzones" of the county and on whose nod the views of the others depend'.[11] The word was an archaic one, but ordinary meetings of the county court, and no doubt of all local courts, were probably guided by the landowners or their representatives and the men of business. Meetings of the court are not well documented but sufficient survives to show that though it was not a 'court of record', by 1300 rolls and files were kept and proceedings were formal with profes-sional pleaders and attorneys representing their clients.[12] As a court of law it had been losing competence to royal courts since the twelfth century, but it was still busy. Its criminal work was not important. Where felonies had been brought to light at the sheriff's tourn or

---

10 Morris, *County Court*, p. 143.
11 Bracton, *The Laws and Customs of England*, ed. S.E. Thorne (Cambridge, Mass., 1968–77), ii. 327. G.L. Lapsley, 'Buzones', in *Crown, Community and Parliament*, ed. H.M. Cam and G. Barraclough (Oxford, 1951), pp. 63–110 (from *EHR*, 1932).
12 Fowler's edition of the county rolls of Beds. and Bucks. in the 1330s gives a good impression of the court at work.

before the coroners, the accused would be awaiting trial before the
justices in eyre or of gaol delivery; such cases might also be brought
forward at the county court or the injured man or his kinsman might
bring an appeal (a private accusation) there, but again the cases would
await the justices. Minor criminal matters such as thefts and petty
assaults which had not been dealt with before a manorial or hundred
court could be brought to the county by the plaintiff and decided.
Most important of all, the county was the court where a man could be
outlawed. The civil jurisdiction of the county court, though greatly
diminished, was important. Complaints of failure of justice in
hundred and manor courts could be brought there. 'Real' actions
could be begun with a royal writ but even if begun in the county court
would be transferred to the central courts. Personal actions such as
debt and trespass where no force was alleged could be heard if the
amount involved was less than 40 shillings. They would be begun by
the old method of verbal (com)plaint or increasingly by written plaint
and the suitors would decide the issue. Slightly greater cases of the
same kind might also be heard if a writ such as *justicies* was bought in
chancery ordering the sheriff to cause judgement to be given. The type
of business done is shown in the roll of pleas for seven meetings of the
county court of Bedfordshire in 1332–33 which records 7 outlawries,
38 cases of debt, 13 of trespass, 10 of illegal distraint (seizing a man's
property to oblige his attendance), 3 of breach of covenant, 2 of
detinue of charters or goods and one case of an order to repair a
bridge. These were cases in progress because procedure here, as in the
central courts, was slow and deliberate, going from stage to stage at
county court after county court. These 74 cases passed through 330
stages at these seven meetings, and at the end of the day many more
cases lapsed or were transferred to a higher court or were settled out of
court than reached a verdict.[13] To use a quite inexact modern analogy,
it was the small-debt court for the country. It was also the assembly of
the county where parliamentary elections took place and other public
business was done.

Courts obviously cannot function without officers to serve them
and carry out their orders, and in the counties a hierarchy of offices
existed to serve the county and the hundred courts and carry out the
considerable volume of orders, judicial, financial and administrative,
that came down from the central courts, the king, the Council and the
departments of central government. At the head was the sheriff, a
man who had a great catalogue of responsibilities (pp. 142–3). He had
an office and a staff without which he could not have coped with the
work, an under-sheriff whom he appointed to deputize for him when

13 Fowler, *Beds. and Bucks.*, p. 50.

necessary, a staff of clerks probably including a receiver of moneys and a keeper of writs, messengers, and under-officers to carry out instructions. He appointed a hundred bailiff for each hundred in royal hands, the same man often in charge of several hundreds. There was also a riding-bailiff for the county, sometimes appointed by the king, sometimes by the sheriff, who had duties such as executing commands of the county court which were not confined to a single hundred. The hundred bailiffs and the bailiffs of private hundreds had their own sub-bailiffs, clerks and servants. Orders, for example to distrain a man's goods, might come down from Westminster to the sheriff, be passed on to the hundred bailiff, and then on to lesser officials, sub-bailiffs, constables, bedels, catcherels or simply 'servants' to execute. Each locality had its own customary arrangements. Matching this officialdom were the arrangements in the townships and hundreds to keep the peace and defend the county. At least since the Assize of Arms of 1181 every freeman had a duty to possess weapons and armour according to his wealth, and by thirteenth-century regulations each hundred and township had one or more constables elected by the community to ensure that these regulations were enforced. The Statute of Winchester of 1285 (13 Edw. I), the great 'peace' statute of the late Middle Ages, gave hundred constables responsibility for inspecting these arms twice a year and for presenting failures to carry out its regulations such as maintaining watches and clearing a strip 200 feet wide on each side of roads to deny cover to criminals. Until the mid fourteenth century, that is before the JPs became established, hundred constables sometimes even received indictments. Hundred or township constables were also called upon for all kinds of semi-judicial duties such as arresting strangers found at large during the night, arresting men illegally bearing arms, raising the hue and cry to pursue criminals, arresting them, keeping custody of seized goods or witnessing the abjuration of a man who had taken sanctuary in a village church. The township constable, the tithing-man and the reeve, the manor 'manager', were villagers and as the lowest members of the hierarchy of considerable importance. Finally, all men had the duty of assisting the constables, for example by raising the hue and cry, reporting the finding of bodies to the constable or the coroner, and of sharing amercements if they failed to carry out these duties. It must be stressed that this customary system did work. Men were arrested and writs were returned and the system survived into quite modern times. But because it depended on unpaid service by local people it was inevitably inefficient and corrupt. At best officials took fees, at worst they took bribes and defrauded and ill-used their neighbours. There are many, many complaints about these officials but supervision was difficult without a paid bureaucracy.

An officer of greater status than any of these save the sheriff and standing apart was the coroner. Villagers probably saw him more often than they saw the sheriff. His task was to record on rolls which were 'of record' unlike those of the hundred or county courts, evidence about unnatural deaths, confessions, private accusations of serious crimes and outlawries so that the justices could check that serious crime was being tackled and that the king was not losing any financial rights arising from it. This was why the office of coroner had been created in 1194. Most counties had two or four coroners, Yorkshire and Kent five, and many boroughs and franchises had coroners performing similar duties. In the counties they were knights or at least gentlemen of substance who held land in fee in the county, resided there and were elected by the county court on the authority of writs from chancery to serve for life or until replaced. Normally they would be selected from different parts of the county so that a coroner would be at hand, but even so it must have been a burdensome job involving a great deal of riding. If a body was found or someone died in unnatural circumstances including suicide or murder, the slayer or the finder, directly or through a local constable or bailiff, should inform a coroner so that he could examine the body and hold an inquest by jury into the cause and the circumstances of death. The coroner should have the accused imprisoned if he could be found, take sureties that everyone connected with the incident would appear in court, and value the land and goods of the suspected killer or suicide and the weapon used (the *deodand*) all of which would be forfeited to the king if he was found guilty or fled. If an accused man took sanctuary in a church a coroner should be summoned to accept his surrender to trial or, much commoner, to receive his confession and arrange for him to quit, 'abjure' the realm. The coroner also had special responsibility in cases of private accusations, 'appeals' of felony. He should be shown the injury and record it, and he should be present in the county court when the appeal was made and record it. The same is true of the process of outlawry. Coroners received confessions and the appeals of felons who turned 'approver' and accused their associates of sharing their guilt. The coroner should record all these things for the king had a financial interest in them. Coroners were also called upon to act with the sheriff in holding enquiries, sometimes to act in place of the sheriff, for example if the sheriff was a party in a case of if the office was vacant. The coroner's responsibility in all these matters was to record the facts and make certain arrangements, not to try cases. He should however attend to record or present his record in court when the cases came up. He did not normally come to the hundred court, but he was likely to be at the county court and the quarter sessions, and before the justices on eyre, other visiting justices and before the King's Bench when it came into the county. For all this work the coroner received no salary and no recognized fees until 1487, but in practice, like most officials, he and his clerks were able to obtain money by fees and favours, for example by refusing to come to view a body until they were given an inducement. Coroners were performing these duties throughout the late Middle Ages, but the creation of Justices of the Peace, men of the same or better social standing, with wide powers to keep the peace, enforce the law and try criminals, meant a decline in their importance.

Private and Town Courts*

Alongside the communal courts in the counties were other officers and courts belonging to private individuals and corporations and also dealing with civil and criminal cases. A lord might hold a court for his tenants by virtue of his lordship. There were seignorial or 'honorial' courts which he had the right to hold for his freehold tenants, those holding by military or semi-military tenures, to determine matters relating to their tenure. Clause 34 of Magna Carta had protected their rights, but by 1300 these courts were unimportant. The scattered nature of holdings and the advantages offered by the king's courts to which it was not difficult to have cases transferred made seignorial courts uneconomic and unnecessary. The manor court however was a different matter. The manor may be thought of as an estate with free and unfree tenants and tenancies, wage labourers and artisans forming an economic unit. A court was necessary to regulate the agricultural affairs of the community, the allocation of strips of land, the enforcement of bye-laws about common land, ditches, crops, and so on, the enforcement of labour services, the transfer of manorial land, petty offences within the manor and the election of the reeve. When the villein tenant became a copyholder, holding land by an agreement made at the manor court and entered on its roll, a 'copy' of which was his title, litigation about the title took place in the manor court until the king's courts began to give it protection in the fifteenth century, and the transfer of copyhold land continued in the manor court for centuries. Lawyers, particularly sixteenth-century lawyers, drew a distinction between the manor court held for the free tenants, the court baron of which they were the suitors, and the court customary for the villein or copyhold tenants of which the lord's steward was

---

* Franchisal jurisdiction in general is discussed in Hearnshaw, *Leet Jurisdiction*, W.O. Ault, *Private Jurisdiction in England*, (New Haven, 1923), Cam, *The Hundred and the Hundred Rolls*, and D.W. Sutherland, *Quo Warranto Proceedings in the Reign of Edward I, 1278–1294* (Oxford, 1963). J. Tait, *The Medieval English Borough* (Manchester, 1936) discusses borough courts.

judge, but in practice there was normally only one court, meeting every three weeks like the hundred court, and presided over by the lord's steward. The court often dealt with petty cases such as assault, trespass and slander involving those who lived on the manor, and the lord had often acquired additional, franchisal rights, by grant from the king or by usage.

The rights which the king had granted or allowed to be assumed varied enormously. At one end of the scale were the thirteenth-century county palatinates of Durham and Chester and that of Lancaster created in 1351 and again in 1377 for dukes Henry and John. They were subject to statute and common law, but the king's writs did not run there; they had their own central courts, justices, coroners, Justices of the Peace, sheriffs, local courts and writs, all closely modelled on those in the rest of the country, but working in the name of the bishop of Durham, the earl of Chester or duke of Lancaster. Though the earl of Chester was the King's eldest son throughout the period and the duke of Lancaster was king after 1399 this separateness was maintained. Only in case of error was there appeal outside the palatinate, to King's Bench and parliament, though the king retained his prerogative to pardon. The other franchises were less massive, ranging from substantial ones such as the abbot of Bury St Edmund's liberty of eight and a half hundreds which was almost a separate county, through the right to hold a hundred court, to the right to hold the view of frankpledge or have the privilege of 'return of writs', that is execute royal writs within one's lands. These were the major and common franchises but there were many more. A great deal is known about them because Edward I launched an enquiry in 1274 into the usurpation of royal rights which surveyed the franchises and then in his *Quo Warranto* 'campaign' sought to oblige those who claimed franchises to prove their right to them.[14] Some exceptional franchises such as Ramsey Abbey had jurisdiction over pleas of the crown or even common pleas but in practical terms what most of them meant was that lords, through their stewards and bailiffs, were executing functions such as holding sessions of the hundred court or exercising its jurisdiction within their own lands, holding the view of frankpledge or executing royal writs which otherwise the sheriff or the hundred bailiff would have carried out. The proceedings were the same; for example a felon might be indicted at a private view of frankpledge and imprisoned until the royal justices came to try him. Sometimes it is difficult to distinguish a manor court from say, a private view of frankpledge because the two jurisdictions were exercised at the same time. Each county was a complex of jurisdictions. Some of the rights

14 Sutherland, *Quo Warranto*.

continued to exist for centuries for they gave profits to their holders, but the rise of the Justices of the Peace and the regular visits of justices from Westminster gradually reduced them to insignificance.

Borough courts were a type of franchise court for they also were dependant on privileges granted by the king or their lord. In origin the borough (or city) was a township, and its courts were developed forms of manor or hundred or, in some exceptional cases, of county courts, while some had additional privileges or exemptions from other jurisdictions granted to them by charter. All boroughs were represented like hundreds before the eyre by twelve men, and most had a court which was the equivalent of the sheriff's tourn or the court leet in criminal cases; it would try the lesser offences but imprison felons for trial by the justices. A borough might also have the right to try criminals caught in the act; it might have a separate commission to deliver the town gaol. It might even have the right to try pleas of the crown. In civil cases there was the same range of jurisdiction, from the petty jurisdiction of the manor or hundred court over cases arising within the borough, through the right to try 'real' actions involving burgage tenements by writ of right to trying all actions involving burgesses wherever they arose. The precise rights and the constitution of the courts varied from borough to borough. London understandably had the most extensive rights.[15] It was a county and more than a county. Its two sheriffs, elected by the citizens, were the sheriffs of the county of Middlesex and the city was divided into 24 wards, the equivalent of hundreds, each with its elected alderman who together in common council elected a mayor each year (p. 153). Londoners had the privilege of being impleaded only in their own courts and these officers held the three major city courts. The oldest, the Husting, was presided over by the mayor with the aldermen acting as suitors or judges. In theory it met every Monday and if necessary on Tuesday to deal in alternate weeks with pleas of land and with common pleas begun by royal writ, outlawries were pronounced there and the sheriffs and coroners held an offshoot of the Husting on Saturdays to hear the possessory assizes. Each sheriff held his own court, daily if necessary, to deal with personal actions such as trespass, debt and account and, at separate session, with the pleas of foreigners by law merchant. The mayor also held his own court with the aldermen as often as necessary to deal with actions begun by plaint not writ, personal actions, complaints against officials and the pleas of foreigners. Criminal justice was done in a fashion similar to that in the counties. The wards held the equivalent of hundred courts and at least twice a

15 H.M. Cam, 'The law-courts of medieval London' in *Law-finders and Law-makers in Medieval England* (London, 1962), pp. 85–94. In general see G.A. Williams, *Medieval London* (London, 1963).

year each alderman held a ward moot at which he put articles to a jury similar to those of the sheriff's tourn and those accused of felonies were imprisoned in Newgate to await trial before the justices of gaol delivery, one of whom after 1327 was always the mayor. In addition to the city courts there were a number of private franchises or sokes within the city with their own courts, and this was also the case in some other towns.

All the courts mentioned so far were secular courts and alongside them was another sophisticated and increasingly professional hierarchy of courts, the church courts with a jurisdiction over both clerics and laymen.[16] A 'criminous clerk', a cleric accused of felony, had 'benefit of clergy, – treason alone was reserved for a royal court. In practice this meant that a jury in a secular court gave a decision on the felony before the cleric was sent to the church court for judgement and, if convicted there, a punishment which did not include the shedding of blood. The ability to read a text had become the test of clerical status, a curious anachronism when lay literacy was increasing fast. Clerics and laymen alike were also subject to church courts on a wide range of matters, on doctrine, sexual offences, tithes, failing to attend church, working on feast days, petty debts, matrimonial, testamentary and other issues. If this sounds very 'medieval', remember much of this jurisdiction existed until the nineteenth century. A hierarchy of courts existed to deal with these matters, from the archdeacon's court, the bishop's or consistory court, the several courts of the two archbishops with the possibility, much less exercised in this period, of appeal to the papal court.

The courts in this section have been mentioned only briefly and others in the same category have not even been mentioned. Most are less well documented than the royal courts and most have been less studied. Yet these were the courts which medieval men and women knew best, where most cases were heard, admittedly many of them lesser issues such as manorial indiscipline, minor assaults and brawls, false weights and measures, failure to pay tithes, working on feast days and the like. There was a maze of courts hearing these cases, but by 1300 royal justices had acquired a virtual monoply of major civil and criminal cases though not of ecclesiastical cases and royal justice was available more and more frequently in the localities. It was this justice which was eventually, over centuries, to drive out all the other courts.

16 See, for example, B.L. Woodcock, *Medieval Ecclesiastical Courts in the Diocese of Canterbury* (Oxford, 1952). William Lyndwood, *Provinciale* (Oxford, 1679) is a distinguished account of canon law in England completed in 1430.

Royal Justices in the Localities*

For a century before 1272 the most effective method of bringing royal justice into the localities was the all-purpose general eyre when visiting justices investigated and determined a wide range of administrative and judicial business. It was a visitation which was feared and up to a point succeeded, but it had become overwhelmed by the work that the king and plaintiffs placed upon it and it was holding longer sessions and visiting each county less frequently. It was little used after 1294 and effectively it was dead by the early 1330s. An alternative took 50 years of anxiety to find though the basis was already there. Royal justices were already making shorter visits with narrower commissions, in particular to hold the assizes, deliver gaols and put issues to juries under the *nisi prius* system (p. 120). After 1272 there was a great increase in commissions to justices to hear and determine (*oyer et terminer*) complaints of injuries to particular complainants, or particular types of offences in specified areas or country-wide and heard by circuits of justices. The most famous of the wider commissions were the *trailbaston* enquiries which came to be as much feared as the eyre. By the early years of Edward III's reign the king and the Westminster judges came to accept with reluctance that they had to rely on panels of local landowners supported as far as possible by lawyers, to arrest suspected criminals and often to try them as well. These new justices were the Justices of the Peace on whom more and more work was loaded. The new system which had emerged by the second half of the century was that the local JPs held regular sessions and the justices came down from Westminster during vacations to hold the assizes several times a year. It was a solution which endured for centuries and, because it relied on local men, it was a momentous one.

The general eyre was the descendant of the eyres of Henry II whose duties can be seen in the Assizes of Clarendon and Northampton. It was authorized *ad omnia placita* to hear 'all pleas' and assizes, all pleas of the crown and of others, and to enquire into virtually everything that concerned the king. It was concerned with doing justice to individuals and checking on the administration of the counties and it

---

* The eyre is discussed by D. Crook, *Records of the General Eyre* (Public Record Office Handbooks, 20, 1982), H.M. Cam, *Studies in the Hundred Rolls* (Oxford Studies in Social and Legal History, 6, 1921) and in editions of eyre records, in particular *The Eyre of Kent* (in 1313–14) and the *Eyre of London* (in 1321) (*Selden Society*, 24, 27 and 29, 1910–13 and 26, 1968–9). The other visting justices have yet to be fully studied. There are short surveys by R.B. Pugh in *Victoria History of the Counties of England, Wiltshire*, vol. v (London, 1957) and *Itinerant Justices in English History* (Exeter, 1967). M.M. Taylor discusses the 'Justices of Assize' in *Eng. Gov. at Work*, iii. 219–57. R.B. Pugh, *Imprisonment in Medieval England* (Cambridge, 1968) deals more fully with gaol delivery, and M. Gollancz's thesis on gaol delivery in the 15th century is summarized in *BIHR* 16 (1939), 191–3.

was conducted by small parties of experienced judges and experienced administrators such as ex-sheriffs. It became so overwhelming an enquiry that by tradition no county was visited more than once every seven years and in practice it was not possible to hold it so often. Eyres were at their most active in Henry III's reign. Edward I used them extensively in the early part of his reign and they were remodelled in 1278 but they were rare after 1294. There was a brief revival in 1329–30 but only ten counties are known to have been visited between 1294 and the 1340s and the eyres begun in London and Kent in 1341 and 1348 were abandoned almost as soon as they were begun. The eyre was dead but its reputation lingered until the end of the century and parliamentary petitions were presented and taxes granted to be free of it. Considering the character of the proceedings this is not surprising. The eyre meant a specially full session of the county court to which all magnates, knights, freeholders, representatives from all townships and boroughs, major officials and former officials were required to come. In Kent in 1313–14 this possibly meant 1,500 to 2,000 people and the proceedings continued through a full year. Other eyres lasted longer and involved more people. While it sat all local courts were suspended and cases that would have come before other visiting justices and before the central courts such as the possessory assizes, real and personal actions and gaol delivery came before the eyre justices. Complaints (*querelae*) from individuals were received and heard. The roll of the previous eyre and the rolls of the sheriff and the coroner were placed in the hands of the justices to supply a check on what was said. Then began an inquisition of juries of twelve men from each hundred to whom the articles of the eyre were read; this catalogue of questions had been steadily growing and from 1278 amounted to 143 items. The justices wanted to know about royal lands and royal rights such as wardships, escheats and presentation to benefices, about encroachment on them by unwarranted private franchises, about the behaviour of all local officials, about false measures, bad wine, illegal hunting and bribes, about those who should be knights and about many other things as well as the names of those suspect of major crimes. Its very comprehensiveness was responsible for its demise because it was cumbersome and slow even though the justices to some extent divided the work among themselves. It had become an occasion when more amercements were levied than criminals punished or suits settled, and its passing was welcomed by the public, though officials such as Chief Justice Scrope in 1329 were partly correct when they looked back to the golden age when the eyre had thoroughly investigated local affairs.

The demise of the eyre left a void in the machinery of justice which a number of measures attempted to fill. The general enquiry into disorder popularly known as *trailbaston* had similarities to the eyre. It was at one extreme of a range of enquiries whereby justices and others were commissioned to hear and determine (*oyer et terminer*) cases of crime and disorder and, less commonly, cases of oppression by local officials, perhaps in a number of counties. At the other extreme were commissions issued to enquire into the grievances of individuals who had petitioned and paid for them. General commissions were most common between the 1290s and the mid fourteenth century, between the demise of the eyre and the giving of wide powers to the JPs, but they were used a good deal in the 1380s after the revolt of 1381 and against disorder and rebellion in the mid fifteenth century. At first the terms varied considerably. For example in 1292–93 there was a widespread enquiry into 'vagabonds' and in 1298, after the political crisis of 1297, a lawyer and a county knight were commissioned in each county to 'hear and determine' grievances such as the seizure of goods and provisions in the king's name.[17] Then in 1304–05 came a large-scale country-wide enquiry by justices in five circuits into murder, arson, robbery and other breaches of the peace, into complicity in these and into confederacies, intimidation, maintenance, bribery and extortions since 1297.[18] In 1305 it was found necessary for the first time to define a crime by statute, the crime of conspiracy, and include it within the jurisdiction of these justices. This was the first of the so-called *trailbaston* commissions – the word comes from a rogue 'carrying a club' – which were not issued regularly but rather in response to unusual disorders. They were as disliked as the eyre and produced a literature of protest which suggests that they were more successful than other commissions. But even in the fifteenth century when magnates were more numerous on general commissions – no longer called *trailbaston* – and the background was often political as well as criminal, they did not depart from common-law practice, an enquiry through local juries into a series of articles, the receipt and hearing of complaints (*querelae*) and the standard process of writs ordering attachments and arrests before eventual trial by jury. And proceedings before the *trailbaston* justices seems to have produced the same high proportion of acquittals and pardons and low proportions of executions as those before other justices (pp. 137–9). There were also thousands of special, particular *oyer et terminer* commissions in this period, to judges, lawyers, magnates and gentry. Chief Justice Shareshull is said to have been appointed to 740 general and special

---

17 *Calendar of Patent Rolls, 1292–1301*, pp. 45 *et seq.*, *A Lincolnshire Assize Roll for 1298*, ed. W.S. Thomson (Lincoln Rec. Society, 26, 1944) contains some of the proceedings in 1298.
18 Cam, *Studies in the Hundred Rolls*, pp. 73–9 and *Select cases in the court of King's Bench under Edward II*, iv, ed. G.O. Sayles (Selden Society, 74, 1957), pp. liv–lvi.

commissions during his career in the mid fourteenth century.[19] A small number come from before 1272, numbers then grew and reached a peak in the second and third decades of the fourteenth century, and then fell back. They were issued by the king or the Council or (often) on the authority of the chancellor alone at the request of a plaintiff and on payment of a fee to enquire into alleged assaults, invasions of property and other trespasses, and after a statute in 1377 into villeins banding together to refuse services. No doubt they provided just remedies for some complaints but they were open to a great deal of manipulation and their recent historian has written that 'on balance the commissions seem to have contributed more to countryside disorder and suspicion of the legal mechanism than to order and confidence in the king's justice'.[20] Their hey-day however was the period before the JPs and the assize justices began to operate together and before the Council and the chancellor began to provide remedy on a large scale for intimidation in the localities. (pp. 133–4).

Another exceptional method of dealing with lawlessness and oppression was to send the court of King's Bench into the counties to deliver gaols, hear complaints and enquire into and determine felonies, trespasses and misdeeds on the basis of articles put to hundred juries in the same way as justices on eyre and justices of *trailbaston*.[21] This was different from the ordinary work of the court and it began only in the last decade of Edward II's reign. After 1318 the criminal work of King's Bench increased and, more important, in 1323 in the aftermath of Edward's victory over the Lancastrians in 1322, it began to act as a court of first instance, questioning juries, and hearing its own indictments when it was away from Westminster. This gave it an important permanent rôle as a court of criminal justice and criminal review which its companion, Common Pleas, never acquired. There was another wave of similar activity in 1328–30 as part of a drive against disorder and during the reigns of Edward III and Richard II King's Bench held sessions in various counties during quite a number of terms. These died out in the fifteenth century; special county sessions were held in only three terms, the last in 1421. It was a device of limited importance. Certainly when King's Bench came into a county virtually all other judicial business was suspended – it was almost omnicompetent, and a strong-minded chief justice could effect a

19 B.H. Putnam, *The Place in Legal History of Sir William Shareshull, Chief Justice of the King's Bench, 1350–61* (London, 1950), p. 26.

20 R.W. Kaeuper, 'Law and order in fourteenth-century England: The evidence of special commissions of oyer and terminer', *Speculum* 54 (1979), 784.

21 *Select Cases in the Court of King's Bench*, iv, pp. lviii–lxvi and v (Selden Society, 82, 1965), pp. 133–5 (where a set of articles are printed). See also B.H. Putnam, *Proceedings before the Justices of the Peace in the Fourteenth and Fifteenth Centuries* (London 1938) and *Sir William Shareshull*.

short, sharp assault on lawlessness. But only a limited time could be devoted to these visits. King's Bench had its normal work to perform at Westminster; unless normal work was temporarily abandoned it could visit only a limited number of counties and few that were far distant from London. There is also doubt about the effectiveness of a short visitation for, as the rolls of uncompleted business before the JPs show (pp. 137–8), King's Bench did not winkle out recalcitrants who would not come into court.

The two last lasting ways in which the king's justice was brought into the localities were the regular circuits of justices of assize and gaol delivery, and the Commission of the Peace. The circuits became established early in this period on a regular and professional footing, and the pattern established lasted with little change for centuries. In 1215 clause 18 of Magna Carta had promised that two justices with four county knights would hear the assizes of novel disseisin, mort d'ancestor and darrein presentment four times a year in each county; in the 1217 re-issue this was reduced to one a year; and during Henry III's reign the assizes were held at irregular intervals by knights, justices, or combinations of both. Early in Edward I's reign circuits evolved, in part by practice, in part by legislation. In 1285 the Statute of Westminster II (13 Edw. I, c.30) provided that two sworn justices with the help of one or two county knights should hear the assizes of novel disseisin and mort d'ancestor and attaints in each county three times a year and at known times, and in order to save labour and expense these justices could also hold inquisitions in the counties into trespasses and straightforward cases that were before the courts of Common Pleas and King's Bench. This is the *nisi prius* system which goes hand-in-hand with the assizes in the late Middle Ages. Cases before the central courts normally required the verdict of a county jury and rather than summon the jurors to them it was convenient to order the sheriff to empanel the jury and send it to Westminster on a given date unless before this (*nisi prius*) justices came into the county; in practice the jurors almost always gave their verdict in their county in the presence of visiting justices, though the verdict had to be sent to the central court and judgement given there. In 1293 this system was said to be failing because visiting justices could not always attend and it was provided (21 Edw. I, st. *De. Justitiariis*) that eight (paid) justices should sit continuously in four circuits covering all the counties to do the work. These can rarely have been justices of the central courts; they were probably trusted lawyers and officials. In 1299 gaol delivery was added to the duties of these justices of assize. Gaol delivery goes back to Henry II's use of juries to find those suspected of serious crimes. The suspects were to be held in gaol – leading to the first spate of gaol-building – and they were tried by commissions of justices, officials or local knights. This procedure also was reformed by Edward I. In the years immediately after 1292 circuits of a sort were organized, and in 1299 the justices of assize were ordered (27 Edw. 1, *De Finibus*, c.3) to deliver the gaols after their civil work was done, replacing any cleric on their commission (who could not take part in the shedding of blood) by a county knight. This linked system was broken during the *trailbaston* visits after 1305 and during Edward II's reign when separate justices were again sent down to the counties but the link was restored by statutes in 1328 (2 Edw. III, c.20) and in 1330 (4 Edw. III, c.2) which provided for justices to take the assizes and deliver the gaols in each county at least three times a year or more often if necessary. The intention was not to call on the justices of the central courts but rather to employ other suitable people if these could be found. In practice the justices were predominantly justices and serjeants practising in the central courts with men who were active in government in the localities, some of whom were probably also lawyers.[22] The assizes like other royal courts were becoming the preserve of professional lawyers. This is a good example of the practical way changes were brought about, and of the fact that statutes must not be accorded the force they have today. For the remainder of the Middle Ages these justices, often a Westminster justice, a serjeant-at-law and a local man, were coming into the counties, normally twice a year, once a year in the northern counties, often in February and July after the end of the Westminster law terms, and were being paid for doing so. They followed six assize circuits formed in the 1330s which lasted in more or less the same form until the nineteenth century. Two good examples of late-medieval 'pure' thinking which were not unfortunately matched by the quality of justice, were provisions that, to avoid favouritism, natives and residents should not sit in their own counties and that, though from 1384 the chief justice of Common Pleas was allowed to sit, his brother in King's Bench was barred because he might have to hear a complaint of error in the proceedings. (8 Ric. II, c.2, 13 Hen. IV, c.2.).

The work of the assizes was first of all hearing the possessory assizes, novel disseisin in particular which was a popular action until the late fourteenth century and extended far beyond its original intention, dealing for example with ejection from life tenures, payments and offices held for life and other things as well as freehold land. The Statute of Westminster II (13 Edw. I, c.25) for example had considerably extended its scope. Other devices such as accepting the formal entry of a child into land as justifying an action for dispossession when he was ejected and thereby testing his right made it into 'a comprehen-

22 Taylor, 'Justices of Assize', pp. 231–4.

sive action for litigating about freehold lands and tenements'.[23] The plaintiff bought the appropriate writ and also (apparently solely for the financial benefit of the king) a special commission to the justices to hear the individual case, and the issue was placed before a jury. From the late fourteenth century however novel disseisin began to decline in importance; other actions, in particular trespass heard in other courts, began to take its place and by 1500 it was probably 'mostly a tradition and memory'. This must have had a drastic effect on the work of the assizes, though the justices had acquired new powers by statute to investigate other cases, for example disorder and abuse of power by officials, and they had *nisi prius* and gaol delivery work to perform. They had become the only judges coming down from Westminster and because of the circuit system they must have become well acquainted with the JPs and the other officials in their counties. This relationship is another aspect of government which badly needs its historian.

The second major change, and in the longer term the more important by far, was the appointment of local gentry, magnates and law-yers as Justices of the Peace to suppress disorder, seek out and try felonies and trespasses and enforce labour legislation.* One result was to draw away responsibility from the sheriff, the coroner and other local officers. The supreme example of this was a statute of 1461 (1 Edw. IV, c.2) which forbade sheriffs and others to arrest, attach or imprison anyone indicted at the sheriff's tourn, and ordered them to bring the indictments before the JPs to be dealt with. JPs with the royal justices sent into the counties became the major means by which the king tried to enforce peace and order in the counties. Their origins lie in an intermittent thirteenth century office, the keeper of the peace (*custos pacis*), an *ad hoc* appointment to raise troops, defend the county and keep the peace, aptly described as local 'commissars' during the Barons' Wars, when both sides appointed rival keepers.[24] During Edward I's reign keepers were appointed in all counties on three occasions to meet particular needs. In 1277 sheriffs were ordered to have a suitable man chosen in the county court to see to the custody of the peace and the arrest of evil-doers during the Welsh expedition which was considered likely to lead to a crime wave in the counties. In 1287 two men were appointed in each county until the king's return from France or until further notice to enforce the Statute of

23 D.W. Sutherland, *The Assize of Novel Disseisin* (Oxford, 1973), p. 165.
* The early history of the keeper is discussed in A. Harding, 'The origins and early history of the keepers of the peace', *TRHS* 10 (1960), 85–109 and B.H. Putnam, 'The transformation of the keepers of the peace into the justices of peace, 1327–1380', *TRHS* 12 (1929), 19–48. Miss Putnam wrote and edited *Proceedings before the Justices of the Peace* (London, 1928) and *Early Treatises on the Practice of the Justices of the Peace in the Fifteenth and Sixteenth Centuries* (Oxford, 1924).
24 F.M. Powicke, *King Henry III and the Lord Edward* (Oxford, 1947), ii. 445.

Winchester of 1285, that is to ensure that felons and robbers were indicted, that every man had arms and that detailed regulations for keeping the peace were observed. They used their own initiative and the traditional method of putting a series of articles to local juries. In 1300 three knights or others were appointed to be 'justices' in every county with still wider powers, to conserve and *punish* complaints about breaches of Magna Carta and the Charter of the Forest. During Edward II's reign there were many commissions to keepers in some or all counties to maintain the Statute of Winchester and enquire into and arrest those indicted or suspected of offences. The commissions vary in detail but the keepership was clearly now a recognized office. The keepers were *not* given authority to try cases, though the same men might be commissioned as justices of gaol delivery to try those indicted before themselves as keepers and before other officers.[25] During Edward III's reign the final stage was reached and the keepers became justices, though only after 25 years of uncertainty. There was disagreement both in and out of parliament about the best way to deal with disorder in the counties; should more authority be given to the keepers or to royal justices and magnates? Sometimes one, sometimes another course was followed; the keepers were given more authority, then it was taken away again; but by 1350 the agreed solution was the one advocated by the Commons in parliament, wider powers for the keepers, that is for men of their own status. They were to *try* those accused of a list of offences which grew and grew, and men with legal experience were associated with them. This came about by experiment and practice rather than by any deliberate act of creation such as the often quoted statute of 1361 (34 Edw. III); there were at first some years when the justices were not permitted to *try* cases; but by the early fifteenth century, after many variations in detail, the office and its duties had taken the form that lasted for centuries.

Justices of the Peace were obliged by statute to hold 'sessions' at least four times a year, the formal 'quarter sessions' which might extend over a number of days.[26] They also held shorter sessions, perhaps merely to hold enquiries with only a couple of justices present, and they might hold them in different parts of the county, sometimes in what amounts to a circuit. Individual justices had responsibilities out of session. Like their predecessors, the keepers of the peace, they were expected to ensure that the peace-keeping provisions of the

25 *Kent Keepers of the Peace, 1316–1317*, ed. B.H. Putnam (Kent Archaeological Society, Kent Records 13, 1933), pp. xx–xxi.
26 Different dates were laid down in statutes of 1351, 1362 and 1414. The intention of the last two was four sessions, in the weeks after Epiphany (6 January), a spring session between late February and April, a summer session between late May and July, and a session after Michaelmas (29 September). In practice these dates were not rigidly observed.

Statute of Winchester and subsequent 'peace' statutes were observed and that disorders were halted. For example a series of statutes between 1391 and 1429–30 placed potentially dangerous duties on JPs and on sheriffs, under-sheriffs and coroners when forcible entries or riots and disturbances were reported. The JPs with the help of the officers and all men of the county were to arrest the wrongdoers and, if the incident was over, have them named by juries and arrested and those dispossessed restored. JPs had also a general authority to arrest men on suspicion or take sureties from them when the peace was threatened. 'Quarter sessions' were like miniature eyre or *trailbaston* sessions to which jurors from each hundred, representatives from the townships, and the sheriff, the coroners and the lesser officials would be summoned and inquisition made through juries of each hundred or of the whole county into a series of articles. Several hundred men might be present.[27] The range of enquiries can be seen from the JPs' commissions, though these vary in detail, and from the statutes, but in practice the justices exercised a wider customary authority than was authorized 'on paper'. The best impression of the range is given in a set of articles probably drawn up for the justices in Lincolnshire in the first years of the fifteenth century and apparently quite typical.[28] This consists of 36 detailed articles of enquiry into felonies, mentioning various types of killing, robbery, arson, rape and those associated with them as receivers, maintainers, procurers, and so on, those imprisoned on suspicion of felony, into trespasses, riots, giving liveries, taking oaths, forcible entries, disturbers of courts, extortion and oppression by officials, menaces, forced purveyance, buying goods on the way to a market or before it had begun to force up the price (i.e. regrating and forestalling), the malpractices of inn-keepers and victuallers, breaches of the assize of bread and beer and weights and measures, a long series of breaches of the labour regulations, and into peace provisions such as whether watches and hue and cry were being carried out. It is a formidable list of both felonies and trespasses and one that grew. It is not surprising that tracts begin to appear to help the JP cope with his load. The hundred juries gave their answers to these enquiries on the basis of their own knowledge and on information given them by officials or representatives of the townships or by private individuals, perhaps in writing in the form of petitions or 'bills' of indictment presented to the JPs. The sheriff was then ordered by writ to summon or seize those indicted. If they did not come to answer at

27 M.M. Taylor, 'Some sessions of peace in Cambridgeshire in the fourteenth century: 1340, 1380–83', *Cambridge Antiq. Soc.*, 55 (1942) suggests that 100–200 attended sessions.
28 Putnam, *Proceedings before the Justices of the Peace*, pp. 10–20. An example of a commission of 1413 is printed in *Select Documents*, pp. 375–8 and see R. Sillem, 'Commissions of the Peace, 1380–1485', *BIHR* 10 (1932), 81–104.

the sessions they were exacted (summoned) and if necessary outlawed in the county court. Enquiry was made into the reputation of those who had been held on suspicion. Trial took place at the sessions, probably a subsequent session, by means of a jury, though cases might be held over for the justices of assize and gaol delivery. Convicted felons were hung; convicted trespassers fined or put in the stocks. At least this was the theory; in practice many of those indicted failed to appear or were pardoned (pp. 137–8).

Giving authority to the JPs to try cases clearly presented a dilemma; the Commons in parliament preferred local men to maintain the peace rather than have potentially burdensome general enquiries by outsiders, but they and the king also wanted legal competence, and for this reason the 'quorum' was introduced. A statute of 1344 (18 Edw. III, st. 2, c.2) seems to originate the principle by giving keepers of the peace 'with others learned and skilled in the law' authority to try felonies and trespasses. The word 'quorum' comes from the commissions which may for example appoint six JPs and empower all or five or four or three or two of them 'of whom' (*quorum*) one must be from a small named group to try felonies; this phrase apparently first appears in commissions in 1344 and becomes common after 1350. Practice, as in all matters concerning the JPs, varied for many years, sometimes there was one quorum of lawyers for felonies and another including gentry as well as lawyers for the remaining offences, but from the early fifteenth century one quorum for all offences was normal. The members of the quorum were royal justices and local gentry, some of the latter were men with legal training or at least experience, say, as stewards, but others apparently with none. The idea of the quorum was a commonsense one but how it worked in practice is obscure, as indeed is the wider question of the JPs as judges. The difficulty is that almost all the surviving records of their activity are exceptional; they are not rolls of proceedings but rolls of extracts from proceedings, cases begun by indictment before the JPs but not concluded, and extracted so that the court of King's Bench could pursue them when it visited the county. In other words they are records of business unfinished before the JPs. Cases certainly were tried before the JPs, some are known and there are records of payments of fines they imposed. As long as King's Bench visited the counties, that is down to 1421, it tried some indictments. More important, so too did the justices of gaol delivery visiting the counties once or twice a year. In the fifteenth century prisoners indicted before the JPs formed the largest group tried before the justices of gaol delivery, and there is a close similarity between sessions to deliver gaols before these visiting justices and sessions held by JPs which included some of these same justices.[29] Probably a working arrangement developed between the county men and the royal justices who were normally on the commission of the peace in those counties where they served as justices of assize and gaol delivery, the local JPs dealing with cases of trespass while felonies were often held over for the justices sitting as justices of gaol delivery or at least sitting with the local men in reinforced quarter sessions. This is certainly what happened in the sixteenth century, but research is required to confirm the practice in the fifteenth century.

To summarize the work of the JPs at the sessions; they received indictments of felony and trespass and they considered the cases of men arrested on suspicion of these crimes. They could not however receive appeals, that is accusations by individuals or approvers (p. 102) even in cases of felony, save pleas of regrating, extortion and offences against the labour laws. And they could not hear civil actions between citizen and citizen, either actions about land or personal actions. It is impossible to be precise about the number of cases they received but considering the numbers extracted for King's Bench to pursue, it was considerable, cases of felony and trespass, including assault, taking goods, resisting officials, forestalling and regrating, extortion, and so on, and, particularly in the fourteenth century and particularly in East Anglia, numerous breaches of the labour laws, for example, labourers moving away from their villages, changing occupation, demanding higher wages and the like. The JPs had clearly quickly established themselves as the major means by which criminals were brought to notice and by which economic legislation could be enforced. In the sixteenth century their rôle was to be even more important.

Who then were the JPs? They were predominantly gentlemen of the county with some magnates and justices. In the first half of the fourteenth century two or three gentlemen were sufficient to be keepers of the peace, but after the keepers became justices numbers steadily grew. Statutes prescribed three or four gentlemen, one magnate and some learned in the law in 1361 (34 Edw. III, c.I), six gentlemen with the justices of assizes in 1388 (12 Ric II, c.10), eight gentlemen besides lords in 1390 (14 Ric. II c.II), and by the mid fifteenth century there were generally 15, 20 or even more on the commission. The gentlemen, and in practice they were the ones who did most of the work, were generally knights and esquires of the county 'establishment' who are to be found serving as sheriff, escheator, MP, or commissioner for this or that purpose. At first no formal qualifications were laid down

---

29 Gollancz, 'System of Gaol Delivery', pp. 191–2. And see the list of gaol deliveries at Worcester in the reign of Henry V in Putnam, *Early Treatises*, p. 89.

but these became defined at much the same time and in much the same terms as those for knights of the shire (pp. 189–91). In 1390 (13 Ric. II, st. 1, c.7) JPs were to be the most sufficient knights, esquires and men of law of the counties; in 1414 (2 Hen. V. st. 2, c.1) all but lords and judges were to be residents of the county; and in 1439 (18 Hen. V1, c.11) JPs were required to have lands or tenements in the county to the annual value of £20. Lay lords within the county were sometimes active at sessions; it was no doubt a matter of temperament whether or not they lived on their estates and took an active part in county affairs. Some clearly were appointed for political reasons. Bishops and abbots began to be appointed in 1424 to act in all cases save those involving the shedding of blood or heresy; perhaps the immediate motive was to strengthen the commissions when many laymen were in France. Judges of the central courts came to be appointed to the commission, each in a number of counties, but they probably sat rarely unless they had a connexion with the county or were assize justices there. One of the JPs was designated 'chief justice' and no doubt presided at sessions and gave a lead to the others, while another was the 'keeper of the rolls'. The justices necessarily had a clerk who no doubt wrote rolls and kept records of fines imposed and orders to summon or arrest or exact those indicted. The clerk and justices who were below the rank of banneret were paid wages for attending the sessions by statutes of 1388 and 1390 (12 Ric. II, c.10; 14 Ric. II, c.11). JPs had received wages intermittently before this but now standard rates of four shillings a day for eight justices a county up to a maximum of twelve days a year, and two shillings a day for the clerk, were laid down, to be paid by the sheriff from the issues of the sessions, and payments duly begin to be recorded. JPs were occasionally appointed in the counties or in parliament, the last occasion being in 1390 when the Commons secured their appointment in parliament, but the normal method of appointment was by the chancellor and the treasurer, sometimes at meetings of the Council. There is some evidence that pressure was brought to bear to have men omitted or included on the commission; some men 'procured' their own election; some magnates 'laboured' over appointments; and to some extent political changes are reflected in the commissions.

The creation of the office of Justice of the Peace was a matter of great significance. A new magistracy effectively composed of the landed gentry in the counties and the leading townspeople in those towns which had their own JPs was set up to work with lawyers of their own area and justices and serjeants sent down periodically from Westminster. The effect of giving them authority to keep the peace and seek out and try felons and lesser criminals was to depress further the status of the sheriffs and the county court and even more of the hundred court and the private court, though the enquiries made at the sheriff's tourn and the private leet courts continued to cover much the same ground as those of the JPs. The fact that indictments before the JPs formed the largest part of the work of justices of gaol delivery in the early fifteenth century is an indication of the change that was taking place, and so is the statute of 1461 (1 Edw. 1V, c.2) which forbade sheriffs and their officers to arrest or attach those indicted at the tourn and ordered them to bring the indictments to the next sessions before the JPs. At the same time a continuous link was formed between this magistracy and visiting justices which must have improved the professional competence of the county men. Moreover what was created was not only a criminal magistracy but a force of officials to enforce royal policy, at this period in particular policy in economic matters, but in the future in all kinds of matters (p. 146). But was this a force for good or evil, for order or disorder? It was obviously dangerous to give authority to local men who could abuse it. Some JPs certainly did abuse it and the increasing numbers on the commissions of the peace show that it soon became a matter of prestige, even of politics, to be a JP. On the other hand the localities had always been at the mercy of local men and it seems that the office meant an attempt on a grander scale than ever before to bring order to the counties. What was required to make it effective was control and support from above. The weaknesses of the JPs were likely to be more the consequence than the cause of political instability.

The Common-Law Courts at Westminster*

Most cases were heard in the counties and towns but the heart of the common-law system and the centre of the legal profession was Westminster, already by 1272 the judicial capital of England. King's Bench (the court *coram rege*) and Common Pleas (the court *de banco*), or Common Bench, were most commonly there, sharing the vastness of Westminster Hall with chancery, their benches and tables merely cut off by barriers from the open and noisy hall.[30] They sat there until 1884. Both courts had developed in the late twelfth century to hear cases within the *curia regis*, 'the king's court', the Household, but

---

* King's Bench is discussed by G.O. Sayles in the introductions to his remarkable seven-volume edition of *Select Cases in the Court of King's Bench* from 1272 until 1422 (Selden Society, 1936–71). M. Blatcher, *The Court of King's Bench 1450–1550* (London, 1978) and M. Hastings, *The Court of Common Pleas in Fifteenth-Century England* (Ithaca, New York, 1947) are clear accounts. M. Neilson provided 'The Court of Common Pleas' in *Eng. Gov. at Work*, iii. 259–85.

30 King's Bench, Common Pleas, chancery and exchequer are shown in four 15th-century illustrations reproduced in colour in G.R. Corner, 'Observations on four illuminations.' *Archaeologia* 39 (1863), pp. 357–72.

since then they had gone 'out of court' and become distinct, each with its own judges, officers and records. They sat for some 15–20 weeks in the year during the four law terms (Hilary, Easter, Trinity and Michaelmas) and probably only in the mornings. Chief Justice Fortescue in the mid fifteenth century wrote that they sat from eight until eleven and the judges could therefore lead a quiet life 'free of all worry and worldly cares'.[31] This must be taken with a large grain of salt because, as we have seen, they were often sent on commissions in the counties out of term and had other work, including private work, at Westminster, though it is true that fifteenth-century judges were professional lawyers and less involved in general administrative business than their predecessors. Both courts sometimes sat outside Westminster. For example there was a period of five years in the 1330s during Edward III's campaigns against the Scots and a term in 1392 during Richard II's quarrel with the Londoners when much of the government including the two courts sat in York. The work of Common Pleas, cases between subject and subject, made it more static. In 1215 Magna Carta (clause 17) had laid down that common pleas should be held '*in aliquo loco certo*', in some certain place, and though this was not yet interpreted to mean literally one corner of Westminster Hall, it sat there almost continuously. King's Bench was however nominally the court *coram rege*, 'in the king's presence,' and this did not become entirely a fiction until about 1300. The court had disappeared completely while Henry III was a minor and though it sat during the first two years of Edward I's reign while he was still abroad, the clerks were unwilling to use the phrase *coram rege* in the records. By 1300 however the fiction was accepted.[32] Edward I did sit there occasionally and so did his immediate successors, but by the mid fifteenth century Fortescue could write that none of the kings of England give judgements themselves though all judgements are his.[33] In Edward I's reign King's Bench was expected to and frequently did follow the king's movements, for example sitting in Wales in 1284 and once at Roxburgh in Scotland in 1292. In 1300 it was laid down (st. 28 Edw. I, c.5.) that it should always be with the king so that he would have legal advice, but in fact after this time, though it was sometimes out of Westminster travelling with the king, at a parliament or operating as part of a drive against crime, it became a Westminster

---

31 Fortescue, *De Laudibus*, p. 129. But see J.R. Maddicott, *Law and Lordship: Royal Justices as Retainers in Thirteenth- and Fourteenth-century England* (Past and Present Supplement, 4, 1978). The terms were approximately 20 January until early February, two weeks after Easter until the morrow of the Ascension, a week after Trinity until about July and 6 October until about 25 November. See *Handbook of Dates*, ed. C.R. Cheney (Royal Historical Society, Guides and Handbooks 4,, 1948), pp. 65–9.
32 *Select Cases in King's Bench*, ii. lxiii–v.
33 Fortescue, *De Laudibus*, p. 23.

institution. In 1365 the Commons petitioned that it meet in a fixed place like Common Pleas and it was away from Westminster only three times in the fifteenth century and never after 1421.

The two courts must be seen as complementary bodies not as rivals, overlapping courts whose work was largely determined by the circumstances of their origin. Common Pleas was the first to be formed – to hear pleas between subjects; 'the "commonness" does not relate to the pleas but to the litigants'; and for this reason it sat conveniently in a fixed place. Its antiquity and its immobility gave it a strong entrenched position. King's Bench was in origin a session to hear cases in which the king himself had an interest and any other difficult or important case. These original functions continued to determine their work in the late Middle Ages. Common Pleas dealt with real actions, those relating to the ownership and tenure of land, though King's Bench could hear the possessory assizes when it was in a county. Common Pleas heard the older personal actions of debt, detinue, account and covenant, for example to demand an account of money collected or recovery of money due; in the later fifteenth century over two-thirds of the actions before it were for recovery of debt.[34] It also heard the mixed actions such as ejectment (from property) which were replacing novel disseisin. Both courts were busy with the flourishing new personal action of trespass which could be extended to cover almost any grievance including the loss of freehold land. It became the most common action in King's Bench – appropriately because the action nominally alleged a breach of the king's peace, but it was numerous also in Common Pleas. Trespass affords an early example of rivalry between the courts for a Commons' petition of 1372 states that writs of trespass were being issued returnable in King's Bench to increase the fees of its clerks and asking that they be returnable in Common Pleas which met in a fixed place and where many lords and commoners retained attornies. The royal answer was that the chancellor should have authority to direct writs to either court as in the past.[35] Their great age of rivalry was in the sixteenth and seventeenth centuries though the device King's Bench used to draw away business to itself, the bill of Middlesex, begins to be used in the fifteenth century.[36] Criminal cases in so far as they came to these courts at all were predominantly a matter for King's Bench. It did not hear them as a court of first instance save when it sat in the counties – and this was rare after 1400 – but cases of major crime could be transferred to it from the counties. Common Pleas exercised a supervision over the

34 Hastings, *Common Pleas*, p. 27.
35 *Rot. Parl.*, ii. 311.
36 Blatcher, *King's Bench*, chapter VII.

county, hundred and private courts; King's Bench heard cases where an error was alleged in the proceedings of any royal justice, in Common Pleas, though not in the exchequer. This was the equivalent of an appeal jurisdiction, though technically it was not.

In terms of numbers of pleas the late Middle Ages was the 'hey-day' of Common Pleas. There are some 6,000 entries each term on its plea rolls in the late fifteenth century and about the same number in the early fourteenth century, whereas there are only about 1,000 a term in King's Bench.[37] These figures are however misleading because they refer mostly to stages in the slow process of cases through the courts, the mesne process during which efforts were made to bring the defendant into court before pleading could begin (pp. 104–5). Many or most of them were probably never heard in open court at all; the plaintiff's lawyer merely bought another writ from the clerks of the court in his pursuit of the defendant who in most cases had failed to appear. In fact the number of cases which reached a verdict seems relatively small. The number of cases respectively before Common Pleas and King's Bench may also be distorted because the latter was apparently more expeditious, though there seems no doubt that the former was the busier. Common Pleas had consistently more judges, though there were no established numbers. Fortescue wrote that it had five or six judges and King's Bench four or five in the mid fifteenth century, one in each court being the chief justice.[38] In Edward I's reign five and three would be typical figures, and later the number in Common Pleas rose at times to seven or eight because of the quantity of business. In 1310 when the number in Common Pleas was increased to six, it was envisaged that the court would meet in two divisions, but this did not happen. Judges were appointed by letters-patent under the great seal to hold office during pleasure (*quamdiu nobis placuerit*) and their appointments lapsed with the death of the king, but in practice they were looked upon as professional officers who were not often dismissed from their posts. Judges were paid annual salaries, £40 to a chief justice, 40 marks to a justice, and after 1346 additional annual sums, increased several times up to 140 marks and 110 marks, to try to eliminate bribery. They received an additional £20 a year for serving as justices of assize. In fact though there was legislation against fees and favours to judges and their oath forbade these in cases before them, the greater part of a judge's income seems to have come from sources other than salaries. They received a share of the fees paid in their

---

37 Hastings, *Common Pleas*, pp. 8–9; Neilson 'The Court of Common Pleas', p. 273; Blatcher, *King's Bench*, chapters IV and V. Blatcher, pp. 167–71 prints tables of the 'profits of the seals' of the two courts from 1358 to 1559 which illustrate their levels of business.
38 Fortescue, *De Laudibus*, p. 127. Sayles lists the judges of both courts in his King's Bench volumes.

courts, they could act as advisors, trustees and the like, and they might receive retainers and favours from, for example, magnates and religious houses. This is foreign to our sense of impartial justice, but fees and favours were a commonplace of medieval government and indeed of government down to quite recent times.

The third of the Westminster courts of common law was the exchequer. It was arguably the oldest of the three and at the very centre of royal justice in the later twelfth century but the expansion and specialization of royal justice in the thirteenth century led it to be confined largely to 'revenue' cases at least nominally related to its administrative work as a finance office.[39] A statute of 1300 (28 Edw. I, c.4) forbade it to hear common pleas and one of the Ordinances of 1311 confined it to pleas concerning the king, his ministers and the exchequer's own officials. In practice it continued to hear other cases, for example those where the plaintiff claimed to be in debt to the king. King's Bench in 1338 claimed the right to remedy errors in the exchequer court but the exchequer successfully maintained that this was a matter for the king alone. In 1348 a commission consisting of the chancellor, the treasurer and two justices was appointed to do so and in 1357 a statute (31 Edw. III, st. 1, c.12) empowered the chancellor and treasurer to do so calling on the judges for advice. This new body was called the Exchequer Chamber because it was to sit in a council room near the exchequer.[40] More importantly this room provided a meeting place and the name for a meeting of judges from all the common-law courts with other lawyers and administrators to discuss difficult cases in the courts. It was not a court of appeal but a high-powered meeting whose opinion was accepted in the court from which the case came.

Council and Chancery*

The Council and chancery also sat as courts at Westminster, supplementing the common-law courts. Like most medieval institutions their

39 The exchequer court like its parent, the exchequer, has been little studied but see *Select Cases in the Exchequer of Pleas (1236–1304)*, ed. H. Jenkinson and B. Formoy (Selden Society, 48, 1931).

40 *Select Cases in the Exchequer Chamber*. ed. M. Hemmant (Selden Society, 51, 1933).

* Neither of these courts has yet been at all fully studied or documented. *Select Cases before the King's Council 1243–1482*, ed. I.S. Leadam and J.F. Baldwin (Selden Society, 35, 1918) and *Select Cases in Chancery* (1364–1471), ed. W.P. Baildon (Selden Society, 10, 1896) are the main printed sources. Baldwin's introduction supplements his own *The King's Council* (Oxford, 1913). M.E. Avery, 'The history of the equitable jurisdiction of chancery before 1460', *BIHR* 42 (1969), 129–44 and 'An evaluation of the effectiveness of the court of chancery under the Lancastrian kings' *Law, Quarterly Review* 77 (1970), 84–97 and N.

jurisdictions were not deliberate creations; they had much in common; and it is only in the fifteenth century that they begin to be
defined at all clearly. They must not be seen in terms of the Tudor
Council or Court of Star Chamber and the Court of Chancery which
developed from them. Their origins go back to the thirteenth century,
probably the late thirteenth century, when petitions or bills seeking
remedies became common and councillors, officials and justices still
provided a pool of experience to help resolve difficult issues. Parliament was one occasion for this (pp. 215–16) and chancery which
issued the original writs to begin actions in court and the Council
which was at the heart of parliament's work were obvious places to
consider requests for remedies in special circumstances. In the fourteenth and fifteenth centuries there were still close links between them.
Councillors and justices could 'sit' in chancery and the chancellor was
the most active member of the Council which the justices also attended
as advisers when they were required. The jurisdiction of the Council
and chancery was still wide-ranging. They heard cases where there was
no remedy at common law or which raised special difficulties, for
example mercantile disputes or piracies involving aliens who could not
sue or be sued there – cases which were only beginning to be a court of
admiralty matter in the fifteenth century. There were cases which the
common law was slow to accept because they were novel and its outlook was conservative, the best example is cases involving 'uses',
where one or more persons held land to the 'use' of another, and
which became a significant part of the work of chancery. There were
cases where there was a common law remedy but this could not be
effective because of local disorder or because one of the parties was
too powerful or too poor to allow a just hearing, and there were cases
where allegations touched the king or his officials. There were a
number of complaints in parliament about this jurisdiction over the
years, that it breached the rules of 'due process' and it was laid down,
for example in 1352 (25 Edw. III, st. 5, c.4), that issues of freehold
land could be determined only at common law. The jurisdiction of
chancery and the Council however remained wide and began to be
formally increased, for example in cases of riot.

The great advantage of the Council and of chancery was that their
entire procedure could be less formal than at common law. Cases
often began with a written petition and they could begin with an
allegation or information which led to an investigation. The parties
were often summoned by authoritative writs (devised in the mid fourteenth century) which did not specify the matter to be considered, for

---

Pronay, 'The chancellor, the chancery and the council at the end of the fifteenth century' in
British Government and Administration ed. H. Hearder and H.R. Loyn (Cardiff, 1974),
pp. 87–103 begin the discussion of the court of chancery.

example the *sub poena* (under pain of a financial penalty) or the *quibusdam certis de causis* (to answer certain matters) and which ran everywhere, for example within franchises. The hearing was also less restricted; traditional methods of pleading and inquest by jury were used but written evidence, replies and counter replies in writing, inter- rogation of the parties and witnesses were commonly used. Most important of all, the Council or the chancellor had greater authority to enforce their orders by fines and imprisonment, and to do so quickly.

A major change took place in the course of the fifteenth century, particularly in chancery. The number of cases it heard increased sharply from at least the 30s and then soared in the Yorkist period so that chancery became a busy, professional law court hearing mercan- tile cases, cases involving 'uses' and many others. This work was to transform it in time from a secretarial and administrative office into the Court of Chancery. The Council meanwhile continued to have a wide-ranging authority, in particular over cases of disorder, riot and maintenance, and it also was to be transformed – into the Court of Star Chamber. The fifteenth century youth of these great Tudor courts and the changes in the executive part of government which was part of it await their historian.

The Quality of Justice*

Maitland's opinion that the main outlines of the new law in England had been drawn by 1272 still has considerable justification, but at the very least these outlines had been greatly filled in by 1461, and in ways which would have seemed strange to Bracton but familiar to lawyers until the nineteenth century and even to an extent today. There were fundamental changes in institutions, in particular in the localities, in procedure, particularly in the use of bills, and in the sophistication and professionalism of legal practice. Good examples of this new maturity are legal literature and legal education. *Glanvill*, the rela- tively simple anonymous treatise of the late 1180s, mirrors the early common law; Bracton's great manual setting down general principles

* This section introduces two principal issues, the quality of the law and the legal profession and their ability to ensure justice and order. Both issues have a large, specialized literature in addition to the works already cited. On the first, Holdsworth, *History of English Law* and T.F.T. Plucknett, *Early English Legal Literature* (Cambridge, 1958) are useful and E.W. Ives, 'The common lawyers' in *Profession, Vocation and Culture in Later Medieval England*, ed. C.H. Clough (Liverpool, 1982), pp. 181–217 is an introduction to his own and others work on the profession and its education in the 15th century.

The second issue is forcefully set out in its modern context in a review article by M.T. Clanchy, 'Law, government and society in medieval England', *History* 59 (1974), 73–8, Bellamy, *Crime and Public Order*, sets out the limitations of the system and S.J. Payling, 'Law and arbitration in Nottinghamshire 1399–1461' in *People, Politics and Community in the Later Middle Ages*, ed. J. Rosenthal and C. Richmond (Gloucester, 1987), pp. 140–60 is a recent qualification of this view with references to other work.

of law and referring to cases extracted from the court rolls shows the change that had taken place by the 1250s; but both are unique texts. From the late thirteenth century however there begins a flood of legal literature for professional lawyers. There were many short treatises and tracts on aspects of the law, collections of statutes – for Edward I's statutes constituted the first major body of legislation in England – registers of writs and Year Books. The Year Books are a good example of the new literature and its time-scale. Bracton had compiled his own *Note Book* of cases compiled from court rolls but the Year Books which survive from 1292 were quite different. They consist of short verbatim reports of significant arguments and rulings in recent cases in court (and sometimes in discussion out of court) noted by those who were present and grouped by year or session. At first they were personal and therefore variant collections by individual lawyers who wished to have a record of recent pleadings; by 1400 they were largely uniform, practical collections of recent pleadings; they began to appear in print by 1520 and were used to build up precedents in the modern fashion, something that had not been done during the Middle Ages. In this period a law library of sorts with statutes, pleadings and tracts became desirable for the student, the practitioner and even the landowner and his steward, and it closed with another great law book, Littleton's *Tenures* of the 1470s. Sir Thomas Littleton was a justice of Common Pleas and his structured text-book on the rights of property in land was in use for three centuries. Coke admired it so much that he annotated it as the first part of his *Institutes* published in 1628. Littleton's contemporary Sir John Fortescue, chief justice of King's Bench, was an even more prolific writer and what is significant in this connexion is his unrestrained admiration for the common law and its profession.

Both Littleton and Fortescue, like all the justices of the two benches in their time, were laymen, knights, educated professional men who had worked their way up to the bench through the grade of serjeant-at-law. Already in Bracton's day there were professional pleaders who spoke in court on behalf of their clients and attorneys who conducted their cases, but the majority of justices were clerics with varied backgrounds in royal service; at best, like Bracton, a cleric, they had learned their law as the clerks of older justices. The great change began in the late thirteenth century. By 1300 most justices and by about 1340 all justices were laymen. They were selected at first mainly and soon exclusively from the pleaders, by then called serjeants-at-law, because of their *legal* experience. This was an important tradition for it enhanced the independence (and narrowness) of the judiciary and encouraged the profession to look to its own education. In 1292 Edward I ordered the justices of Common Pleas to ensure a sufficient number of attorneys and apprentices to serve the needs of the counties; he thought 140 would suffice and they were to follow the court and have a monopoly of the work.[41] No doubt the apprentices sat in court to learn (and perhaps compose their Year Books) in special seats – in Common Pleas called the 'crib' in 1309. By the early fourteenth century these apprentices were hiring houses in which to live and from these came the Inns of Court where by the fifteenth century an organized legal education was available. According to Fortescue, who may have exaggerated but who certainly did not invent his description, the young apprentice might study the elements of the law in one of the lesser inns and then proceed to one of the four greater inns called Inns of Court – Lincoln's, Gray's and the Middle and Inner Temple – where he would attend lectures, read his books, engage in disputation and attend the courts. After a time he began to take clients and practice in the lesser courts. He proceeded from 'inner barrister' to 'outer barrister', to bencher and reader, the terms derive from the mock trials or moots where the juniors pleaded cases 'at the bar' before their seniors on the bench. After 16 years he might be called to the grade of serjeant-at-law which had a monopoly of appearing in Common Pleas. He might then serve as a justice of assize and in time be appointed a justice of one of the two benches or a baron of the exchequer. There is still much that is uncertain about the early history of the legal profession but in essentials it was created by the fifteenth century and its members were practising not only at Westminster but also in the counties and the towns.

There was also a greater respect for justice and humanity, both inside and outside the courts. Justices in the thirteenth century were still actively involved in all aspects of royal government; by 1400 they were professional lawyers who for example had become legal advisers rather than full members of parliament and the Council. There was greater emphasis on the independence of their judgements; they swore an oath to do justice to rich and poor alike and to accept nothing for doing so. In 1346, following complaints about their venality, Edward III ordained that justices and barons of the exchequer should take fees and robes only from the king, that they should take no gifts save food and drink of small value from those before them, and he reiterated their duty to do justice to all without interference. More surprisingly he increased their salaries to compensate for the losses they would suffer as a result – and this was apparently the reason for another increase in their salaries in 1389. In practice they often fell short of all

41 *Rot. Parl.*, i. 140.

these ideals. They were commonly retained with fees as advisers to individuals and institutions and 'labouring' justices and interfering with the course of law were widespread. Kings were as guilty of seeking 'justice with favour' as others.[42] Yet justice and humanity were more respected. For example, the principle that no man should be injured or punished save by 'due process of law' was reiterated and a number of fourteenth-century statutes extended the famous clause 39 of Magna Carta to give it greater effect. Violence was common during the period but lynch law was unusual and even the killing of an outlaw on sight was made illegal in 1329. Torture was rare and Fortescue eloquently condemns it. Mutilation and amputation, common before, were little used. They were used much more in Tudor England. Fortescue wrote at length about the virtues of the English jury and declared that he would 'prefer twenty guilty men to escape death through mercy, than one innocent to be condemned unjustly'.[43] Fortescue and his contemporaries made, I think, an important contribution to the first-formulation of some of the traditional English and British traditions of justice and government, though practice, I admit, often fell short of principle. There was no professional police, no standing army, no local government in our terms, communications were much more difficult, the bonds of society were different and people had to rely for protection much more on their communities and their connexions (Chapter 7). The law had to be a compromise in practice between the ideal and the possible. Two good examples of this are the failure to convict criminals and the expense, delays and low success rate of civil proceedings.

The problem of convicting criminals is highlighted in the rolls of indictments made before the JPs and extracted for consideration by royal justices or King's Bench, that is, cases unfinished before the JPs, not all cases. In a high proportion the accused did not appear or produced a pardon and only a small proportion were convicted. Miss Putnam concluded in her edition of twenty such rolls 'that of the four rolls in which trials are recorded only in the latest Southamptonshire roll (1475) is there a substantial proportion of convictions for felony, but that in all of them there is a fair number of fines for trespasses. Of the cases in the sixteen rolls for which the sequel must be sought in gaol delivery or in King's Bench the results are as follows: a large propor-

---

42 Maddicott, *Law and Lordship*. The *Paston Letters* contain a deal of evidence about the value of a favourable judge and the difficulty of obtaining a fair hearing against a powerful opponent. And there were many complaints in parliament about royal privy-seal and signet letters interfering with cases in court. The original letters that survive seem innocent enough but one in a formulary (Cambridge University Library, MS, Dd. 3. 53, p. 92) ordering justices to ensure equal justice to the parties in a trespass case has the rubric that they do 'justice with favour'!

43 Fortescue, *De Laudibus*, p. 65.

tion of the accused are never taken but are merely noted as outlawed or are not mentioned at all; a large number of those indicted for trespasses and for economic offences who appear in court are convicted either by jury or by their own confession and are entered as paying fines, some are acquitted and a few produce pardons; in gaol delivery there are some convictions for felony, far more acquittals; in King's Bench very few examples of conviction for felony, but almost always either acquittal or the production of a pardon'.[44] Editions of other rolls produce the same conclusion. For example, the figures for Lincolnshire rolls of the late fourteenth century and Shropshire rolls of the early fifteenth century of indicted men summoned before King's Bench are as follows:[45]

			Felonies		
	Summoned	Appeared	Acquitted	Convicted	Pardoned
Lincs.	410	61	46	0	13
Shrops.	156	14	0	0	14

			Trespasses		
Lincs.	468	223	28	195	0
Shrops.	118	29	0	28	1

These figures, and they are quite typical figures, show that the machinery of the law was operating; accusations were being made and pursued through the courts; but a high proportion of the accused were failing to appear. The contrasting figures for felonies and trespasses are particularly significant. Those accused of felony were much less likely to appear and, if they did, they were unlikely to be convicted. Jurors were apparently unwilling to see a neighbour hung for felony though they were prepared to see him fined for a trespass or an economic offence. It seems to have been easy to hide away or 'go on the run', as landowners found when their tenants and labourers deserted them for better terms. This helps to explain why, in addition to continuing to grant personally large numbers of individual pardons of crime, kings from the late fourteenth century proclaimed general pardons every few years. These offered letters of pardon of all save a few specified offences merely on payment of a fixed fine in chancery. Large numbers were bought; for example a general pardon was offered within a few months of the revolt of 1381 to those who had taken part in all but a few heinous incidents, and 616 were bought. A

44 Putnam, *Proceedings before the Justices of the Peace*, pp. cxxvii–viii. Gollancz, 'System of Gaol Delivery', p. 192 and Payling, 'Law and arbitration', p. 158, note 4 confirm this.
45 *Records of Some Session of the Peace in Lincolnshire, 1360–1375*, ed. R. Sillem (Lincolnshire Record Society, 30, 1937); *The Shropshire Peace Roll, 1400–1414*, ed. E.G. Kimball (Shrewsbury, 1959).

general pardon was an act of royal clemency and probably a convenient security for the better-off, but it was also probably a practical way for the king to offer a settlement to some of those who would otherwise abscond. This does not necessarily mean, as has sometimes been said, that there was a breakdown of law and order or an unusually high level of crime during the late Middle Ages. There is more evidence about crime than ever before but there are also more legal records.[46] Contemporaries in every reign from Edward I to Henry VI complained about the level of crime but this is true of most periods. There is just not enough solid evidence yet to enable comparisons to be drawn between different periods in the Middle Ages. What is certain is that during this period the king's government made more sustained efforts to identify and punish crime on a regular basis than ever before.

The same question-mark hangs over civil proceedings in the Westminster courts. King's Bench and Commons Pleas were busy, increasingly professional courts and men of property were ready to begin actions there even though proceedings were protracted and expensive and though only a tiny minority of actions were brought to judgement. What this seems to mean is that men of property, even small amounts of property, were litigious about their rights and had become accustomed to take their disputes to court if only to set down markers or promote a settlement or to have it formally recorded. The courts were however only one avenue to be exploited. Litigants resorted to self-help, to force, influence, gifts, labouring of juries and any other way, in or out of court, when it seemed advantageous. Sometimes, perhaps often, actions begun in the courts were settled as the result of mediation or formal arbitration or some other form of negotiation, sometimes with the help of a justice.[47] The fundamental problem in both criminal and civil matters was that while a sophisticated and formal legal system had been created, the king lacked the force and the officers in the localities to make it work independently. He had to work with the power structures of society in the counties and towns and rely on the co-operation of even relatively humble people. This is the theme of the next chapter. It is of course a problem which is not unique to the Middle Ages. Law and order are never as effective as they should be. Charles Dickens and others wrote bitterly about crime and venality and the delays in the courts in the early

---

46 There are some trenchant remarks in this vein by K.B. MacFarlane in *The Nobility of Later Medieval England* (Oxford, 1973) pp. 14 *et seq.*, and he was the scholar who introduced us to 'bastard feudalism'.

47 E. Powell, 'Arbitration and the law in England in the late Middle Ages', *TRHS* 33 (1983), 49–67 and 'The restoration of law and order' in *Henry V – The Practice of Kingship*, ed. G.L. Harriss (Oxford, 1985), 53–74 are excellent discussions of arbitration and of how an able king might cope with disorder.

nineteenth century – in the last days of the system which in significant part was the creation of the late Middle Ages. And we today complain about the level of crime, the number of unsolved cases, about the expense and delays of litigation and the advantages the well-to-do enjoy in the courts. The truth is that the kings of the later Middle Ages did not govern the local communities. They moderated government there – largely through the legal system, but government there was and could only be in the hands of the leaders of these communities, the landowners and the men of property. This is the theme of the next chapter.

7

Royal Authority in the Local Communities*

The last three chapters have shown the considerable scale of English government in this period. It was able to collect heavy taxation, raise and support large armies and maintain an extensive legal system throughout the country. These things were done remarkably readily though not always exactly as planned; for example the burden of taxation and its distribution was often altered and the law bypassed by local 'arrangements'. The achievement is remarkable because the king had neither significant coercive power nor a bureaucracy of his own in the localities. There were no royal governors in the counties or towns, no extensive royal estates in most counties and royal castles which did not face foreign enemies came to be rarely garrisoned or even maintained. Royal officials, apart from the visiting justices, were almost all local men serving for limited periods and for relatively little payment. In the main royal authority was enforced *directly* through the legal machinery described in the last chapter. But it was also enforced *indirectly* in more subtle ways. Kings could rely on the fundamental loyalty of their subjects and their willingness to obey his personal orders in most circumstances. The loyalty shown to the young Richard II personally during the great revolt of 1381 and to the pathetic Henry VI as late as 1460 is striking – though there were limits to that loyalty, both were subsequently removed from the throne! But while kings had majesty and prerogative and could normally have their way in great matters in parliaments and councils, their authority over the local communities was exercised largely through the local landowners and the wealthier townsmen and their power structures. This was the tradi-

---

* H.M. Jewel, *English Local Administration in the Middle Ages* (Newton Abbot, 1972) is a general survey of a large topic which is otherwise discussed mainly in specialized studies. The second volume in the *Eng. Gov. at Work* Series is sub-titled 'Local Administration and Justice' and has useful studies in the decade 1327–1336. R.B. Pugh's article 'The king's government in the Middle Ages.' in *Victoria County History of Wiltshire* vol. 5 (London, 1957), pp. 1–43 gives a valuable insight into the character of government in one county.

tional way and by and large kings accepted its limitations. They were content if their rights and dignity were respected, their dues paid, a reasonable level of order and justice maintained as they had promised in their coronation oaths, and if they had the resources and support necessary to maintain their increasing standards of living and defend their territorial rights. They certainly did not attempt to set up any new system of government in the localities.

In the counties – the towns will be considered later (pp. 152–5) – the significant developments during this period were the increased number of royal officials and the increased authority given to the gentry. The sheriff continued to be the principal royal official with a great variety and volume of duties, though he lost responsibilities to more specialized officials such as escheators, tax collectors, arrayers, commissioners and, most important of all, to the Justices of the Peace. By the fifteenth century the 'Sessions' of the Justices were beginning to rival the county court as gatherings of the county. The Church was often a major owner of property and important churchmen had an important voice in county affairs but most royal officials were now laymen, either landowners, some of them peers but most knights, esquires and gentlemen, or professional men, lawyers or estate officials. It is not difficult to describe their duties; the difficult thing is to describe how the duties were carried out. They were local men, subject to only limited supervision from Westminster, but subject to the pressures of the locality such as family and kinship, friendship, lordship, self-interest, force, bribery and influence. The publication, over 200 years ago, of many of the Paston Letters opened a window into this society in the fifteenth century and in the last generation there have been studies of society in a number of counties.[1] Evidence is much fuller from the latter part of the period, each county had its own character and the pattern of authority could quickly change because of factors such as forfeiture, minority or the failure of male or any heirs among the greater landed families, but it is possible and permissible to generalize.

Sheriffs were by far the most important royal officials in the counties. They did not have the independent authority of their twelfth century predecessors, they were rarely outsiders sent in to control a county, but they retained a wide range of duties. They normally presided over the county court every four or six weeks and over the large, twice-yearly meetings of those hundred courts which were not in

---

1 For example N. Saul, *Knights and Esquires: The Gloucestershire Gentry in the Fourteenth Century* (Oxford, 1981), S.M. Wright, *The Derbyshire Gentry in the Fifteenth Century* (Derbyshire Record Society, 8, 1983), and articles in collected volumes published by Alan Sutton and in journals. C. Given-Wilson, *The English Nobility in the Late Middle Ages* (London, 1987) is a convenient guide to the literature.

.private hands. They prepared for the coming of the eyre or the visits of the justices by ensuring the presence of the necessary jurors, the officials concerned with indictments and the accused. They prepared the courts and attended them. They were responsible for the custody of prisoners and were normally the keepers of the county gaol. The Justices of the Peace were given some of their criminal responsibilities but the Justices depended on the sheriffs to summon and seize the accused. The Westminster courts depended on them to execute original and judicial writs to summon defendants, take pledges and attachments, distrain chattels and empanel juries. A roll of the writs and returns of Ralf Wedon, sheriff of Bedfordshire and Buckinghamshire, records that he received and executed almost 2,000 writs between May 1333 and November 1334.[2] It was the sheriffs' task to collect the fines imposed by the central courts and the sums due in chancery and the exchequer, the so-called 'summons of the green wax' listed and sent down by the exchequer. They collected the items in the shire farm, the revenues from lands and goods committed to them by the king and many small debts, and they answered for them in the exchequer. It was burdensome, detailed work though the receipts were now only a minor part of the king's income. Sheriffs also paid out money by royal order, for example instalments of annuities, wages for soldiers raised in the county, payments for war provisions, supplies for the Household, for royal building work, for royal deer, hounds, birds of prey and their keepers and for many other purposes. Every volume of the *Calendar of Close Rolls* contains many letters under the great seal to sheriffs and similar letters were sent out in increasing numbers under the privy seal. For example they ordered MPs to be chosen and their wages paid; proclamations to be made in the county court and in the principal towns – of new statutes, truces, a stop on pensions, war news, not to believe rumours or a summons to come out to suppress a rising or join a campaign; men or property to be seized or released; coroners or verderers to be chosen. Sheriffs might be ordered to raise or supervise the raising of troops, if necessary to lead them, and to assemble or forward military supplies. It is true that much of the sheriffs' work (or rather the work that is recorded) was carrying out instructions, most of them of a routine kind, but the impressive thing is the quantity and diversity of the work. It is not surprising that sheriffs had under-sheriffs, an office staff to write and file documents, a receiver to handle money, and a gaggle of messengers and other officers to carry out their instructions (pp. 109–10).

2 *Rolls from the Office of the Sheriff of Beds. and Bucks., 1332–1334*, ed. G.H. Fowler (Beds. Hist. Record Society, Quarto Memoirs, 3, 1929), p. 27. See also *supra* p. 109 and the bibliography on p. 106. The *List of Sheriffs for England and Wales* (Public Record Office, Lists and Indexes IX, 1898) contains their names and service by county.

A list of the sheriff's duties is only the bare bones of the story. It was often difficult to carry out instructions because there was obstruction or force or insufficient money. Sheriffs themselves had many opportunities to show favour or ill-will. The many complaints made against them by the Commons in parliament in the fourteenth and to a lesser extent in the fifteenth century, complaints which led to a number of statutes, show how apprehensive the counties were about sheriffs who could demand fees before they would act – a complaint that was made against most officials – or delay the execution of writs, pack juries, seize property or goods on a pretext or make false returns, for example of parliamentary elections. The ideal sheriff from the county point of view was set down in the Provisions of Oxford in 1258 – a loyal, prudent landowner of substance in the county, a man who would treat the county well and take no fees, and, most important of all, who would hold office only for one year at a time.[3] The Commons' petitions repeat these requirements, particularly for annual appointments, and add others such as that lords' stewards should not be appointed. The counties would have preferred to appoint their own sheriffs and for a few years after royal concessions in 1300 and 1338 they were permitted to do so, but the normal practice was for sheriffs to be chosen at a meeting of the chancellor, the treasurer, the barons of the exchequer and the justices – or at least some of them – in the exchequer or the Council on 3 November each year.[4] These officials had direct dealings with sheriffs and had knowledge of the circumstances and personalities in the counties. There was certainly lobbying and influence as there was for most offices. One well-known case is the sheriffdom of Norfolk and Suffolk in 1450, admittedly a year of great political tension.[5] John Heydon, esquire and a lawyer, was said to be willing to spend £1,000 to ensure a favourable sheriff to protect his interest while other gentry were lobbying the duke of Norfolk to tell the king and the Council that a sheriff of birth and property was necessary to ensure justice in the counties and proposing Sir Miles Stapleton. After John Jermyn, esquire, was appointed sheriff, the talk was of the need for a good under-sheriff who was not favourable to Heydon. The information may be prejudiced but the apprehension was genuine. Kings, however, seem to have been remarkably complacent or content with the existing order. They did not even insist on appointing all the sheriffs. They did not do so in the county palatinates of Durham, Chester, Cornwall or Lancaster, nor for long periods in the counties of Westmorland,

3 *Select Charters*, p. 382 – *EHD*, iii. 365.
4 Sir John Fortescue describes the procedure in his *De Laudibus Legum Anglie*, ed. S.B. Chrimes (Cambridge, 1942), p. 55.
5 *Paston Letters*, i. 158, 159, and 171.

Rutland and Worcester where the office belonged hereditarily to a magnate and was performed by his deputy, nor in further counties for the period of several life grants of shrievalties made to magnates by Edward III. Moreover in nine cases the same sheriff served in two counties, Essex and Hertfordshire for example, and this must have reduced his ability to control his shires. Only Richard II in his later years and Henry VI in the 1440s and 1450s seem to have made significant efforts to place their own men as sheriffs, and they did so for the wrong reasons. Kings were content to appoint substantial knights and esquires of the county as their sheriffs and allow the traditional ways of the counties to operate.

The other principal royal administrative official in the county was the escheator.[6] In simple terms his duty was to maintain the king's rights as the ultimate lord of all land. For example, if a royal tenant-in-chief died, the escheator, on his own initiative or on receipt of a writ of *diem clausit extremum* from chancery, would take his lands into custody. He would hold an inquisition *post mortem* with a jury to determine the extent of the lands and who was the heir, and send it to chancery. If the heir was of age the escheator would in due course be informed by writ that his homage and fealty had been taken and that the inheritance should be released to him. If not, the escheator might have to make an extent of the land as the basis for a grant of the wardship or the division of the land among heiresses. He might have to assign dower to the widow. He had to account for the profits of the land while he had it in custody. He had other duties connected with royal rights in land, for example the custody of forfeited estates or of church lands during vacancies and he might hold an inquisition to determine if there was anything prejudicial to the king in a proposed grant of land into the 'dead hand' (*mortmain*) of the Church or of a right such as holding a fair. He was routinely making valuations of land. These duties had originally been performed by sheriffs but from 1232 they were transferred to escheators, at first to two, one for the lands north of the Trent and one for those south of it, while the sheriff or a deputy escheator served under them in each county. Practice varied thereafter but from 1341 there was an escheator for each county. At first the sheriff held both offices but soon separate escheators were appointed – in the same way as sheriffs and with the same sort of qualifications, each administering one, two or three counties. They were required to be landholders in the county, from 1368 (42 Edw. III, c.5) with £20 of land in fee, and to hold office for only one year. In practice they were likely to be knights or esquires of the county but men of not quite the same substance as the sheriffs.[7]

6 See E.R. Stevenson, 'The Escheator', *Eng. Gov. at Work*, ii. 109–67.
7 *The List of Escheators for England and Wales* (List and Index Society, 72, 1971) contains their names and service by county.

The Close rolls and the files of chancery show that escheators were busy officials within a narrow field, and, like all officials, they had the opportunity to show favour or ill-will.

The only other royal administrators resident in the counties with an authority which was at all broad were the Justices of the Peace. The origins of the office and its essentially judicial duties were described in the last chapter (pp. 122–8), but from the mid fourteenth century JPs were required to enforce what may be described as social policy, laid down in statutes beginning with the Ordinance of Labourers, restraining wages and prices and the movement of workers, and soon extending to subjects such as dress, livery and maintenance, beggars and vagabonds and heresy. They were local gentry and lawyers often enforcing the policies which they or their fellows had petitioned for in parliament. This was the beginning of the 'stacks of statutes' which Tudor and later JPs had to enforce. Lambarde's *Eirenarcha*, a guide to hard-pressed JPs first published in 1581, listed 309 statutes relating to their duties, 133 enacted before 1485 and 125 before 1461.[8] There were also many *ad hoc* officials. Coroners had their recording duties in connexion with crime, normally exercised in the part of the county near their homes (pp. 111–12). There were the officers of the king's own estates, surveyors of his works, forresters and warreners and keepers of his hunting dogs and birds. There were constables and porters of castles. There were commissioners to collect taxes, array troops, supervise weights and measures, survey embankments and dikes or to hold enquiries into particular complaints and disturbances. The Patent and Fine Rolls contain many such appointments and commissions. There were certainly more officials in the counties than ever before but they did not constitute a royal bureaucracy. In practice the counties were largely self-governing by groups within each community.

Most English people lived on the land, in the manors and townships, working it as tenants or labourers with the support of servants and others such as blacksmiths, bakers and inn-keepers whose outlook was very similar to their own. They were subject to the control of officials of the manor, the township and the parish, men such as the steward, the constables, the ale-tasters and the priest who governed the conduct of work and religious observance, settled most of the petty crimes and disputes, maintained the policing regulations, saw to the payment of taxes and so on. Authority there lay principally with the landowners, their officers and the group of leading men who

---

8 W. Lambarde, *Eirenarcha, or the Office of the Justices of the Peace* (London, 1607).

emerge in every community. Royal authority impinged very little. The hundred however had 'public' responsibilities; the sheriff appointed its bailiff and came there twice a year but most hundreds had been granted by the king to landowners and were administered by their officials. A landowner might also have special privileges such as 'return of writs' which meant that his officials executed royal writs on his lands; writs still came to the sheriff but he would send them on to the landowners' officials to execute and report back to him. Some landowners, particularly ancient religious houses, had privileges over extensive areas such as the Liberty of St Edmund covering eight and a half hundreds in West Suffolk or the three hundreds of St Oswald, Oswaldslaw, belonging to the cathedral monastery of Worcester. A county or a hundred was often a mosaic of detached portions of other counties or other hundreds and a multitude of manorial, township and hundredal rights and privileges coexisted, each jealously guarded as a source of profit and power. The utmost privilege was the county palatinate, a virtually autonomous county.[9] Durham was the extreme case for in the county and in his lands in Northumberland and in some of those in Yorkshire the bishop of Durham exercised most royal rights. He had his own courts and administrative officers, central and local, including sheriffs and JPs. Durham was not represented in the Commons and levied only its own grants of taxation. The earl of Chester had similar rights and institutions in the county palatine of Chester but the earl was the king's eldest son, and if he had no son or the son was a minor, the county was in the king's hands. In 1337 Edward, earl of Chester, was created duke of Cornwall with similar rights in that county. Lancaster was a new county palatine in this period created first for Duke Henry in 1351 and then for his son-in-law, John of Gaunt, in 1361 with rights similar to those of the earl of Chester. Lancaster had its own courts and offices but it continued to be represented in parliament and taxed there. In 1399, when Gaunt's son became king, the duchy and the county palatinate of Lancaster came to be held by the king himself. The royal connexion of Chester, Cornwall and Lancaster still remain to-day. All these privileges, great or small, were held to derive from royal grant and therefore in theory did not deny royal authority. They had to be exercised and exercised properly or they would be over-ridden or recovered. In practice most were exercised, and continued in altered forms for centuries.

9 For Durham see G.T. Lapsley, *The County Palatine of Durham* (New York, 1900) and R.L. Storey, *Thomas Langley and the Bishopric of Durham 1406–1437* (London, 1961); for Chester, G. Barraclough, *The Earldom and County Palatinate of Chester* (Oxford, 1953); for Lancaster, R. Somerville, *History of the Duchy of Lancaster* (London, 1953), i.

Government and the exercise of authority was a matter of these institutions and officials but it was also a matter of social structures and status and personalities. Each community within the county had its own structure, families had changing fortunes and personalities and these determined how its institutions worked. Manor court rolls for example may show how an enterprising man might build up a large holding and become an official and leader in the manor and township. A good marriage or a relative who had made good might be the means of acquiring status and influence. Even the smallest communities saw bitter disputes about lands and rights which parallel those of the best people in the county. This period was a time of great social change and redefinition. Serfdom more or less died out by the late fifteenth century and freemen became very conscious of their status. At county and national level the social hierarchy became more defined and more complex. At the highest level under the king there emerged an hereditary nobility or peerage of five grades, lords, viscounts, earls, marquises and dukes, with the right to be summoned to parliament (pp. 177–82). These titles were loosely associated with income from land, for example an income of at least £1,000 a year, properly from land, was considered to be necessary for an earl to maintain his dignity. Some noblemen were stay-at-homes who came reluctantly to Westminster but most were well-known to the king; they were his natural counsellors, the men to whom government belonged if the king was incapacitated (p. 22). Many felt an obligation to join the king on campaigns; dukes and earls were likely to be the commanders of expeditions. A nobleman had wealth, status, influence and power. Where he had estates in a county he had influence. Where he was the greatest landowner he had power. He would not normally hold county office though it is striking how many peers came to be appointed JPs in their own county, great noblemen in a number of counties. They probably rarely attended the Sessions but they could influence them through their dependents; their appointment was a sign of status and, from the king's point of view, of their obligation to ensure its good government. It was the lesser nobility, the gentry, the knights, esquires and gentlemen, who were the county office-holders and MPs and dominated its day-to-day affairs – and continued to do so until the nineteenth century.

The term 'gentry' is a convenient though not contemporary term for the three degrees of lesser landowners who shared or aped the military and social ethos of the nobility exemplified in the right to have their own coats of arms.[10] The élite of the group were the knights, some of

10 Given-Wilson, *English Nobility*, 69–83 and *Gentry and Lesser Nobility in Late Medieval Europe*, ed. M. Jones (Gloucester, 1986) are valuable guides on the gentry.

whom owned as much land as the poorer lords. Next came the esquires, a step below the knights, paid only half a knight's war wages and permitted to have coats of arms only from the mid fourteenth century. Thirdly in the last years of the fourteenth century references begin to an entirely new degree, the 'gentlemen' (*generosi*), who were a step below the esquires and permitted coats of arms only from the mid fifteenth century. The important thing for the gentlemen, even though the status came to be given to officials and even merchants, was that they were recognized to be a step above yeomen and petty husbandmen. Status mattered a very great deal in this society. The statutes regulating the parliamentary franchise are good examples of this (pp. 190–3). There were no absolute qualifications for the three degrees of gentility but ownership of land was the fundamental basis for the distinctions – by the fifteenth century normally worth £40, £20 and £10 a year in income for the three degrees. As one would expect, the number of knights declined as the status and numbers of esquires grew and the numbers of esquires declined with the advent of the gentlemen. The consensus of recent studies is that by the mid fifteenth century there were perhaps 2,500 gentry families throughout England who were prominent in the affairs of their counties and perhaps three times as many who were 'parish gentry' and active only in their own part of the county. In each county, and each county had its own unique character and political tradition, it was knights and esquires of the county gentry families who provided most of its sheriffs, Justices of the Peace, members of parliament and some of the escheators. The parish gentry, esquires and gentlemen, provided most of the coroners, tax collectors and jurors. What lies behind these distinctions was a complicated and long-lasting social structure at county, hundred and parish level. The county had a unity of its own formed by centuries of common activity centred on the county court and common county responsibilities; and so too had the hundreds and parishes. It was not exclusive because lands and families extended across boundaries but long-established families in particular had a special stake in their county or part of it. Bonds were formed within it by marriage, friendship, service in war and administration. It is striking how often a young man's career was advanced by his neighbour's influence. There were also deep rivalries and contentions. Litigation about inheritances and rights were pursued to extremes by law and force by all levels of society.

The king faced the problem of preserving order and justice and maintaining his rights in the counties where his resident officials were the leaders of society, deeply involved in its affairs and ready to take advantage of their offices. The exchequer and chancery with their excellent archives were able to maintain his financial and feudal rights quite well; the legal system functioned but, as the last chapter showed, often only within limits determined by local people; and the king had to rely on loyalty and good-will for political support. He could use the traditional bond of good lordship. The king was the lord of all England and of all men – and more than a lord. He had a direct, personal relationship with his noblemen. They were fundamentally loyal and they looked to him for patronage in forms such as land, wardships, offices, marriages and good-will in their affairs. National politics was largely the relationship of the king with these men. It demanded good judgement. Too much or too little favour was dangerous; outright favouritism was likely to lead to outright conflict. Noblemen were in turn lords to their men, to lesser peers, to the gentry and to lawyers and officials. They offered access to the king's patronage, opportunities for profitable service which was the road to advancement, assistance in the courts and offices, support in disputes, and perhaps annual fees or even land. In return they expected respect, service and support. This bond of mutual advantage began to replace 'true' feudalism and from the late thirteenth century came often to be formalized in written retaining indentures.[11] This 'bastard' feudalism was a new form of an old relationship with a similar ethos. A nobleman was necessarily a major landowner with estates and retainers in his own part of the kingdom, his 'country', for example the Percies and Nevilles in the North, the Courtenays in Devon, the Beauchamps in Warwickshire and Worcestershire, the Fitzalans in Surrey and Sussex, Rank, landholding, personal knowledge and retinue gave him a duty and the means which the king did not possess to bring a measure of order to his own 'country'. Bishop Russell, a man with considerable experience in royal government, set out this duty in a sermon he prepared to deliver in parliament in 1483.[12] He likened noblemen to islands among the unstable and wavering running water of the 'lower people' and he declared that 'the polityk rule of every region wele ordeigned stondith in the nobles'. This represented what both kings and noblemen knew to be common practice but did not express so eloquently. A nobleman did not however *control* his 'country'; his lands were never so extensive nor the loyalties of his men so certain for this. A nobleman had rather *influence*; he could guide the choice of the county MPs (pp. 195–7) and even of the king's officials there, he could lead out his men in the county on campaign, provide material support to the suppression of crime and take a possibly decisive part in

11 The classic article which made the unfortunate phrase 'bastard feudalism' common is K.B. McFarlane, 'Bastard Feudalism' reprinted in his *England in the Fifteenth Century* (London, 1981) from *BIHR* 20 (1945).

12 S.B. Chrimes, *English Constitutional Ideas in the Fifteenth Century* (Cambridge, 1936), pp. 169 and 172. The text is reprinted there.

the settlement of disputes. He had a strong voice but on the one hand the authority of the king, his officials and justices was never negligible and on the other the opinions and the status of the county gentry and the lawyers who administered the county day-by-day had to be respected. The gentry in turn had their own connexions, even their own retainers, in the hundreds and parishes whose status had equally to be maintained. Each county had its unique and changing social and political structure which had to be carefully tended and cultivated if a nobleman's or a gentleman's 'worship' and influence was to be maintained.

Kings had also direct links with men lower down the social hierarchy. There were always knights and esquires of the royal Household and others whom the king knew from campaign and other service.[13] The first three Edwards retained bannerets, knights and esquires, sometimes in large numbers, primarily to be leaders of cavalry (pp. 27–8). Richard II and Henry IV retained knights and esquires with fees on a much larger scale, partly for military reasons but primarily to secure support in the counties, and Henry V did the same on a smaller scale. An explicit statement of what might be expected from this policy is contained in advice given to Henry IV in 1400 in a Great Council held immediately after a failed counter-coup by supporters of the deposed Richard II.[14] Henry was advised to issue commissions to the Justices of the Peace and the sheriffs throughout the realm and to other persons of substance in each county to oblige evil-doers to stand to the law. He was also advised to retain a number of men of substance and good fame in each county with annuities, to associate them with the commissioners and charge them to apply themselves in their own countries (*paiis*) to save the estate of the king and of his people from robbers and other evil-doers.

The king personally had majesty and authority, even from afar, but the successful exercise of that authority in the counties depended ultimately on the support of the men who had always counted most there, the landowners, the noblemen, the increasingly potent gentry and the men of business, the lawyers and the administrators. Institutions channelled the authority of local men and limited its abuse; the regular visits of the justices from Westminster moderated it in the king's name through the processes of the law; but if the king himself did not take an interest or failed to control his noblemen, force would increasingly pervert justice. The only effective answer to this was greater force. The court of King's Bench was sometimes sent into the counties and because it retained a special authority as the king's own court it had

13 C. Given-Wilson, *The Royal Household and the King's Affinity* (London, 1986) is a good guide to the subject and the literature.
14 *Procs. & Ords.*, i. 109.

some limited success. The king's Council could summon offenders and impose fines or imprisonment or take bonds or sureties; the chancellor could do the same; but when the king's own authority was weak, so too was the authority of his institutions. A more effective response was to commission noblemen to go with justices and gentry to hold sessions of *trailbaston* or *oyer* and *terminer*. More effective still was for the king himself to go with them. Most kings did so on occasion and even Henry VI had some success on an extended judicial progress in 1452–53. Kings of this period however could not do so regularly. Overseas campaigns, the demands of bureaucratic government and a new life-style in the castles and manors around London meant that many parts of the kingdom, particularly the more distant parts which were in general the most disorderly, would not see a king for decades unless he was on campaign. Henry V is the best example of what a strong-minded, hard-working king could achieve, Henry VI of the reverse.[15]

The problem of authority was less severe in the cities and boroughs, over 600 of them by the fifteenth century.[16] Each was unique, but most were of only local importance. London had perhaps 30–40,000 inhabitants, York and Bristol about 10,000, Plymouth and Coventry about 7,000, but only some 40 had more than 1,000 and many were little more than privileged townships. By 1300 most of the larger towns were self-governing. They had once been governed by reeves or bailiffs appointed by the king or their lord – like a township – but in the twelfth century traders had often been allowed to set up their own organizations, the gild merchant, and from the last years of the century charters giving them self-government began to be granted. In this period hundreds of these were granted. Town rights can be equated with those of townships or hundreds or, in a few cases, of counties, sometimes with special privileges similar to those of franchises. In the larger towns the common pattern was for an elected mayor or, less commonly, bailiffs to govern with the help of a council of 12 or 24 burgesses, sometimes called aldermen, elected by the burgesses. They collected the town's farm, saw to its defence, held its court and acted as its justices, regulated its trade and carried out orders that came from the king. It was self-government by the leading burgesses with some regard for the views of all burgesses. Townsmen however became as status conscious as the men in the counties and disturbances over 'citizens' rights' and constitutional change became common.

15 *Henry V: The Practice of Kingship*, ed. G.L. Harriss (Oxford, 1985) provides excellent examples of royal leadership.
16 S. Reynolds, *An Introduction to the History of English Medieval Towns* (Oxford, 1977) provides a good background. There is no general book on town government. J. Tait, *The Medieval English Borough* (Manchester, 1936) is indeed authoritative but brief on the period after 1300.

London is the best documented town but its size, wealth, trade and proximity to Westminster makes it quite untypical.[17] It was in all but name the 'capital' of the kingdom with a significant rôle in national politics throughout this period. For example the period ends with London's gates closed against Henry VI's victorious troops, its inhabitants resisting any temporizing by the more cautious city authorities, and the entry and acclamation of Edward IV who could probably not have become king without its support. London's wealth and independence and its stormy internal politics often led it into conflict with the king and its privileges were confiscated several times and restored only at a price. It became a county in the twelfth century; it chose its two sheriffs who were also the sheriffs of Middlesex; it came to have its own coroners, escheator – who after 1327 was the mayor – and Justices of the Peace. Government was in the hands of the mayor and a council or court of 24 aldermen chosen by the 'good men' of its 24 wards which were the equivalent of hundreds. The mayor, who was almost always an alderman, and the sheriffs were elected annually in an assembly representing the wards; in the fourteenth century this meant about 300 of the better citizens. The mayor, the aldermen, who often served for long periods, and the sheriffs held the city courts (pp. 114–15) and took most of the decisions. In practice they were the wealthier citizens, in the early part of this period most of them wholesale merchants, but London's social structure, like that of other large towns, was changing. The number of citizens, those who shared the city's privileges and responsibilities including taxation and were eligible for office, increased significantly, and trade or craft organizations called gilds or misteries or companies multiplied and flourished. The greater misteries such as vintners, fishmongers, grocers, mercers and goldsmiths and lesser ones such as butchers, sadlers and tilers which regulated the practices of their trade or craft played a large part in the social and religious life of their members and gave them an opportunity to organize themselves. Men from the trades began to break into the ranks of aldermen after the monopoly of the merchant families was broken during a 13-year dispute with Edward I from 1285 during which city government was in the hands of officials appointed by the king. Citizens' rights became a live issue, particularly at times of national political troubles, for example in the years after 1327 and 1376. In 1376 the crafts were able to have aldermen elected for only a year at a time and to have regular meetings between assemblies called 'common councils', composed of representatives of the crafts, and the

17 G.A. Williams, *Medieval London: from Commune to Capital* to 1338 (London, 1963) is excellent and S. Thrupp, *The Merchant Class of Medieval London, 1300–1500* (Chicago, 1948) and R. Bird, *The Turbulent London of Richard II* (London, 1949) and the introductions to the volumes of London city records are valuable.

mayor and aldermen. After 1384 these changes began to be dismantled and in practice a narrow circle of wealthy merchants monopolized authority though it was possible for members of less important trades or even incomers such as 'Dick' Whittington to break into the governing circle.

London's politics were complex and at times bitter. Its social structure was becoming more stratified; even within the companies there came to be a distinction between the 'liverymen', the more prosperous members entitled to wear its colours, and the rest; wealth meant power at most times. London was unique but the same tendencies can be seen in the larger towns. Bristol became a county in 1373 with a sheriff chosen by the king's Council from three names submitted by the burgesses, and by 1461 York, Newcastle-upon-Tyne, Norwich, Lincoln, Coventry, Hull, Nottingham and Southampton were also counties with their own sheriffs, escheators and Justices of the Peace. By 1461 19 towns had acquired the status of a legal corporation with common rights such as the power to sue and be sued by the name of the corporation, to hold land and issue by-laws, to be effectively separate from the surrounding county. Institutions and privileges varied from town to town but the general pattern was a mayor and aldermen or bailiffs holding courts and governing the town. Trade or craft misteries or companies were often at the heart of town life and struggles among the 'better' townsmen to enter the governing oligarchy and demands for citizens' rights and common councils were common. Shrewsbury for example, an ancient county town with a population of about 3,000, saw three elaborate agreements made after periods of dissension.[18] In 1389 in the presence of the earl of Arundel and the abbot, the two bailiffs who governed the town and twelve representatives of the 'commons' agreed on a number of provisions about its government including that each year the bailiffs should choose 25 loyal, resident and tax-paying burgesses who would choose the two bailiffs for the following year from resident burgesses with £10 a year in land or rents or £100 of possessions. Dissensions continued and further long and detailed agreements were made in 1433 and 1444. The first included a council of 12 burgesses, now called aldermen, supported by a body of 24 burgesses serving for life who were to report to the bailiffs and aldermen through one of their number called the 'speaker' the views of any meeting of the commons. This is only one layer of elaborate agreements. Clearly there were pressures within the body of townsmen for better and wider government. Nominally more townsmen were to take part but there were tight property qualifications and control of the town must have remained within a limited circle of

18 *Calendar of Patent Rolls*, 1396–99, pp. 472; *Rot. Parl.*, iv. 476–80 and v. 121–7.

prosperous men. In 1445 a new charter gave the bailiffs and burgesses new privileges. The bailiffs were to act as escheators and Justices of the Peace in the town and its suburbs and have jurisdiction over its pleas about lands, debts, trespasses, etc. 'so that no sheriff, coroner, or any minister shall in any way inter-meddle in any jury or panel touching lands or tenements within the said town and suburb'. Each town had its own story and its own governmental arrangements but the same common themes recur.

The king exercised less control over the affairs of the larger towns than over the counties. The towns had their own commercial life regulated by their own trade and craft organizations and their own social life, though the distinctions between the rich townsman and the landowner were beginning to break down. Most of the larger towns were self-governing by councils and officials chosen within the town. The king was content with this as long as the towns paid their (higher) direct taxes, conformed to any trading restrictions or regulations he imposed, lent him money, provided troops and supplies and maintained a decent order. My impression is that, London apart, the number of royal letters sent to towns on matters such as escheats, the arrest and release of prisoners, disorders and sanitation – quite a common issue in the towns – was relatively small. The king's greatest check on the towns was through the visiting justices; his great weapon was a fine or the revocation of the town's privileges.

England was a kingdom of many communities, each one jealous of its distinctiveness, yet not cut off one from another. News could travel remarkably fast and the French wars encouraged a sense of being one nation. The king himself was the major force for unity; in some ways he was almost the landlord of all England. Bearing in mind how little force of his own he could deploy and his reliance on the visiting justices to bring his authority into the localities, it is remarkable how much his orders were respected, for example how readily taxes were collected. This was the result of centuries of kingship, the increasing exploitation of royal rights over a long period and the personal links between the king and his leading subjects. In this period a major new link was formed – parliament – to which all the active political community came either in person or by their representatives. This is the subject of the next three chapters.

8
The Development of Parliament*

A great deal has been written about the medieval English parliament, too much some would say in relation to its contemporary importance, but no major history of parliament has yet been written and there has been debate, sometimes angry debate, about issues as fundamental as what was a parliament and when it became a recognized institution. Because of this and because parliament changed so much during the period, it is helpful to consider first the pattern of its development and so give a perspective to the subject before analysing its membership, organization and authority in the two following chapters.

The word 'parliament' is found in several west-European languages from about 1100.[1] At first it was not a technical term; it could be applied to a private conversation or to any kind of discussion or meeting; but it came to be used particularly for special, full meetings of a sovereign's court or council, meetings which might equally be called a *curia, tractatus, colloquium* or *consilium* (court, treaty, discussion or council). By the fourteenth century in a number of

* There are historiographical surveys of the medieval parliament by G. Templeman, 'The history of parliament to 1400 in the light of modern research', *Univ. of Birmingham His. J.* 1 (1948), 202–31 and G.P. Cuttino, 'Medieval parliament reinterpreted', *Speculum* 41 (1966), 681–7. Most studies have appeared as articles in journals and a number are reprinted with an introduction and annotation in *Historical Studies of the English Parliament*, ed. E.B. Fryde and E. Miller, 2 vols. (Cambridge, 1970) – cited here as *Hist. Studies*. No articles by H.G. Richardson and G.O. Sayles, the greatest modern writers on parliament, were included but most of them have now been reprinted in *The English Parliament in the Middle Ages* (London, 1981) – cited here as *English Parliament*, and there is a short, general account of their views in G.O. Sayles, *The King's Parliament of England* (London, 1975). The most comprehensive recent study is the planned series of articles in *The English Parliament in the Middle Ages* ed. R.G. Davies and J.H. Denton (Manchester, 1981). One should never overlook W. Stubbs, *The Constitutional History of England* (5th ed., Oxford, 1891). Its judgements have often been overtaken but its content is still remarkable and useful.

1 The history of the term is discussed in H.G. Richardson, 'The origins of parliament', *English Parliament*, I, 146–78 (from TRHS, 1928 as amended in *Essays in Medieval History*, ed. R.W. Southern, London 1968). A. Marongiu, *Medieval Parliaments: A Comparative Study* trans. S. Woolf (London, 1968) is a good survey of European parliaments.

countries, including England, it had become a technical term for institutions with largely defined membership and functions. In England, the first example so far discovered of its use in an official source is in November 1236, when a case about an advowson, the right to present a parson to a parish church in Wiltshire, was adjourned from the King's Bench to the 'parliament' at Westminster at the octave of Hilary (20 January) 1237.[2] This was a special meeting of the king's court, nominally at least including archbishops, bishops, abbots, priors, earls and barons, to treat of the state of the king and the kingdom, and this is the type of meeting the word 'parliament' came to denote in official circles, though it is difficult to believe that many magnates considered the advowson case; presumably it was dealt with by a group of justices and ministers during the parliament. The word was common in this technical sense from the 1240s, and an indication of this is its use in the Provisions of Oxford of 1258 for the meetings ordained to be held three times a year, at stated days, at which the king's 15 councillors and 12 magnates chosen by the community (of barons) would, with the king and his ministers, treat about the business of the king and the kingdom. Parliaments of this kind were a baronial ideal during the following seven years and the word occurs often. It survived the defeat of the baronial movement and in the last years of Henry III's reign, meetings described as parliaments were often held three times a year and with some attempt at regularity.

During the first 20 years of Edward I's reign, twice-yearly parliaments, around Easter and Michaelmas, were the norm (p. 162) and 'parliament' was a common and recognized term for special, full meetings of the king's Council. True, the word was sometimes used, even by royal clerks, for other meetings, but this was its normal meaning and when meetings take place with considerable regularity, when matters can with confidence be referred to the next 'parliament' and when records of business done in 'parliament' begin to be written, it is difficult to deny that a recognized institution called parliament existed. Recognition need not however mean uniformity and these meetings were regular in neither composition nor function. They consisted normally of the king, councillors and ministers, and important clerical and lay magnates. It seems this often meant less than 50 people, though occasionally there were many more and on a few occasions, several hundred representatives of the counties and towns were also summoned. This is very different from the parliament of the mid-fourteenth century when membership was almost completely regularized, when, for example, the county and town representatives

2 H.G. Richardson and G.O. Sayles, 'The earliest known official use of the term "parliament" ', *English Parliament*, II, 747–50 (from *EHR*, 1967).

were invariably summoned, when procedure was much more formalized and when parliament's rights and authority over, say, taxation begin to be defined. By 1450, there was much greater definition still, for example, of the proper procedure for legislation or of parliamentary rights. Parliament changed considerably in the late Middle Ages, and the historian must understand and explain the changes. The great danger is reading back changes, even by decades.

The existence of these meetings in thirteenth-century England is not surprising. There was a tradition in England and elsewhere of meetings between the king and great men. Medieval kings were not absolute rulers; they were expected to take important decisions with the counsel of great and wise men. Vassals had a duty to counsel their lords and they to listen. In England before and after the Norman Conquest, there were gatherings for ceremonial and governmental purposes, though it would be wrong to see in these a continuous institutional development. Counsel and consent were ideas both pre-feudal and feudal, and good sound political sense as well, and they flourished in the thirteenth century. Henry III for example met repeated demands from his barons that he should consult them before taking important decisions, even from time to time demands that he should constantly have at his side councillors *they* nominated. The principle of consent was a topical subject. For example, the maxim of Justinian that 'what concerns all should be approved by all' was quoted with approval by popes, emperors and kings. Edward I used it in the writs of summons to parliament in 1295. Moreover, 'all' began to have a broader meaning. In Magna Carta consent to scutage and aids was required from tenants-in-chief, but in the so-called statute *De tallagio non concedendo* put forward by magnates in 1297, consent to tallage and aids was required from 'archbishops, bishops and other prelates, earls, barons, knights, burgesses, and other free men'.[3]

The change coincides with changes in the burden of taxation (Chapter 4), in the way armies were raised (Chapter 5) and in society itself. The king's great vassals, the earls and greater barons, were less dominant; economic wealth and power was in more hands. Knights for example were now largely a gentry settled on the land and with the wealthier town merchants served on juries and in local offices and came to the king's court on legal or administrative business. Kings negotiated to tap the wealth of towns, many of which sought and received privileged borough status in the thirteenth century. It is not surprising that 'counsel and consent' came to embrace many more people and became more institutionalized. It is no coincidence that

3 *Select Charters*, p. 493 – *EHD*, iii. 486.

this was also the time when provincial assemblies became normal in the Church and representation of *all* the clergy, not merely the prelates, became common.

'Counsel and consent' and sharing power are ideas with which our age sympathizes, but the medieval conception of them was not ours. Rights were based on property and status, not on egalitarianism. True, all men had rights, but in practice in the country as a whole, in the counties and the towns, the men whose voice counted in government were drawn from a restricted circle of 'substantial', propertied men numbering at most ten or twenty thousand. Early parliaments were also as much administrative and judicial as deliberative occasions. Many more hours must have been spent in them on the details of government than on general discussion. Government was already a matter of offices and officials and documentation, but it depended greatly on the king himself and the king's Court was still the centre of government. Important or difficult matters and those which touched the king's own rights were referred to the king himself or his Council, and parliament was still a specially full meeting of his Council. When parliament's records begin in Edward I's reign they relate mostly to petitions and cases, and early references to it are largely to this kind of business. The fact that most parliaments during the first half of Edward I's reign were held after Easter and Michaelmas must be related to the great sessions of the exchequer and the beginning of the law terms, times when officials and justices were gathered in force at Westminster. Jolliffe in an important article linked this with the practice from the middle of Henry III's reign of deferring matters, and in particular matters relating to the royal investigation into franchises, to be heard in the exchequer or before the justices or the king and his Council a fortnight after Easter or Michaelmas, or , less often, Trinity.[4] The king and his councillors were often present and sometimes a number of magnates were summoned at the same time. This is the likely explanation of many of the characteristics of the late-thirteenth-century parliament, and it is unfortunate that Jolliffe's thesis has not been further investigated and tested. Another strand in the story is the many occasions in the thirteenth century, beginning in 1212, when representatives were summoned from some or all the counties to meet the king, to bring information or receive instructions. The evolution of a parliament is in no way surprising but it was not planned, it did not proceed logically, and a variety of circumstances formed it.

4 J.E.A. Jolliffe, 'Some factors in the beginnings of parliament', *Hist. Studies*, i. 31–69 (from *TRHS*, 1940).

The Records of Parliament

A major difficulty in understanding the medieval parliament is the
severe limitation of evidence. No journal of proceedings in the Commons survives and almost certainly none was ever written. Copies of
a few fragments of lord's journals survive from 1449 onwards,
including a record covering eight days in the parliament of 1461, and it
is likely that they were written regularly in some form from 1449,
though unlikely from much if at all earlier.[5] They are also unfortunately completely untypical of the medieval evidence as a whole;
indeed until the 1290s there is little evidence of any kind about parliament. A meeting may be known only from a reference that a case had
been heard in a given parliament; sometimes it is only that a case is to
be heard in a coming parliament, and there is no evidence that the
parliament was held. Only a few memoranda of business before parliament survive, perhaps 30 printed pages from before 1290. There are
rather more in the following years, probably because of the initiative
of the new clerk of parliament, Gilbert Rothbury, but they are a
miscellaneous collection, rolls of summaries of petitions presented to
the king and Council with their answers, reports of pleas heard by the
Council in parliament, and some memoranda of decisions about public business. The record of the Lent parliament of 1305, the most
complete of the early rolls, consists only of memoranda that certain
men were appointed to receive and hear petitions, the proclamation
that the representatives of the counties and towns might return home,
memoranda of a discussion and decision about how Scotland should
be represented at the next parliament, summaries (beginning 'ad peti-
tionem . . .') of 469 private petitions with the replies, and accounts of
16 cases before the Council. This is the type of record that it was
considered worthwhile to write; it is not a case of many records having
been lost.[6] The major change in the records took place early in the

5   H.G. Richardson and G.O. Sayles discuss the early records of parliament in several articles
    republished in *English Parliament* and summarize their views in the introduction to *Rotuli
    Parliamentorum Hactenus Inediti, 1279–1373* (Camden Series, 51, 1935). The first substan-
    tial part of a journal to survive is *The Fane Fragment of the 1461 Lords' Journal*, ed. W.H.
    Dunham (New Haven, 1935). Several earlier fragments survive from 1449 onwards and are
    surveyed in G.R. Elton, 'The early journals of the house of lords', *EHR* 89 (1974), 481–512.
6   The major collection of parliamentary records, the rolls of parliament, is *Rotuli Parlia-
    mentorum* 6 vols. (1777) and index volume (1832), supplemented by *Rotuli Parliamentorum
    Hactenus Inediti*. The roll of the Lent parliament of 1305 was re-edited by F.W. Maitland
    with a famous introduction, reprinted several times, as *Records of the Parliament holden at
    Westminster . . . 1305* (Rolls Series, 1893) and normally cited by its half-title *Memoranda de
    Parliamento, 1305*. A 14th-century collection of extracts from the rolls, the *Vetus Codex*,
    contains little that does not survive to-day and suggests that little more survived then and
    that little more was ever written. Writs of summons and returns and writs for payment of
    expenses to 1327 are printed in *Parliamentary Writs and Writs of Military Summons*, ed.
    F. Palgrave 2 vols. in 4 (Record Commission, London, 1827–34). Writs of summons for the
    whole period are printed in *Reports from the Lords' Committees . . . Touching the Dignity
    of a Peer* (London, 1820–29), ii–iii.

*In 1341 a more orderly type of roll began to be kept.
— initiative of Thomas of Drayton.

reign of Edward III, reflecting a change in parliament itself. About 1332 rolls of *private* petitions, a large part of the records until then, ceased to be written, and in 1341, a more orderly type of roll began to be kept, again probably on the initiative of a new clerk of parliament, Thomas of Drayton. This records the opening proceedings, the appointment of receivers and triers of petitions, any grant of taxation, some of the proceedings before the king, some pleas, and the *common* petitions presented to the king with his answers. It is a very incomplete record. It is formalized and compiled for governmental convenience; some rolls, particularly at first, are brief; they tell virtually nothing about *proceedings* in the lords or the Commons, but they give a more complete impression of parliament than the earlier records, and they continued to be written in the same form until the close of the Middle Ages.

*very incomplete record.

*Evidence of parliament in other sources.

There is of course evidence about parliament in many other sources. Copies of writs of summons to members were regularly enrolled on the Close rolls in chancery from 1295; so too from 1300 until 1414 were writs ordering payment of the expenses of members of the Commons. Thousands of original private petitions presented to the king in parliament survive, and many led to the issue of royal letters. Pleas heard in parliament are mentioned in judicial and other records. Statutes, which at first were not necessarily considered in parliament, were enrolled on the Statute rolls which begin in Edward I's reign, and taxes granted in parliaments are inevitably mentioned in other sources. There are references in chronicles to parliaments though distinctly fewer than one might expect, particularly in the early period. Contemporaries did not give the attention that historians (and this book) give to parliament!

*Evidence = fragmentary and restricted.

The evidence, always fragmentary and restricted, mirrors changes in parliament itself, an early phase down to the 1290s, another from then until around the 1330s, and from the mid fourteenth century a parliament already showing the characteristics that it would have for centuries, indeed in some respects right down to the present day, but one which continued to develop and had developed considerably further by 1461. The changing character of parliament largely explains the difficulties historians have found in writing about it.

*Parliament already showed the characteristics it would have for centuries.

*Change in character of parliament — explains the difficulties historians have found writing about it.

The Early Parliaments of Edward I

*1272 to 1290s — form a distinct group.

The parliaments of the first twenty years of Edward I's reign, from 1272 to the early 1290s form a distinct group. They are poorly documented but if all the references to parliaments in record sources are

✗ pattern is clear. — held parliament after Easter and Michaelmas.

collected, then a pattern does emerge.[7] Edward came to the throne in
November 1272, but he did not return to England until August 1274
and, whenever possible, each year from Easter 1275 until the 1290s, he
held parliaments after Easter and after Michaelmas (29 September) –
on the feast or a few days or weeks after it, and almost always at
London or Westminster. He did so in 1275, 1276, 1278, 1279, 1280,
1281, 1285 and after Easter 1286. He was in France from May 1286
until August 1289 and his lieutenant held only one parliament, after
Easter 1289. Edward held parliaments after both feasts in 1290; the
affairs of Scotland and Wales halted the pattern in 1291 and 1292; it
was resumed in 1293 and 1294 but, apart from 1299, this was the end
of regular parliamentary sessions for 400 years. In other years a parliament was held after one of the feasts and references to forthcoming
parliaments show that officials expected parliaments to be held after
both feasts in 1277, 1283 and 1284, but Welsh campaigns made this
impossible. There is no doubt however that until the 1290s it was
considered desirable and normal to have parliaments after Easter and
Michaelmas in every year. Indeed, in a letter to the pope after his first
parliament Edward declared, apparently quite wrongly, that an
annual Easter parliament was customary.[8] He was to make it customary but his later commitments were to destroy the custom. Besides 23
such parliaments, Edward held at least five others, in July and August
1278 at Gloucester, about Christmas 1289 at Westminster, in January
1291 at Ashridge, in January 1292 at London, and after Christmas
1293 at London. They were apparently held to meet immediate needs;
in 1291 and 1292 for example, there was probably no other time in the
year that was convenient because of the proceedings about the succession to the kingdom of Scotland.

✗ destroyed the custom

use of the word parliament is significant!

The significance of this list depends of course on the validity of the
assumption which underlies it, that the use of the word 'parliament' is
significant, but this does seem to be justified by the pattern which
emerges and by the confident way in which the word 'parliament' was
used in the records. Men were released or the custody of land was
given until a decision by the king and his Council in the next 'parliament' after Easter or Michaelmas. In 1279, for example, Nicholas
Weston landed in trouble for failing to obey a royal order; he put

---

7 Richardson and Sayles in their articles of the late 1920s and early 1930s (reprinted in *English
Parliament*) assembled references to parliaments and produced lists of them by this
criterion. Corrections and further material will be found. For example M. Prestwich, 'Magnate summonses in England in the later years of Edward I', *Parliaments, Estates and
Representation* 5 (1985), 97–101 is an important qualification of the evidence on summons.
But the balance of evidence is unlikely to change much and this is the basis of the pattern set
out in this chapter. The *Handbook of British Chronology*, ed. E.B. Fryde *et al*, 3rd ed.
(Royal Historical Society, 1986) includes a list of English parliaments.
8 *Parl. Writs*, i. 381–2.

himself at the king's will and was told to appear at the parliament after Easter; he did so but the king did not have time to deal with him because of more important business and the case was adjourned until the parliament after Michaelmas. This is known because Nicholas failed to appear and a royal letter was issued explaining the circumstances and ordering his arrest.[9] There seems moreover to be a distinction between assemblies described as 'parliaments' and those which are not. The Winchester annalist who describes the assembly of magnates, prelates, knights and townsmen which took an oath of loyalty to the absent king and settled some matters of government in January 1273, does not use the word, nor does Edward himself when he ordered a 'council' of magnates and others to meet in his absence in 1274, and the word 'parliament' seems deliberately avoided in references to the series of gatherings which the king's lieutenant held during Edward's absence between 1286 and 1289. At this period, the presence of the king was perhaps necessary for a parliament, though the assembly which the king's lieutenant held after Easter 1289 was described as a parliament in at least two record sources. The status and name may have been given to it because it was given special competence to deal with accumulated business and because the king wished it to make a grant of taxation. It is also possible that evidence of further parliaments may be found, but few other assemblies of this period seem likely candidates; gatherings such as those of magnates in November 1276 and May 1282 which agreed to campaign in Wales or that at Bristol after Christmas 1284 which a chronicler with unusual precision describes as 'non universali seu generali sed tanquam particulari et speciale parliamento'[10] or the simultaneous meeting of county and town representatives at York and Northampton in 1283 which agreed to a tax, or the four meetings of Scots and English in 1291–92 to discuss the matter of the Scottish crown. The evidence is not strong enough to warrant absolute confidence about all these assemblies but they seem to be *ad hoc* gatherings, not 'general' parliaments like the 28 others.

Little is known about the membership or the business of these parliaments. Representatives from the counties and the towns are known to have been summoned to only three or four, and with no regularity of numbers.[11] They were clearly not a necessary nor an important part of parliament. Even less is known about the magnates

9 *Calendar of Fine Rolls, 1272–1307*, p. 120.
10 *Annales Monastici*, ed. H.R. Luard (Rolls Series, 1869), iv. 300.
11 Four knights and four or six townsmen from each county and town were summoned in April 1275, two knights in October 1275 and two knights and two townsmen from each of only 21 towns in September 1283. Two or three knights were summoned at the end or just after a parliament in July 1290 to assent to a grant of taxation. The evidence in the first two cases is the chance survival of original writs, in the second two there are enrolled writs.

in parliament. Only one set of writs of summons to them is known, to 10 earls and 99 barons to decide the fate of David of Wales at Shrewsbury in September 1283.[12] No ecclesiastics were summoned and the number of barons is large by the standards of the second half of the reign, no doubt to encourage them to fight alongside the king in Wales. It is not typical of Edwardian parliaments and it cannot be assumed that writs of summons were issued to magnates on other occasions during this period but were not enrolled. Parliaments held at regular intervals, almost always at Westminster, may not have required writs of summons, particularly if attendance was normally comparatively small and largely ministerial and courtier. In the baronial 'plan' of 1258, twelve men were to represent the community at parliaments, and a memorandum of May 1290, tells how a feudal aid was granted in 'full parliament' by six bishops, one of them the chancellor, by the king's brother, his cousin and four other earls, by eleven barons who have been described as 'all officials or close members of the household' and 'other magnates and leading men in parliament'.[13] Bearing in mind the wide variation in the number of magnates summoned to parliaments after 1297 and the difficulty in making them attend, it is likely that in this early period parliament often consisted of the king, his councillors and ministers, some of the earls and other prominent laymen and ecclesiastics, and that only when the king saw advantage in doing so, to obtain wider support for a policy or a decision, were larger numbers of magnates and sometimes even commoners summoned to be present.

The work done in these early parliaments is also problematical. The considerable regularity of sessions at Easter and Michaelmas suggests that it was administrative and judicial business which gave them their character though in the records it is petitions to the king or the king and Council which predominate. The written petition or 'bill' was a major innovation of the thirteenth century and in particular of the second half of the century. It had a great effect on the legal system (p. 103) and on government (p. 19) and the right to petition in parliament was a privilege apparently granted only in the 1270s. Soon special arrangements had to be made to handle the flood that resulted (pp. 216–17). In 1280 Edward announced arrangements to sift these petitions 'because people coming to the king's parliament are often delayed and disturbed by the multitude of petitions placed before the king, to the great grievance of them and the court' and to enable the king and Council, without the charge of other matters, to 'attend to

12 *Parl. Writs*, i. 15–16.
13 *Rot. Parl.*, i. 125. The comment is made by J.E. Powell and K. Wallis, *The House of Lords in the Middle Ages* (London, 1968), p. 213.

the weighty matters of his realm and his foreign lands'.[14] These matters might be diplomatic relations, disputes with the pope, trading rights, piracies, the maintenance of the peace, homages and individual pleas and processes. A schedule of 37 items before the Easter parliament of 1279 is the best indication of the range of such matters.[15] A legal treatise of the 1290s called *Fleta* gives the only contemporary general statement about parliament. 'The king has his court in his council in his parliaments in the presence of prelates, earls, barons, magnates and others learned in the law, where the doubts of the judges are concluded and new remedies are provided for new injuries that have arisen, and where justice is done to each according to his merits.'[16] This is part of an account of the courts by a lawyer and it is not a balanced account of *all* the work of parliament, but it seems to be accurate as far as it goes. A narrow line, difficult to draw, separates this work from the administrative work which the Council handled with the help of chancery and exchequer. This is all in the tradition of 'business' sessions inherited from Henry III to which Jolliffe drew attention. The other tradition, the consultative tradition, was also maintained. Sometimes taxes were approved or legislation considered though parliament had no *right* to do so.

The character of the early Edwardian parliaments is inevitably somewhat uncertain for lack of evidence. My impression is of largely regular, working meetings where administrative and judicial cases were decided, where petitions were handled and where wider issues of policy and government were discussed, often in the presence of small numbers of magnates, councillors and officials, occasionally with considerably larger numbers specially summoned.

The Later Parliaments of Edward I

In the 1290s and certainly from 1295, there was a marked change. Easter and Michaelmas parliaments were held in 1290, 1293, 1294 and 1299, but the king was often away from Westminster at these feasts and regular sessions ceased. This was probably a major reason why it became normal practice from 1295 to enrol and possibly for the first time regularly to issue writs of summons. Initially, these writs normally announced that the king wished to have a 'colloquium et tractatus' without using the word 'parliament', but the rubric in the margin of the roll, the note which clerks wrote so that they could find

14 J.G. Edwards, ' "Justice" in early English parliaments', *Hist. Studies*, i. 284 (from *BIHR*, 1954).
15 *Rotuli Parliamentorum Hactenus Inediti*, pp. 1–7.
16 *Fleta*, ed. and transl. H.G. Richardson and G.O. Sayles (Selden Society 72, 1953), ii. 109. See Edwards, 'Justice', pp. 281–2.

documents quickly, was normally 'De tenendo parliamenti' or 'De summonicione parliamenti'. Between 1295 and the end of the reign in 1307, 15 assemblies were described as 'parliaments' in the writs (7) and /or the rubrics (15). There were four other assemblies where neither writ nor rubric uses the word; two (in June/July 1297 – for which there are no writs – and in March 1298) were probably parliaments, two (in May 1298 and May 1306) were probably not.[17] There were also a few meetings of knights or burgesses or councillors and four wider meetings on which there may be room for doubt, but these 17 assemblies are all or at least almost all the parliaments of this period. A striking feature is their lack of uniformity. They met at varying times of the year. Membership varied considerably. The king himself was abroad on campaign and represented by a lieutenant at the September parliament of 1297 though this was an unusual assembly intended to make peace and grant taxation after the great 'crisis' of the summer. No churchmen were summoned to the February parliament of 1297 because the king had outlawed them in a dispute over clerical taxation, and only two bishops and no lay magnates are known to have been summoned to the March 'parliament' of 1298 because they were supposed to be with the army in Scotland. The numbers recorded as summoned varied from 14, an archbishop, four bishops, four earls, and five barons, in October 1299 to some 600 on five occasions, when magnates, commons and proctors of the clergy were summoned. In 1305, over 600 were summoned to the February parliament while under 40 were summoned to the September parliament. The selection

17 These four cases are worth documenting to illustrate the nature and difficulty of the evidence. In the case of most parliaments the evidence is clear cut, but in a minority it is problematical – in part because contemporaries themselves were uncertain or made mistakes. There are no writs or proceedings known for the 1297 parliament but Edmund Mortimer was ordered to appear at 'parliament' on the octave of Trinity (17 June), a royal letter refers to a decision on 21 June 'in full parliament' and a memorandum in the exchequer records a decision in parliament on 22 July. All were king and Council matters. (*Calendar of Close Rolls, 1296–1302*, p. 107: *Documents Illustrating the Crisis of 1297–8 in England*, ed. M. Prestwich (Camden Series, 24, 1980), pp. 99 and 108.) The assembly of March 1298 to which two bishops and 20 royal clerks and officials were summoned by writs with the rubric 'de consilio summoniendo' would not be considered a parliament but for a memorandum of four decisions headed 'De parliamento apud London' at Easter 1298. (*Parl. Writs*, i. 65; *Rot. Parl.*, i. 143). The meeting in May 1298 at York to which six earls, such barons in the army in Scotland as the commander thought fit and two knights and two townsmen from each county and town were summoned was an unusual assembly called a 'colloquium speciale' in one writ. (*Parl. Writs*, i. 65–7). The assembly of 1306 to which prelates, lords and commons were summoned by writs which do not use the word 'parliament' and for which there is no rubric was called a 'parliament' in a note to the enrolment of the writs for the commons' expenses and in an exchequer source. (*Parl. Writs*, i. 177–8; Thomas Madox, *Firma Burgi* (London, 1726), p. 100–1). The unusual character of the writs and other evidence however makes it very doubtful if this was a parliament and I have excluded it. H.G. Richardson and G.O. Sayles, *Parliaments and Great Councils in Medieval England* (London, 1961), pp. 24–30 (*English Parliaments*, XXVI) discuss it fully and see Prestwich, 'Magnate Summonses', pp. 99–100.

Barons — who were summoned were astonishingly variable & hap-hazard.

of barons who were summoned was astonishingly variable and hap-hazard (pp. 179–80). The numbers present is another matter; there is an annotated list of those summoned to Edward's last parliament, at Carlisle in 1307, from which 'it would appear that perhaps no more than forty-one, almost certainly no more than fifty-seven' of the 167 prelates and magnates summoned were present.[18] Representatives of the counties and towns came to nine, a distinctly higher proportion than earlier in the reign, but they were clearly not an essential part of parliament. The nucleus of a parliament was still the king, his council-lors and officers, some of them prelates and magnates. They could do business in parliament before others came or after others had gone. Others were summoned in larger or smaller numbers, apparently as the business in hand demanded. This lack of uniformity in ter-minology and membership may seem surprising if parliament was a clearly established meeting, but contemporaries, though they were well aware of legal rules in, say, matters of property, did not think in 'constitutional' terms. For example, consent was considered necessary for general taxation, but the precise form of consent was not defined for almost a further hundred years (pp. 224–8).

Parliament was certainly changing radically. It ceased to meet with regularity and Edward's constant campaigning and the consequent taxation and complaints about the burdensomeness of his government made it more an assembly and less an administrative occasion.[19] Par-liament was also becoming larger because the king thought it desirable to involve a wider community in his business. Its work is now better documented though there are still few memoranda of proceedings and the overwhelming bulk of the records are of petitions and pleas. Par-liament was still the great occasion for clearing administrative and judicial business. The best illustration of this is the record of the February parliament of 1305 which Maitland edited and brilliantly analysed.[20] By contemporary standards, it was a large parliament, and apparently, though the evidence on length of sittings is slight, at three weeks, a long parliament. The 'greater part' of its roll is taken up with petitions from subjects and communities addressed to the king or to the king and the Council – not petitions *by* parliament, not petitions *to* parliament, but petitions in time of parliament. They sought

18 J.S. Roskell, 'The problem of the attendance of the lords in medieval parliaments', *BIHR* 29 (1956), 161.

19 There is apparently a reflection of the change in a law tract, *The Mirror of Justices*, ed. W.J. Whittaker (Selden Society, 7, 1895), p. 155 which complains that 'it is an abuse that whereas parliaments ought to be held for the salvation of the souls of trespassers, twice a year and at London, they are now held but rarely and at the king's will for the purpose of obtaining aids and collections of treasures'. The tract was probably written in the reign of Edward I and it would apply well to the 1290s.

20 *Memoranda de Parliamento, 1305.*

favours and remedies of many kinds, and there was a machinery to handle them (pp. 216–17). Receivers took them in; committees of auditors considered and sifted them; and only the most important came to the king and/or the Council. Often the petitioner did not receive a final answer but was sent to chancery, exchequer or the courts to obtain his decision, though with the authority of the king or the Council behind him. 'In these parliaments, the whole governmental force of England is brought into a focus', the king, the great officers, their subordinates, the Council, the records.[21] Maitland stressed the importance of the Council. Men were promised a hearing before the Council in parliament. In 1305, the chancellor, treasurer, and others of the Council were instructed by the king to deliver as many petitions as they could before he arrived, while three weeks after it had begun all those who were not members of the Council or had no business in hand were sent home, leaving the councillors to carry on for some further weeks in what could still be described as 'full parliament'.[22] The Council was equally active in judicial business. The Segrave case, a case of baronial treason, was heard before the barons and the Council, and others such as the case of the citizens of Winchester who had allowed a prisoner to escape or of the bishop of Salisbury who claimed to tallage the men of Salisbury were probably heard before the Council alone. It is not at all clear why such cases came to parliament at all. 'Seemingly all that we dare to say is that the causes heard in parliament are important causes, important because they concern the king, or because they concern very great men, or because they involve grave questions of public law, or because they are unprecedented'.[23] Much less conspicuous were the consultative functions of parliament; in 1305, no tax was asked and no statute was placed on the Statute roll though what became the Statute of Carlisle in 1307 received 'the consent of the prelates, earls, barons, and others of the realm'. Several general decisions were taken, for example about delays in inquests to which the king was a party, about setting up *trailbaston* enquiries (p. 118), and the king's vassals were allowed to levy a scutage and a tallage from ancient demesne in their hands. There probably was some general discussion about the export of money by monks and about establishing a settled form of government in Scotland, though the practical solution, a parliament to which representatives of Scotland were to come, was decided after 21 March when only a small number remained. Parliament was an occasion for subjects to

21 *Ibid.*, lxxi–ii.
22 *Ibid.*, lvii, 4, 293 and 297. B. Wilkinson, *Studies in the Constitutional History of the Thirteenth and Fourteenth Centuries* (Manchester, 1937), pp. 7–14 maintains that only the commons were sent home.
23 *Memoranda de Parliamento, 1305*, p. lxxxv.

petition, for difficult issues and cases to be heard and for the king to seek advice and consent. The Lent Parliament of 1305 cannot stand as a model for all Edward I's later parliaments, but it was probably not untypical of many.

Early-Fourteenth-Century Parliaments

The 30 or 40 years after the death of Edward I in 1307 saw a rapid change in parliament. From an ill-recorded and ill-defined assembly it became one with consistent though not highly informative records, almost regular composition, developing procedures and the beginnings of recognized rights. It became absolutely distinct from any other assembly. The lords summoned as individuals *and* the representative knights, townsmen and lower clergy together made it the recognized assembly of the whole community. By mid-century it possessed a number of the classic features of the English parliament. The changes are beyond dispute; the reasons for them are much less clear.

It soon becomes easier to identify parliaments in the enrolled writs of summons though it was some time before these became standardized completely. During Edward II's reign (1307–27), there were a variety of specially summoned meetings, for example of merchants or county knights with the Council and small and large meetings of councillors, but 29 larger assemblies stand out clearly. In 25 cases where men were summoned to have 'discussion and treaty' (*colloquium et tractatus*) with the king, the writs or the rubrics use the word 'parliament' – in 17 cases both do so; in three the writs do but there is no rubric; in four the rubrics do so but the writs do not; and in one case, in November 1325, the writs do so but the rubric refers to the assembly as a *tractatus*. In all but this last case the writs for the expenses of the commons or other royal documents refer to the assemblies as parliaments, and all must be considered parliaments. After 1310 in all but one case – November 1322 which may not have been a parliament – the writs of summons use the word 'parliament'.[24] The four remaining cases seem to show contemporaries seeking to differentiate between assemblies. Two were in 1309. The first, on 23 February, was different in various ways from contemporary parliaments. It was smaller – only 11 bishops, no abbots and priors, 9 earls, 42 barons and 17 councillors were summoned by writs which were unusually brief; the rubric calls it a *tractatus* and no source calls it a parliament. Little is known about its work; perhaps it led to the

24 The phrase 'colloquy and treaty' was used in most writs of summons to assemblies and has no evidential value. The word 'parliament' was rarely used in writs before 1300 but was then used frequently. The assembly of November 1322 is mentioned below, p. 171 n. 30.

summons of an undoubted parliament, several hundreds strong on 27 April where a series of articles seeking reforms were presented to the king by the commonalty as a condition of making a grant. He gave no immediate answer and another assembly was summoned to meet at Stamford on 27 July. This was smaller than the April parliament but larger than the February *tractatus*. The writs of summons do not use the word parliament and the rubric refers to it as a *tractatus* but the king's answer to the articles and at least two later royal letters call it a parliament. Those summoned to it were virtually the same men who were summoned to a campaign in Scotland for the same day by writs which refer to it as a *tractatus*. The best one can say is that it came to be considered a parliament.[25]

Two assemblies in May and October 1324 were clearly 'treaties' (*tractatus*), not parliaments. The first, on 27 May, was unusual because privy-seal writs, not the customary great-seal writs, summoned the bishops, earls and barons of the kingdom, though great-seal writs at only three weeks notice summoned 15 justices for 27 May and all (*sic*) the knights of the counties for 30 May. The object was to gain support for a campaign in France. The second, on 20 October, had the same purpose; bishops and lay magnates were summoned in normal parliamentary numbers but only eight abbots and county knights but not townsmen were summoned. In both cases the writs do not use the word 'parliament' and the rubrics use *tractatus*.[26] This is the word which seems to be used deliberately at this time for large assemblies which were not considered to be parliaments. For example, a letter to the archbishop of Canterbury ordered him not to molest the archbishop of York coming to the *tractatus* in October 1324 and recalled disputes between them 'ad diversas tractatus et parliamenta' and an agreement about their behaviour 'ad parliamenta et (alios) tractatus'.[27] The terms 'parliament' and *tractatus* may be used here and in other sources as synonyms, but it is more likely that a distinction was being drawn. Two abortive meetings add weight to the argument. A meeting of earls, barons, councillors, knights and burgesses in normal parliamentary numbers was summoned for 20 January 1324 but only a few clerics were summoned because the Canterbury convocation was to meet on the same day and the York convocation a little later. The writs do not use the word 'parliament' and the rubric is 'De tractatu habendo'. The arrangements were then changed; the meeting was postponed until 23 February and bishops,

25 *Parl. Writs*, II, ii 23–4 (February); *ibid.*, 24–36 and 38–9 and *Rot. Parl.*, i. 443–5 (April); *Parl. Writs*, II, ii. 37–8 (July).
26 *Parl. Writs*, II, ii. 316 (May) and *ibid.*, 317–25 (October).
27 *Ibid.*, II, ii. 318–19.

abbots, priors, clerical proctors and barons of the Cinque Ports as well as those called to the *tractatus* were summoned to a meeting called a parliament in both writs and rubric.[28] A meeting of bishops, abbots, priors, earls and barons in normal parliamentary numbers summoned in March 1325, postponed until April, then cancelled, and intended to meet on the eve of a Gascon expedition, seems also to have been deliberately a *tractatus* not a parliament. For example, the writs postponing the meeting refer to the 'diem tractatus predicti', the rubric uses the same word and, very significantly, the Council advised that magnates be summoned to this assembly 'to advise etc. and not for parliament'.[29] *Tractatus* was the word commonly applied to the assembly in November 1322 including both knights and burgesses which Richardson and Sayles classified as a parliament on the grounds that the rubric uses the word.[30] The *Vita Edwardi Secundi* complains that parliaments, treaties (*tractatus*) and councils 'decide nothing these days', and there is further evidence of the same kind.[31] Contemporaries seem to be seeking to identify large assemblies which they knew were not parliaments.

The problem continues into the early years of Edward III's reign. Briefly, again ignoring smaller councils, between 1327 and 1340 there were 21 assemblies which the writs of summons, the rubrics and other evidence call parliaments, but there were also five assemblies of very similar composition to which other names were given. The assembly of September 1327 was called a parliament in the rubric but a *tractatus* in other sources; and the rubric calls that of July 1328 a *tractatus* or a council; that of September 1336, a council or great council; that of September 1337, a council, though the writs for the common's expenses call it a parliament; and that of July 1338, a council or a great council. In the 21 cases, the writs use the word parliament, in the five they do not. There was some confusion but the great weight of documentary evidence is consistent. An unusual testimony comes from an abbot who claimed that he had petitioned in all the parliaments since the coronation and listed the first six undoubted parliaments but omitted the assemblies of September 1327 and July 1328 and a small

---

28 *Dignity of a Peer*, iii. 342–4 and *Parl. Writs*, II, ii. 289–315.

29 *Parl. Writs*, II, ii. 325–8. *The War of Saint Sardos (1323–1325)*, ed. P. Chaplais (Camden Series, 87, 1954), p. 134. 'Item qe les grants soient somouns dy estre pur conseiller etc. et noun pas pur parlement.'

30 H.G. Richardson and G.O. Sayles, 'The English parliaments of Edward II', *English Parliament*, XVI, 83–4 (from BIHR, 1928). They concluded 'somewhat doubtfully' that this was a parliament because the rubric (and several proxies and sheriffs' returns) use the word though most references are to a 'tractatus'.

31 *Vita Edwardi Secundi*, ed. N. Denholm-Young (London, 1957), p. 136.

assembly in July 1329.[32] In the 1330s 'Council' becomes the preferred term rather than 'treaty' for these 'non-parliaments' and from the 1340s there was unquestionably a distinction between parliaments and Great Councils. The latter could advise but they lacked the authority of parliament to act in the name of the community, for example to approve a statute (pp. 218–20). The difficulty is to define the distinction at an earlier date. Membership may at first have played a part but not by Edward III's reign. The rights of parliament over taxation and legislation were not yet formulated. The most likely explanation, that of Richardson and Sayles, is that only in parliament did subjects have the right to present petitions and receive answers, or, from the king's point of view, in other assemblies only the business of the king and the kingdom was considered. This would explain why the Council advised in 1325 that the *grantz* be summoned 'to advise etc. and not for parliament'. The wider context is the major change in parliament which began in the 1290s under pressure of war, taxation and common grievances, pressures which continued through the miserable reign of his son. Parliaments saw political confrontations and settlements, discussions about war, grants of money and men and the presentation of common grievances. In the early years of Edward III's reign politics and war led to an unusually large number of short parliaments. Parliament became less and less an enlarged session of the Council in which many individual issues were decided and more and more an assembly of the community to deal with common issues, and this was its future rôle. Two well-known documents from Edward II's reign illustrate the change. The Ordinances of 1311, forced on the king by magnates and published during a parliament, contain many references to parliament. Some are to the older type of parliament. It must meet once a year, twice if necessary, to hear pleas in which the king's interest was involved or which arose from complaints against royal officers or pleas about which the judges differed, and petitions presented in parliament must be answered. Others refer to the newer type of parliament. The assent of the baronage was necessary for a number of things 'and this in parliament' – if the king wished to make war or leave the country or appoint a lieutenant; to his choice of ministers and castellans at home and abroad; a committee consisting of a bishop, two earls and two barons would investigate complaints against officials in parliament and doubts in Magna Carta and the charter of the Forest would be clarified there. When military victory enabled Edward II to revoke the Ordinances in 1322 he did so in parliament and went on to lay down in the Statute of York that

32 Richardson and Sayles, *Parliaments and Great Councils*, pp. 4–5. (*English Parliament*, XXVI). There is a very different view in T.F.T. Plucknett, 'Parliament 1327–36, *Eng. Gov. at Work*, i. 82–128 (*Hist. Studies*, i. 195–241).

important political decisions affecting the king and the kingdom could only be made in parliament.[33] Under pressure of circumstances it would not be surprising if private petitions which are so large a part of the early records of parliament were squeezed out, and this is indeed what happened. Edward I had complained that they held up his business; there were complaints in 1309 and 1311 that Edward II had made no arrangements to handle them; they were not dealt with in three successive parliaments in 1332 and from this time the rolls of private petitions ceased to be written. They ceased to be an important part of parliament, driven out by the affairs of the community, and common petitions become important (p. 218). What this suggests is that in the 1320s and 1330s some of the older functions of parliament, in particular answering petitions, differentiated parliaments from other large assemblies, and that from mid-century the newer functions of parliaments differentiated them from Great Councils.

The rolls of parliament do not often contain much evidence about proceedings and procedures before the 1340s (p. 161). It is not possible for example to trace the origins of the division into two houses, lords and Commons, which certainly became normal in the 1330s, or precisely how business was handled. The clearest evidence that major changes were taking place is in the writs of summons which show that the membership of parliament became largely regular in the course of Edward II's reign. Archbishops, bishops and earls were always summoned if they were available; barons were summoned with fair regularity on the basis of lists which were revised from time to time, though the numbers still varied and complete regularity only came later in the century (p. 180). Abbots and priors were not summoned at all in 1310 but this was unusual and their numbers also were becoming standardized. The lower clergy were summoned to most parliaments and to all from 1334. Representatives of the counties and towns were summoned to all but two parliaments after 1312, those of January 1320 and June 1325, and after 1325 they were invariably summoned. By the 1330s membership was largely defined – though by custom and practice not by enactment. Parliament now visibly and regularly represented the whole community; the lords no longer spoke for the community; and the Commons now had a substantial but subordinate and different rôle to that of the lords. The physical evidence of this from the 1330s is the separate meetings of lords and Commons,

33 The Ordinances of 1311 are in *Rot. Parl.*, i. 281–6 – *Select Documents*, pp. 11–17; *EHD*, iii. 527–39. The Statute of York is in *Statutes of the Realm*, i. 189 – *Select Documents*, pp. 31–2, *EHD*, iii. 543–4. The precise meaning of the phraseology of the Statute of York is still uncertain, but it certainly lays down that the most important political decisions must be reached in parliament by the king with the assent of the prelates, earls and barons and the commonalty (*communalte*) of the realm as has been accustomed in the past'. The changed status and the place of the commons in parliament is clear.

a highly unusual arrangement which, like the other changes, must have arisen from the circumstances of the previous 30 years.

One piece of evidence which confirms these remarkable changes is the existence and contents of a curious anonymous tract called the *Modus Tenendi Parliamentum* (The Manner of Holding Parliament) which most scholars now date to the early 1320s, though no manuscript earlier than the reign of Richard II is known.[34] It purports to describe how parliament was held in the reign of Edward the Confessor and combines invention with apparently accurate observation. It is a puzzle why it was written and why with a group of other procedural tracts it later became popular. So little is known about parliamentary procedure in the 1320s that it must be used with great caution, but it was written, and two features in it are striking. It ascribes an apparently well-developed order to parliamentary proceedings; the detail may be suspect but it does suggest that procedure was much more developed than we know (pp. 208–9) And it gives surprising emphasis to the representatives, the clerical proctors, knights and burgesses. They ought to be summoned; they have a greater voice in granting taxes than the magnates because they represent not themselves alone but the whole community of England; and they are in a clear majority in the (entirely notional) committee of 25 which might be chosen to resolve disagreements in parliament. This is in large part make-believe but there are accurate observations and anticipations of attitudes and features of later parliaments which make one suspect that parliament of the 1320s was a more developed institution than we can document.

Parliament after 1350

From the 1340s parliament is better recorded and there is no longer a problem of definition. There was another assembly, the Great Council, but it was quite distinct from parliament.[35] For example a Great Council met at Westminster on 23 September 1353. It was summoned by great-seal writs similar to those for a parliament; but they do not call it a parliament, the rubric calls it a Council and the roll of its proceedings a Great Council. The lords were summoned in parliamentary numbers but no representatives of the lower clergy, only one knight from each county and two townsmen from each of 39 towns were summoned. Its business and proceedings were similar to those

---

34 N. Pronay and J. Taylor, *Parliamentary Texts of the Later Middle Ages* (Oxford, 1980).
35 Great Councils have not been systematically studied but see J.F. Baldwin, *The King's Council in the Middle Ages* ((Oxford, 1913); Richardson and Sayles, *Parliaments and Great Councils*; and T.F.T. Plucknett, 'The place of the Council in the fifteenth century', *TRHS* 1 (1918), 157–89.

of a parliament; the two houses met, customs duties were granted, ordinances were approved and answers given to some common petitions. But its members knew that it was not a parliament and asked that the articles touching the estate of the king and the common profit of his realm should be entered in the roll of the next parliament because 'the ordinances and accords made in councils are not of record as if they were made by common parliament' and parliament in 1354 affirmed the ordinances as statutes in parliament to ensure for ever and to be changed only in parliament.[36] This Great Council had much in common with the treaties and councils of the 20s and 30s but after the 50s Great Councils quickly changed – probably because there was no place for an assembly at all like the increasingly authoritative parliament. Great Councils began to be summoned by privy-seal writs and serviced by privy-seal clerks, a sign that they were now related to the Council rather than parliament. On occasion large numbers were summoned. For example in June 1371 a selection of the members who had served in the February parliament including one knight from each county and one townsman from each town were summoned to a Great Council to approve an increase in the rate of a parish tax granted in parliament. And in 1401 prelates and lords and over 200 knights and esquires from the counties were summoned to a Great Council to discuss the military threat to the kingdom.[37] Normally however a Great Council was an assembly of 30, 40 or more prelates, lords and others summoned to meet the king and consult on important issues. For example in February, 1392 the king and at least 43 others discussed an embassy to France, war preparations, wool exports, proposed modifications to the Statute of Provisors, and exchanged promises of benevolence and loyalty.[38] Two Great Councils considered Henry V's proposal to renew the war in France. Great Councils were clearly useful occasions for the king to discuss important issues with important people without the formality and the other business of parliament and between 1350 and 1461 there were apparently more Great Councils than parliaments. A Great Council may be seen as an enlarged session of the Council or a meeting of the active members of the 'house of lords' outside parliament.

Parliament itself was now better recorded, more organized in its business, regular in its composition. It acquired the right to assent to all taxation and all statutes. It became in theory the assembly of all the people in the kingdom and the occasion where political conflicts were expressed and settled. By the death of Edward III in 1377, certainly by

36 *Dignity of a Peer*, iv. 598–601, *Rot. Parl.*, ii. 246–53 and 257. The reference (ii. 253) to parliament as a court of record is significant.
37 *Dignity of a Peer*, iv. 605–3. *Procs. & Ords.*, i. 155–64.
38 Baldwin, *King's Council*, pp. 493–6. See above p. 40.

1400, most of these things had been achieved. By 1461 many of the features and surprisingly many of the details of procedure of the classic English parliament were already in existence – for example the 40 shilling freehold franchise, the terminology of legislation and the readings of bills, and some of the mythology of parliament such as the three estates and the High Court of parliament. The next two chapters examine these changes in some detail – in terms of parliament's membership and then its work. They provide a further evidence of the time-scale set out in this chapter.

9
The Members of Parliament

The members of parliament fall into two groups, those summoned individually – the lay and spiritual lords, justices, councillors and clerks; and those chosen locally to represent their communities – the county knights, citizens and burgesses, barons of the Cinque Ports and representatives of the lower clergy. The laws and customs relating to each group were distinct and must be considered separately. It is remarkable how much and how quickly they changed. In 1272 there was little established custom, by 1461 there were firm customs which lasted for centuries. Two other features stand out which confirm the pattern of parliamentary development set out in the last chapter. There was a remarkable regularization of membership between the 1290s and the 1330s and from the 1370s there was a striking growth of interest in parliament among the 'political community'.

The Lords Temporal*

The late Middle Ages saw the creation not merely of a 'House of Lords' but also of the concept of an hereditary peerage with several grades and privileges. In 1272 there were only two grades of lay lords, a small number of earls whose titles were hereditary, and a large number of military tenants of the crown called 'barons' who did not form a coherent group and whose numbers were uncertain. By 1461 there were five grades of peer, dukes, marquesses, earls, viscounts, and a modest number of barons who had the title 'lord'. All were normally summoned to parliament, and passed the privilege to their heirs.

'Earl' was in origin an Anglo-Saxon office with a definite responsibility for a shire. It had become a mark of distinction held in 'fee simple' by a dozen or so great landowners with no meaningful respon-

* J.E. Powell and K. Wallis, *The House of Lords in the Middle Ages* (London, 1968) is an excellent, critical history, parliament by parliament, and K.B. McFarlane, *The Nobility of Later Medieval England* (Oxford, 1973) is a magisterial study of the lay lords.

sibility for the government of the shire from which the title came, though they normally drew the traditional 'third penny' from 'their' shire in the form of a £20 annuity. During the late Middle Ages it became more than ever a dignity, to maintain which the new earl might have to be endowed with land or even money. In 1272 there were 13 earls. New creations were made for members of the royal family and important and favoured magnates such as the Percy earls of Northumberland in 1377 and the Neville earls of Westmorland in 1397. Edward III in 1337 as an act of policy created six earls because 'among the marks of royalty we consider it to be the chief that, through a due distribution of positions (*ordines*), dignities and officers, it is buttressed by wise counsels and fortified by mighty powers'.[1] Earldoms however also became extinct and the number rarely rose higher than 13. Nine earls were summoned to Henry VI's parliament in 1460, omitting one in sanctuary and one abroad. Baronial preference had gradually caused all earldoms to be held in 'tail male' rather than in 'fee simple', that is they descended to male heirs in preference to all female heirs.[2] The same rules of descent were applied to three further dignities introduced in imitation of grades that existed on the continent. In 1337 Edward III's eldest son was created duke of Cornwall (with echoes of King Arthur), the first English duke, with a status above the earls. There were more than 20 such creations before 1461, mainly members of the royal family, but there were rarely as many as five dukes at any time. On a number of occasions creations were for life only, for example the dukedoms of Bedford, Gloucester and Exeter given by Henry V to his younger brothers and his uncle, Thomas Beaufort. In 1385 a new dignity, that of marquess ranking between duke and earl, was created for Richard II's favourite Robert de Vere. Only two more marquesses were created before 1461 and it is an indication of the early distaste attached to the title that in 1402 when the Commons asked that the marquessate granted to John Beaufort in 1397 and taken from him in 1399 be restored, Beaufort, the king's half-brother and close to him, begged to be excused because it was 'a strange title in this realm'.[3] The dignity of viscount, ranking between earl and baron, was created in 1440 for John Beaumont, apparently on the ground that he was already a comte and vicomte in the kingdom of France, and the same was true of the only other viscount in the period, Henry, Viscount Bourchier. The dukes, marquesses, earls, and viscounts were almost invariably summoned to parliament if they could come and if they were of age; this is true of the

1 Powell and Wallis, *House of Lords*, p. 326.
2 McFarlane, *Nobility*, pp. 270–4. This is a more complicated subject than the text suggests.
3 *Rot. Parl.*, iii. 488. Powell and Wallis, *House of Lords*, pp. 434–5.

earls even in Edward I's reign. Their wealth, their importance and the status of the title demanded they be summoned.

The story of the barons was quite different. Their status was defined only during this period, and slowly. 'Baron' is one of many status words which changed their meaning drastically. In origin *baro* meant a man, the vassal of a lord, but in the twelfth century it came to be used in the more restricted sense of a military tenant-in-chief of the king or perhaps of a great lord; 'earls and barons' became a stock phrase for important laymen. Magna Carta (clause 14) laid down that archbishops, bishops, abbots, earls, and 'greater barons' (*majores barones*) must be summoned individually and all tenants-in-chief by a general summons through sheriffs and bailiffs to give their consent to scutages and extraordinary aids. Clause 2 shows how the term was narrowing by prescribing the same relief of £100 to be paid by the heir of an earl or a baron to succeed to his inheritance, his barony, while prescribing only a £5 relief for the heir of a tenant-in-chief holding one knight's fee. In the thirteenth century however no more specific qualification to be a baron with the minor privileges which went with it, was known than to be a tenant-in-chief by military service who held land 'by barony'(*per baroniam*), and this was proved not in terms of size of holding or of rights but by acceptance, say, by evidence that an ancestor had paid the higher relief. It had become a question of record, not a living fact.[4] Matthew Paris recounts that Henry III was able to name 250 baronies in England in 1257, and this figure is probably roughly accurate for the 'greater barons'.[5] It was summons to parliament which reduced it, at first to about 100 and then by 1400 to around 40, and gave a new basis for the status of barons. The enrolled writs of summons after 1295 show that at first the names and numbers of barons summoned varied considerably. In 1295 11 earls and 53 barons were summoned to the August parliament but only 8 and 41 to that in November, and the number of barons summoned to subsequent Edwardian parliaments varied from 46 to 100.[6] The word 'baron' was indeed scarcely appropriate because all who held 'by barony' were not summoned and a good many who were summoned are not known to have held baronies. Summons were 'haphazard'. For example it has been suggested that the 'barons' summoned for August 1295, were taken from a list of men mainly from the Scottish and Welsh marches drawn up for an earlier parliament or more probably from a list of

4 I.J. Sanders, *Feudal Military Service in England* (London, 1956), p. 13 and *English Baronies: A Study of their Origin and Descent: 1086–1327* (Oxford, 1960).
5 Powell and Wallis, *House of Lords*, p. 225.
6 This section is heavily indebted to Powell and Wallis, *House of Lords*. The figures necessarily come from the enrolled writs of summons though these are not necessarily complete. See M. Prestwich, 'Magnate summonses in England in the later years of Edward I', *Parliaments, Estates and Representation* 5 (1985), pp. 97–101.

tenants summoned for military service.[7] For the remainder of Edward I's reign 'a list of addresses compiled for one purpose was used again, with or without alteration, in different circumstances; a military list was made to do duty for parliamentary summons and *vice versa*. In fact, as long as a chance selection of fifty to a hundred of the sort of substantial people who were regularly called on for service had been summoned, that was enough for parliamentary purposes!'.[8] Numbers continued to fluctuate widely in the first years of Edward II's reign when parliaments were frequent, but from 1314 until 1321 a basic list of over 80 barons was in use, then a shorter list, and after the royal victory in 1322 the number did not exceed 50 for the rest of the reign, and the same men were summoned more regularly. Repeated summons is likely to lead to greater regularity of summons and the disputes between Edward II and his magnates must also have encouraged it. For example the Ordinances of 1311 repeatedly laid down matters on which the king must act with the advice of the 'baronage' – and that in parliament; political trials raised the question of where and by whom great men should be tried; and significantly this is the time when a concept of a body of 'peers of the realm' with special privileges begins to be formulated.[9]

During Edward III's reign it was unusual to find a baron summoned only once, though there were three cases as late as 1371. A man once summoned was likely to continue to be summoned and his heir after him. New men were frequently added and twice, in 1332 and 1349, the list was deliberately reinforced on a substantial scale. The newcomers were normally men of substance whose ancestor had been summoned or who had acquired, by inheritance or marriage, the land of a man who had been summoned. A baron was coming to be the holder of particular lands of which an earlier holder had been summoned. It was a convenient but not historically accurate rationalization. It meant that because of failure of heirs and other reasons numbers fell; to 50 or just below from 1322 until a rise to 67 in 1332; to below 50 by 1337, a number not exceeded until a rise to 56 in 1349. Within a few years it was below 50 again, and for the rest of the century the number summoned was rarely above 50, normally in the 40s, and not

---

7 Powell and Wallis, *House of Lords*, pp. 227–9.

8 *Ibid.*, p. 231.

9 The concept of the right to judgement by one's equals or peers is an ancient one which began to be seen in particular relation to the magnates in the 13th century and to trials in parliament in the reign of Edward I. The political trials of Edward II's reign and the growing definition of lay magnates who should receive an individual summons to parliament led to an equally rapid growth in the concept of 'peers of the realm' or 'of the land' applied to the earls and barons and their right to trial in parliament. The political crisis of 1340–1 contains explicit statements of this right, in particular to the right of the higher clergy to the same privilege as the lay lords. L.W. Vernon Harcourt, *His Grace the Steward and Trial of Peers* (London, 1907) is still the best documented account of the subject.

infrequently less because of war service. In the fifteenth century the normal number was in the 30s. A small, defined group of hereditary 'barons' had been formed. In the late fourteenth century the group became self-conscious and a distinction was made between the notionally 'old' barons and newcomers. The title 'banneret', which had come into currency a century earlier for an experienced warrior knight entitled to higher war wages and to have a banner rather than a pennon carried before him, came to be used instead of 'baron' for those more recently summoned who could not claim to have directly inherited their summons. A baron whose status was ancient (more than fifty years!) was considered more dignified than a new man, and the two groups were frequently differentiated in documents. This usage died out in the early fifteenth century, probably because there was by then an order of precedence among barons. The first reference to this is in March 1405 when the king and Council ruled that Lord Grey (of Codnor) should have precedence over Lord Beaumont in parliaments and councils, perhaps on the grounds of antiquity of summons, which certainly became the test later.[10] Disputes about precedence within all the grades of lay lords became common from this time. The next and most important stage was reached in the 1430s and 1440s when baronies began to be created without any claim to be reviving an earlier barony, indeed without any connection with land. There is an even earlier example, in October 1387 when Richard II 'preferred' John Beauchamp, Steward of the Household, by letters-patent 'to be one of the peers and barons of our realm of England' with the status for himself and his heirs male of 'lords Beauchamp and barons of Kidderminster', but this was a special case. It was a time of acute hostility between king and some of the magnates and Richard's intention was to give Beauchamp, a leading loyalist, an unquestioned status, probably as against other new men who were bannerets. Beauchamp did receive an individual summons to parliament a few weeks later, but in it he was impeached and executed without recognition of his new status. It was probably not considered a 'good' precedent, but it is significant of a movement of opinion towards a barony as a matter of status, though in this case still linked with land. Half a century later there was no doubt. In July, 1432 John Cornwall was given the 'name, style, title and honour of baron of Fanhope' with 'his seat and place in the parliaments and councils of the king among the other barons of the realm of England' with all their rights and privileges. In 1441 Ralph Butler was created baron of Sudeley, described as 'a noble of our realm', and he and his heirs male were given an annuity to maintain their status.[11] Other creations followed. Baronies had

10 *Procs. & Ords.*, ii. 104–5.
11 Powell and Wallis, *House of Lords*, pp. 402–4, 460–2 and 470–1.

fallen into line with the higher grades of 'nobility'; they were hereditary dignities, no longer necessarily linked with tenure of particular
lands, and closely bound up with a place in parliaments and councils.

By the 1440s the terminology and appearance of the 'House of
Lords' was well-formed in its modern fashion. 'Lords' had come into
use in the 1340s as the term for all those individually summoned to
parliament, and by the end of the fourteenth century it was the normal
description for the men and the meeting and the terms 'lords spiritual'
and 'lords temporal' were common. 'House of Lords' has not been
found in this period but 'Lower House', 'Upper House', and 'Common house' were certainly in use in the fifteenth century.[12] The general
seating plan of meetings of the lords goes back to the early fourteenth
century if not earlier (p. 209), the order of precedence within the
grades and the scarlet robes with from two to four bands of white fur
to distinguish the several grades and other features of their dress to the
late fourteenth century and early fifteenth century.[13]

The Lords Spiritual

The summons of the lords spiritual, archbishops and bishops, abbots
and priors, is a much less complicated subject. All were summoned by
writs similar to those of the lay lords, but 'by the faith and love' (*in
fide et dileccione*) which bound them to the king, not 'the faith and
allegiance or homage' of the laymen because they did not do homage
to the king. The bishops were also ordered with increasing frequency
and invariably from 1334 by a clause, the *premunientes* clause, to have
their cathedral deans, their archdeacons and representatives of the
lower clergy in their dioceses 'forewarned' to come to the parliament
(p. 206). The familiar time-scale is found here again. Numbers varied
considerably in the reign of Edward I, became much more regular
under Edward II and became almost completely stable by the close of
the reign of Edward III. In the case of the bishops uniformity came
quickly. None at all were summoned to the February parliament of
1297 because the king had outlawed the clergy for refusing to pay
taxation, and only a few were summoned to the small parliaments of
October, 1299 and September, 1305, but it then became normal to
summon all or most of the 21 English and Welsh archbishops and
bishops on every occasion. The *premunientes* clause probably

12 A list of the sanctioning clauses in statutes from 1377 printed in S.B. Chrimes, *English
   Constitutional Ideas in the Fifteenth Century* (Cambridge, 1936), pp. 101–4 illustrates the
   change in terminology. The terminology of the 'houses' is discussed there on pp. 126–30.
13 *The English Parliament in the Middle Ages*, ed. R.G. Davies and J.H. Denton (Manchester,
   1981), pp. 115 and 159. The robes can be seen in drawings depicting the members of the lords
   and Commons on two royal charters of 1446. Powell and Wallis, *House of Lords*, plate
   XIV.

hastened the practice that when it was known that a bishop could not attend, the writ was addressed to him *or* his vicar general, and, if the see was vacant, to the keeper of its spiritualities, in both cases ecclesiastical officials who could represent the diocese in parliament and summon the lower clergy. This practice was common but not invariable and cases did arise, for example when Thomas de Lisle went into exile in the 1350s or when St Asaphs fell into rebel hands in Henry IV's reign and even after a new bishop had been consecrated, where the diocese was apparently unrepresented.

In the case of the abbots and priors only a proportion, ultimately only 27 out of over 300 heads of English and Welsh houses of monks and canons were summoned.[14] None at all were summoned to three early parliaments, February 1297, October 1299 and February 1310, and numbers varied from three in September 1305, to 83 in January 1301. After 1310 two lists of abbots and priors were in use, a longer of some 50 used when representatives of the lower clergy were summoned, and a shorter of a little over 30 used on other occasions. From 1324 the shorter list was always used, and, save for a drop to less than 20 summons between 1327 and 1329, this continued to be the basis of summons in Edward III's reign. A further 'shake-down' came after 1340. That year a tax of a ninth was granted in parliament but lands already paying the clerical tenth were exempted, and in 1341 to clarify the issue the king conceded that only those clerics who held by barony and who ought to come to parliament by summons should pay the ninth.[15] This led a number of religious houses to claim that they did not hold by barony and should not be summoned; some were successful, and by the 1360s a standard list existed of 25 abbots, the prior of Coventry, and the prior of the Hospitallers, though for various reasons one or two might be omitted on any occasion.[16] It had evolved almost accidentally and was certainly not based on tenure, wealth, antiquity, royal foundation, or any other principle. Probably it was a combination of royal or chancery discretion, and the lack of desire or success on the part of the religious house to escape summons which produced the final list. It was Cistercian and Premonstratensian

---

14 See H.M. Chew, *The English Ecclesiastical Tenants-in-chief and Knight Service* (Oxford, 1932), pp. 167–79, D. Knowles, *The Religious Orders in England*, ii. The End of the Middle Ages (Cambridge, 1955), pp. 299–308 and Powell and Wallis, *House of Lords*. A.M. Reich, *the Parliamentary Abbots to 1470* (Univ. of California Pubns. in History, 17, 1941) is a poor book.

15 *Rot. Parl.*, ii. 130.

16 The Benedictine abbots were from Peterborough, Colchester, Bury, Abingdon, Shrewsbury, Gloucester, Westminster, St Albans, Bardney, Selby, St Benet's of Holm, Thorney, Evesham, Ramsey, Hyde, Glastonbury, Malmesbury, Croyland, Battle, Winchcomb, Reading, St Augustine's Canterbury and St Mary's York, the Augustinian abbots from Cirencester and Waltham, the Benedictine prior from Coventry and the prior of the Hospitallers.

houses, on the longer list in the early fourteenth century probably because of their interest in wool and wool-taxation, which escaped most successfully, and it was principally old, substantial Benedictine houses which remained. They may have looked on the summons as a matter of status, and an entry to parliament which might be useful at times for the business of their houses. They could in any case ignore it or fulfil it by proxy. Most did so and it seems to have been common for only three or four abbots to be present in person while others appointed one or more monks, local clerks, or more commonly royal clerks as their proxies. The king was unconcerned as long as the absentee abbots did not dispute decisions taken in parliament. Abbots were rarely national figures and their absence made so little difference to parliament that during a vacancy no substitute was demanded from their house.

The Officials

A fourth group, justices, administrators, and royal clerks also received individual writs of summons to be with the king 'and others of our Council', *not* to be 'with us and with the other prelates, magnates and chief men' as in the case of the lay and spiritual lords. The number varied, particularly at first, for none had a right to be summoned and it dropped sharply in the course of the fourteenth century. In Edward I's reign numbers varied from 39 (in 1295) to 15 (in 1307) but were often in the 30s; in Edward II's reign they tended to be high at first (43 in 1313) but dropped to the 20s at the close; and in Edward III's reign they dropped still more and rarely reached 10 in the later years. Ten to twelve were normal numbers thereafter with a slight rise in the mid fifteenth century. The explanation is the radical change that was taking place in parliament and in the Council. In February 1305 for example among the 33 who were summoned were the chancellor of the exchequer, barons of the exchequer, 13 masters of chancery or clerks attending the king's Council, justices of the two benches and others who served as justices on eyre.[17] These, with the chancellor and treasurer who as a bishop and a dean were summoned in their own right, were the leading royal officials and councillors. They were useful and indeed necessary members of parliament when it was primarily an enlarged session of the Council handling a great deal of administrative and judicial business, but as it became less an administrative and more a political occasion and as membership of the Council became more exalted second-grade officials and clerks ceased to attend either body, though they were always available if they were

17 *Memoranda de Parliamento, 1305*, p. xxxvii.

required. By the later fourteenth century only the justices of King's Bench and Common Pleas, the occasional serjeant-at-law, perhaps the chief baron of the exchequer, and a few clerks who were canon lawyers were summoned. By the end of Henry V's reign only the justices and serjeants remained. They gave advice on matters of law but they were not full members of the lords. The Fane Fragment of 1461 does not list their attendance and a number of references suggest that they were brought in to be consulted and retired to prepare their answers. There was an immense difference between the world of Chief Justice Hengham in Edward I's reign who boasted that the judges had 'made' a statute and who brought his difficult cases to parliament for resolution and that of fifteenth-century justices with their views of the omnicompetence of the 'High Court of parliament' and their unwillingness to meddle in its affairs.

The Commons*

By 1272 it was already customary to represent the local communities at the king's court by knights from the counties and townsmen from a number of towns. This was the method used when it was considered desirable to represent them in parliament but it took time before it settled into the classic two knights, two burgesses form. Until the 1290s representatives were rarely summoned to parliament – knights alone in October 1275 and July 1290, knights and townsmen in April 1275 and September 1283 – and the number of knights and townsmen varied. It was the so-called 'Model' parliament of November 1295 which proved a turning point. The sheriffs were ordered to send two knights from each county and two citizens or burgesses from each city or borough, and the writs were enrolled.[18] This was the standard formula thereafter whenever representatives were summoned to parliament save in October 1297 when two knights only were summoned, and May 1306 when smaller boroughs were allowed to send one

---

* The principal books on the Commons (additional to those on p. 156) are J.S. Roskell, *The Commons in the Parliament of 1422* (Manchester, 1954) which covers much more than its title would suggest and M. McKisack, *The Parliamentary Representation of the English Boroughs during the Middle Ages* (Oxford, 1932)). D. Pasquet, *The Origins of the House of Commons*, transl. R.G.D. Laffan (Cambridge, 1925) and L. Riess, *The History of the English Electoral Law in the Middle Ages*, transl. K.L. Wood-Legh (Cambridge, 1940) are old works with limited value apart from the examples they cite. Some of the many articles written on the Commons are cited in the footnotes.

18 The writs are printed in *Select Charters*, pp. 441–2 (April 1275), 460–1 (1283), 481–2 (1295) and W. Stubbs, *the Constitutional History of England* (4th ed., Oxford, 1896), ii. 234–5 (September 1275). When the April 1275 writs were first printed it was thought that the knights were to be chosen from those 'more discreet in the law' but this was corrected to the conventional 'more discreet and lawful'. H. Jenkinson, 'The first parliament of Edward', *EHR* 25 and 58 (1910 and 1943), pp. 231–41 and 462–3.

burgess only. They were not yet summoned to every parliament; this became almost invariable after 1310 and invariable after 1325; and soon after 1325 it must have been considered customary to summon them to parliament though no enactment laid this down.

. The major determining factor in regularizing representation was the tax on movables. The 90s was the first time of heavy, repeated taxation and Edward I tried both obtaining the consent of the counties and towns together in one assembly and negotiating separately with the towns (p. 224). The former became the accepted method and the two knights/two burgesses pattern became standard even when no tax was requested. This is not to say that the representatives were summoned *only* to grant taxation; this is demonstrably false; but taxation was undoubtedly a major factor, probably *the* major factor in the development. A striking confirmation of this is the experimentation which took place down to 1295 to find a form of words in the writs which bound the men of the counties and towns to the decisions of their representatives. The final form, which remained substantially the same until 1872, was that the knights were to come with 'full and sufficient power for themselves and for the community of the county aforesaid and the said citizens and burgesses for the communities of the cities and boroughs. . . . to do what shall be ordained then by common consent in the aforementioned matters, so that for lack of the same power the business aforesaid shall not remain undone in any way'.[19] The most compelling reason for this demand was surely full power to bind their communities to pay taxes.

The remainder of the writ also became standardized at this time; minor variations occur later and clauses were added rehearsing the provisions of legislation about elections, but the framework remained much the same.[20] The writ began by stating in general terms that a parliament was to be held at a given place and date and ordered the sheriff to have chosen two knights and two citizens or burgesses from each city and borough in the county. They were to have full power, not to 'discuss' and 'treat' like the lords, but to 'do' and 'consent' to the things ordained by common consent; this was an advance on the writs of summons to the *colloquia* of 1290 and 1294 which had summoned them merely to consult and consent to what the earls, barons, and magnates had agreed.[21] Finally the sheriff was ordered to return the names of those elected and the writ itself. He normally complied by

19 J.G. Edwards, 'The *Plena Potestas* of English parliamentary representatives', *Hist. Studies*, i. 136–49 (from *Oxford Essays in Medieval History* to H.E. Salter, 1934).
20 The variants are discussed in Stubbs, *Constitutional History*, ii. 263–5 and iii. 410–6. Examples of writs of summons, returns and writs to pay expenses are printed in *Select Documents*, pp. 361–5.
21 *Select Charters*, pp. 273 and 477.

writing his return on the back of the writ, sometimes continuing on another sheet of parchment attached to it. He gave the names of those chosen and normally the names of two others who were sureties (*manucaptores*) for the attendance of each member, and he might add when and where the county election had taken place. Not much importance should be attached to the use of sureties; it was a frequent practice at common law; it proves nothing about willingness or unwillingness to attend, and quite soon the names were sometimes fictitious. A simple return like this was open to fraud by the sheriff and in 1406 a new type of return for the counties was introduced by statute (7 Hen. IV, c.15). *All* the electors were required to seal an indenture with the sheriff stating who had been chosen, and one part was to be attached to the writ as the return for the county. The indentures were duly made and the practice was extended to the boroughs. They should be a boon to the historian but their usefulness is limited because normally only a small number of electors, presumably the more important, sealed (pp. 190–1).[22]

At the close of parliament members could obtain writs (*de expensis*) in chancery ordering the sheriff or the officers of their town to pay their expenses. The earliest writs speak only of 'reasonable expenses', but after 1315 they specify the daily rate and the number of days to be counted, including travelling-time calculated on a customary scale related to the distance involved. The rate varied slightly at first but by Edward III's reign four shillings a day for knights and two shillings for burgesses was standard. Many members, particularly burgesses, failed to buy the writs or at least to have them enrolled, and this has led to the suggestion that many members failed to attend.[23] It can however be shown from other sources, in particular town archives, that a good many members for whom no expense writs are enrolled were present in parliament or were paid wages. The small size of town communities probably often made a writ unnecessary. The sheriff was supposed to make a levy to raise the money to pay the county knights, and a statute of 1445 (23 Hen. VI, c.10), which probably merely confirmed existing practice, sets out how an assessment was to be made – in the county court on each hundred and then on each township. Complaints about dishonest sheriffs and about who should contribute show that this assessment was often a source of discontent. Towns which sent

22 Lancashire and Lincolnshire lists are printed by J.S. Roskell. *The Knights of the Shire for the County Palatine of Lancaster, 1377–1460* (Chetham Society, 96, 1937) and A. Rogers, 'The Lincolnshire county court in the fifteenth century', *Lincolnshire History and Archaeology* 1 (1966), pp. 64–78.

23 A.F. Pollard, *The Evolution of Parliament* (2nd ed. London, 1926) was a strong exponent of this view but it was firmly disproved by J.G. Edwards, 'The personel of the commons in parliament under Edward I and Edward II', *Hist. Studies* i. 150–67 (from *Essays in Medieval History presented to T.F. Tout*, 1925). The writs ceased to be enrolled in 1414.

members to parliament, peers who were summoned personally and their tenants, free and unfree, were exempt from contributing, so too were tenants in gavelkind in Kent, and apparently tenants of ancient demesne of the crown; probably each county had its own customs. Cities and boroughs were left to their own devices over expenses. London and a few large towns paid over the prescribed rate, no doubt for the honour of the town; others paid less. By the fifteenth century many towns were not paying the full rate and some were already accepting offers from outsiders to serve without payment.[24]

The writs of summons, the returns and the writs *de expensis*, supplemented by many other sources, provide a mass of hard information about the representation of the communities. The information is patchy but the medieval volumes of the *History of Parliament* series will one day provide a 'Namierization', a thorough survey of the electorate and the elected.[25] The questions to be asked here are more modest. At first representation was regulated by few instructions and no laws. As in the case of the lords, it was sufficient that there was representation. When and why did it become in part regulated? How did the system work in practice? And is there a pattern in time of these changes which matches the development of parliament as an institution – which is the subject of the next chapter? These questions must be asked first about the county and then about the town members because their history was different, significantly so, and this remained true until the nineteenth century.

The County Members

There were 74 county members, two from each English county, excluding Chester and Durham which were county palatines before representation became common and were not represented in parliament until 1543 and 1673 respectively, but including Lancaster which continued to be represented after it became a county palatine in 1351. In addition a number of important towns, ten by 1461, were granted the status of counties and received writs addressed to their sheriff or sheriffs ordering two (in the case of London four) citizens or burgesses to be elected to parliament, but their members were in effect burgesses rather than county knights. For long no instruction was given to the sheriffs on how the knights were to be chosen but the intention was clearly that expressed in the writs for the parliament of October

---

24 McKisack, *Parliamentary Representation*, pp. 82–99.
25 *The Return of the name of every member of the Lower House, 1213–1874* (Parliamentary Papers, 1878), vol. i provides a valuable list of members for each parliament. It has been supplemented by McKisack, *Parliamentary Representation*, Roskell, *Commons in 1422* and many other local studies.

1275 – election 'in full county court by assent of the same county' – and returns frequently state that the election took place in full county court at a given date and place.[26] What lies behind this is another matter. For a start, the court met on a fixed day every four or six weeks and the schedule must sometimes have been tight or even impossible, particularly in the more distant counties. In 1297 for example the writ reached the sheriff of Northumberland only on 28 September for members to be at Westminster on 6 October.[27] Moreover attendance at the court was often small and selective (p. 108). What probably happened was that the county 'establishment', the governing circle, determined the choice, no doubt often before the court met. A study of Essex elections in Edward I's reign concludes that the procedure worked smoothly and that a consensus chose the two representatives from knights 'or men of equivalent status, mature in years, experienced in local government, and well reputed by the (county) court', and that such men were willing to serve.[28] This conclusion would probably apply to most county elections throughout the Middle Ages but there are few descriptions of how the consensus was achieved.

Complaints about malpractices and legislation against abuses suggest that attitudes to elections changed appreciably and that the second half of the fourteenth century was a turning point. There were a few complaints from the early fourteenth century onwards of sheriffs making false returns. The most interesting is in parliament in 1318 by Mathew Crawthorne, a well-known Devon gentleman, who was in fact sitting as one of the members for Exeter city, that he had been chosen as one of the county knights for Devon 'by the bishop of Exeter and Sir William Martin, by assent of the other good men of that county . . . and presented to the sheriff in full county court' and that the sheriff had returned another in his place 'against the will of the said community'.[29] The selection had presumably been delegated to these two major county landowners, but it is not known if this was normal practice or what lay behind the incident. During Edward III's reign there is indirect evidence of sheriffs manipulating returns in the increased number of sheriffs who returned themselves and in 1372 an ordinance barred from election sheriffs and lawyer with business before the courts (pp. 193–4). The initiative in 1372 seem to have come from the king rather than the Commons, but in 1376 the Commons themselves petitioned that county knights be chosen 'by common

26 Stubbs, *Constitutional History*, ii. 235.
27 *Parl. Writs*, I, 60.
28 J.S. Illsley, 'Parliamentary elections in the reign of Edward I', *BIHR* 49 (1976), 40.
29 *Parl. Writs*, II, ii, App., p. 138. Crawthorne served on commissions in the county, acted as attorney for the bishop, and sat for Exeter at least four times and twice for the county.

election of the better people (*les meillours gentz*) in the counties'
and not returned by the sheriff alone without proper election.[30]
Presumably 'lesser' people were interfering. The royal answer was
that election should be 'by common assent of all the county (court)',
the traditional method. From this time evidence and complaints of
malpractice increase. Richard II was accused of sending sheriffs the
names of men to be chosen as knights, and though this cannot be
accepted at its face value, it shows at least that the practice – and the
advantage in it – was now in men's minds.[31] The sheriff or his under-
sheriff was a key-figure in electoral manipulation. In 1404 the sheriff
of Rutland was accused of returning William Ondeby though Thomas
Thorpe had been elected 'in full county (court)'; this was confirmed by
a lords' enquiry and the sheriff was dismissed and imprisoned.[32] In
1406 one of the 31 articles accepted by the king in parliament complained of improper returns by sheriffs and laid down that the date
and place of election should be proclaimed in each market town in the
county 15 days in advance so that qualified (*suffisiantz*) persons living
in the county could be present. This was overtaken by a Commons'
petition against county elections made by the favour (*affeccioun*) of
sheriffs and otherwise contrary to the writs, and it led to the first
statute (7 Hen. IV, c.15) regulating elections. It did not provide for 15
days notice, which might have been difficult to give, but merely that at
the first county court after the arrival of the writ 'proclamation be
made in full county court of the day and place of parliament, and that
all those present, both suitors duly summoned for this purpose and
others, proceed to the election of their knights for the parliament . . .
freely and indifferently, notwithstanding any prayer or command to
the contrary' and that the return of the result be in the form of an
indenture sealed by *all* those who took part.[33] In 1410 justices of assize
were authorized to enquire into election returns and punish sheriffs in
breach of the statute of 1406 with a fine of £100, while county members
improperly returned were to lose their wages (11 Hen. IV, c.1). In 1413
these statutes were confirmed and it was laid down that county members and those who elected them, 'knights, esquires, and others', must
be resident in the county on the date of the writ of summons (1 Hen. V,
c.1).[34] In 1429–30 came the most famous of these statutes (8 Hen. VI,
c.7) establishing the 40 shilling freehold franchise which lasted until

---

30 *Rot. Parl.*, ii. 355 – *Select Documents*, p. 111. K.L. Wood-Legh, 'Sheriffs, lawyers and
belted knights in the parliaments of Edward III', *EHR* 46 (1931), pp. 372–88.
31 *Rot. Parl.*, iii. 420 – *Select Documents*, p. 189. The chronicler Thomas Walsingham
accused John of Gaunt of packing the first parliament of 1377.
32 *Rot. Parl.*, iii. 530 – *Select Documents*, p. 214.
33 *Rot. Parl.*, iii. 588 and 601 – *Select Documents*, pp. 225–7; *EHD* iv. 459–60.
34 *Select Documents*, pp. 233 and 237.

1832.[35] It arose out of a Commons' petition and began 'whereas the elections of knights of the counties chosen to come to the king's parliaments in many counties of England have lately been made by too great and excessive a number of people living in the same counties, of which the greater part were people who owned little or nothing, each pretending to have an equivalent voice in making such elections with the most valiant knights and esquires living in the same counties, as a result of which homicides, riots, batteries, and divisions between the gentlemen and others of the same counties truly have and will arise if a suitable remedy is not provided' and it laid down that electors and those elected be living in and resident (*demurantz et receantz*) in the county, that the electors must have free-tenements to the annual value of 40 shillings at least over and above charges, that the sheriffs have authority to make electors swear on the gospels how much they might expend a year, that those supported by the majority of such electors be returned, and it laid down penalties for breach of these provisions. It would be unsafe to accept the statements in the statute at face value, and it was probably prompted by a few recent cases of interference with elections. Nevertheless it was enacted and it was applied for 400 years. It marks the end of the tradition that the whole county court elected and the establishment of a property-in-land qualification.

No comprehensive attempt has yet been made to find out precisely how many and what condition of people could and did take part in elections after 1430. The election indentures normally include only some names, presumably the most important ones. In Yorkshire between 1435 and 1460 the numbers varied from 24 to 451 with an average of 90, or more representative an average of 45 if the exceptional 451 in 1442 is omitted. In Lincolnshire between 1407 and 1478 the number varied between 16 and 116 with an average of 38. In 1450 almost 200 freeholders and a larger number of commoners were present at the election in the relatively small county of Huntingdon. Taking these figures with Gray's estimate from the income tax of 1436 that there were some 7,000 in the counties with incomes from lands, rents, and annuities in excess of five pounds a year, a potential electorate of some ten to fifteen thousand, a few hundred in each county, is probably a fair estimate.[36] It ranged from knights and esquires, some of them wealthy men, through gentlemen, to yeomen. Some impression of the men at the lower end of this group may be obtained by

35 *Select Documents*, p. 267; *EHD* iv. 465. See Roskell, *Commons in 1422*, p. 15.

36 A. Gooder, *The Parliamentary Representation of the County of York, 1258–1832* (Yorkshire Arch. Society, Record Series. 91, 1935), p. 238. Rogers, 'Lincolnshire county court', p. 69. J.G. Edwards, 'The Huntingdonshire parliamentary election of 1450' in *Essays in Medieval History presented to Bertie Wilkinson*, ed. T.A. Sandquist and M.R. Powicke (Toronto, 1969), pp. 383–95. See H.L. Gray, 'Incomes from land in England in 1436', *EHR* 49 (1934), 607–39.

noting that an income of 40 shillings a year was the qualification of a juryman in an assize, that a statute of 1390 (13 Ric. II, st. 1, c.13) laid down that no artificer, labourer (such as butcher or tailor), or labourer without lands or tenements worth 40 shillings a year should keep hunting dogs, that Fortescue wrote that five pounds was 'a fair living for a yeoman'.[37] Forty shillings would have rented 100 or more acres, dependent of course on the quality of the land. The land in question was freehold but this suggests that the franchise extended to yeomen and even husbandmen, landowners on a modest scale, though it did exclude the overwhelming majority in the shires. Bearing in mind the hierarchical nature of society and the sort of men who were elected it is difficult to believe that those excluded in 1430 had ever had a meaningful voice in elections – though they may have taken part in disturbances and disputed elections, and after 1430 it is likely that most freeholders acquiesced in what their betters decided.

The spate of legislation continued for a short time after 1430. An act of 1432 (10 Hen. VI, c.2) laid down that the freehold land must be in the county concerned, and in 1445 a statute (23 Hen. VI, c.14) began by declaring that these earlier statutes had recently been broken by sheriffs who for their own profit did not hold proper elections or make true returns, and laid down a further series of penalties for the offences of sheriffs (and town officials), even enacting that the proper hours for elections were between eight and eleven in the morning.[38] This was the last of the statutes governing county elections in this period and, it is important to stress, virtually the last for centuries.

Complaints and enactments about elections are parallelled by others about who should be elected. From the first the writs had ordered the election of knights (*milites*) and of the county. This was to be expected; knights had traditionally been singled out for the more responsible duties such as serving on the Grand Assize. The demand was however impossible in practice for the number of knights had dropped to only about 1,500 in the late thirteenth century and was fewer in the fifteenth century. It has been questioned if more than a third of the county members in the 'Model' parliament of 1295 were knights,[39] and it is easy to find county members who were landowners but not knights, or were lawyers, royal officials, or even clerks. This situation was accepted by the king, instructions were issued in some cases in Edward II's reign to pay *valetti* lower wages than knights for attending parliament; the writs of summons in November 1330 ordered knights or *serjeants* to be chosen; and in 1372 an ordinance

---

37 Sir John Fortescue, *The Governance of England* ed. C. Plummer (Oxford, 1885), p. 151.
38 *Select Documents*, pp. 280–2. T.E. Hartley, 'The statute 23 Henry VI c. 14: the problem of the texts', *EHR* 82 (1967), 544–8 clarifies the hours of election.
39 K.L. Wood-Legh, 'Sheriffs, lawyers, and belted knights', p. 383.

provided that 'knights or serjeants from among the more valiant in the countryside be returned in future as *knights* in parliament'. 'Knight of the shire' had become a technical term.[40] In 1445 a statute (23 Hen. VI, c.14) laid down that 'knights' of the shire be 'notable knights of the counties where they shall be thus elected or otherwise such notable esquires, gentlemen of birth of the same counties as are able to be knights; and no man to be such knight who is of the degree of valet or below'.[41] The ideal was the landed, armigerous, valiant county man.

Edward III tried to insist on this ideal against, at least at first, a certain indifference in the counties. In October 1339 the Commons, unwilling to grant taxation for the war until they had consulted their communities and perhaps merely delaying, asked that another parliament be summoned to which two of the more valiant knights be sent from each county and not sheriffs or other officials.[42] The writs for the January parliament of 1340 therefore demanded that the county knights should be 'girt with the sword' (*gladio cinctos*). The phrase was then included intermittently in the writs until the 70s when it became a matter of common form, always used. In 1371 and 1373 the additional words, knights 'more approved by feats of arms' were added. The king's motive seems to have been to have men returned who had some experience and enthusiasm for war. The Commons' complaint in 1339 was justified though perhaps hypocritical. It was quite common in the early years of Edward III's reign for sheriffs to return themselves; their numbers fell after 1339 but rose again in the 60s; and it was apparently on the king's initiative that the matter was settled by ordinance in 1372. Sheriffs 'who are common ministers to the people' and ought to remain at their posts, and lawyers with cases before the courts who present common petitions for the benefit of their clients were barred and denied wages if elected.[43] There was apparently no Commons' petition behind this and it seems the negative side to the king's demand for valiant knights. Sheriffs and lawyers were seeking election, presumably to further their own affairs and be paid wages while doing so, and were not attending to the king's business, and were even impeding it with private matters. The writs of summons thereafter contained a clause barring sheriffs and they were rarely elected, though as they were normally gentlemen of the county, they were commonly elected in other years. In four parliaments in the 1350s 'professional pleaders (*perlitatores*), maintainers of pleas, and

40 *Rot. Parl.*, ii. 443 (1330) and 310 (1372) – *Select Documents*, p. 92.
41 *Select Documents*, p. 282.
42 *Rot. Parl.*, ii. 103 – *Select Documents*, p. 49. Wood-Legh, 'Sheriffs, lawyers, and belted knights' discusses this whole issue.
43 *Rot. Parl.*, ii. 310 – *Select Documents*, p. 92.

men who live by such litigation' had been barred in the writs, but no
similar phrase was added after 1372, perhaps because it was difficult
to formulate, and the number of lawyers in fact increased. Most
however were not the sort of men who were the target in 1372; rather
they were administrators or lawyers in the service of the king or
a magnate, often landowners and gentlemen, and active in their
county's affairs as Justices of the Peace, commissioners or sheriffs.
Twenty of the 74 county members were lawyers of this type in 1422.[44]

This evidence of complaints and legislation has been cited at length
because it is the best general evidence available. It is eloquent about
the social structure and the social pressures in the counties. Obviously
it would be unsafe to build much on one statute or the repetition of the
same statute, but the succession of statutes in the first half of the fifteenth century, sometimes regulating elections in precise detail, must
surely have arisen from a perceived need. There must have been resentment at manipulation, concern about disorder, and a fear among the
'better' people that lesser folk were interfering with their privileges.
The timing is also significant. The first complaint is in 1376 and the
bulk of the evidence is from the fifteenth century. This accords with
the evidence of the development of the Commons as an institution,
with its vocal rôle in parliament, and with the 'invasion' of borough
seats by outsiders (pp. 204-5). It all seems part of a pattern.

Unfortunately there is little precise evidence of how members were
chosen to place beside the general evidence of legislation, and virtually
none before the fifteenth century. What exists is of particular value
for it alone gives something of the character and atmosphere of
elections and of county society in general and I offer no apology for
setting it down at length.

The best evidence is in the Paston letters, a collection of letters to
and from members of the Paston family, a gentry family in Norfolk
whose fortune was founded by William Paston (d. 1444), a justice in
the court of Common Pleas. The first election they mention was for
the November parliament of 1450.[45] Cade's rebellion had taken place
in the summer, the duke of York had returned without permission
from Ireland and parliament was certain to see a confrontation. On 6
October a friend in London, William Wayte, a justice's clerk, wrote to
John Paston in Norfolk encouraging him to seek election for the
county. 'Labour ze for to be a knyth of the shire and speke to my

---

44 Roskell, *Commons in 1422*, p. 66.
45 *The Paston Letters, 1422-1509*, ed. J. Gairdner (Edinburgh, 1910), i. 150-3 and 160-1 –
Select Documents, p. 292 prints York and Oxford's letters. The four-volume Gairdner
edition is cited because it is the most common. *Paston Letters and Papers of the Fifteenth
Century* ed. N. Davis 2 vols. (Oxford, 1971-6) is a more accurate edition. K.B. McFarlane,
'Parliament and bastard feudalism', *TRHS* 26 (1944), 53-79 is a classic discussion of the
Paston evidence on elections.

Mayster Stapulton (Sir Miles Stapleton, a well-known county man from East Norfolk) also that he be yt. Sir, all Swafham (in West Norfolk), and they be warned, wyll zeve yow here voyses'. – 'Labour' that some lawyer friends be returned for Norwich and Yarmouth. 'Ordeyne ze that Jenneys mown ben in the Parlement, for they kun seye well . . . In good feyth, good Sir, thynke on all these maters'. What was uppermost in Wayte's mind was that the duke of York's good lordship should be used to win a victory for Paston and their friends over Lord Moleyns and the late duke of Suffolk's faction in Norfolk. Paston was encouraged to seek York's lordship, and membership of parliament was probably considered a sign of Paston's standing in Norfolk. Ten days later however the Duke of Norfolk wrote to Paston that he and the Duke of York 'have fully appoynted and agreed of such ii. persones for to be knightes of shire of Norffolk as oure said unkill and we thinke convenient and necessarie for the welfare of the said shire, we therfor pray you . . . as ye list to stonde in the favour of oure good lordshipp, that ye make no laboure contrarie to oure desire'. Two days later the earl of Oxford wrote to Paston that one of his yeomen had received from one of York's gentlemen a token and schedule of the two nominees, and his advice was 'me thynkith wel do to performe my lordes entent'. One of the nominees, Henry Grey, esquire, was elected but Sir Miles Stapleton was chosen instead of the other, Sir William Chamberlain. Stapleton also had been advised to seek York's lordship and the change may have been approved by York in deference to county feeling. This possibility is suggested by the second election documented in the Paston letters, that for the July parliament of 1455 soon after the Yorkist victory at the battle of St Albans.[46] The duchess of Norfolk wrote to Paston that as 'it is thought right necessarie for divers causes that my lord have at this tyme in the Parlement suche persones as longe unto him, and be of his menyall servauntz . . . (we desire) ye wil geve and applie your voice' to John Howard and Sir Roger Chamberlain. Paston himself hoped to be returned and two letters from a friend and fellow-lawyer, John Jenny, show him sounding out the duke through Jenny while not revealing his ambitions. Jenny wrote that he had told Norfolk he had laboured divers men and they would have Chamberlain but not Howard 'as he hadde no lyvelode in the shire, nor conversaunt' but that they would have Paston. Norfolk's answer was that if they would not have Howard he would write to the under-sheriff that they might have a free election as long as neither Tuddenham nor anyone who favoured the duke of Suffolk be chosen. Howard was furious, but Jenny added 'It is an evill precedent for the shire that a straunge man

46 *Paston Letters*, i. 337 and 340–2 – *Select Documents*, pp. 303–4.

shulde be chosyn, and no wurshipp to my lord of Yorke, nor to my Lord of Norffolk to write for hym; for yf the jentilmen of the shire will suffre sech inconvenyens, in good feithe, the shire shall not be called of seche wurshipp as it hathe be'. In the event both Howard and Chamberlain were elected. In 1461, in the elections for Edward IV's first parliament, there was certainly a contest in Norfolk.[47] The under-sheriff wrote to Paston, after the shire court, 'there hath ben moch to do' but John Berney, Henry Gray and you 'had grettyst voyse' and he proposed to return Gray and Paston. 'Nevertheless', he added, 'I have a master'. The master was the sheriff, Sir John Howard, the outsider of 1455, who later complained that Berney and armed men had pre-vented the election being held. Howard seems to have attempted to hold a second election when the meeting of parliament was postponed for four months. Howard alleged that on this second occasion Paston brought armed and unqualified supporters to the county court and prevented the return of the properly elected candidates, Sir William Chamberlain and Henry Gray, but it was Paston and Berney who were returned and according to Paston's wife, they were the heroes of the county. These cases and those of 1470, when there was a contest between local gentry with the earl of Oxford playing a part, and of 1472, when the dukes of Norfolk and Suffolk decided on the mem-bers, demonstrate a number of things about Norfolk elections in this period. Lords with a stake in the county often sought to determine or influence the choice of members. Their motive was no doubt in part to have support in parliament on national issues, in part to increase their 'worship', their status. In 1449 or 1450 the duke of Norfolk ordered John Paston to come with him to parliament 'in youre best aray with as many clenly people as ye may gete for oure worship at this tyme; for we will be there like oure estate in oure best wise without any delay'.[48] A lord's wishes would be respected but he could not just command; he had to ask the suffrance of the county gentry – some of whom would wish to be elected – and he had to contend with strong county senti-ments. If the lords did not give a lead, the gentry might contest the seats and victory might be decided by 'voices', presumably by acclamation, at the county court, though the sheriff or his deputy might manipulate the proceedings or the returns.

The problem is to know how far 'politicking' and sentiments like these were typical of other counties and other times. East Anglia was certainly faction-ridden at this period and the factions were connected with the exceptional struggle at Court for royal favour and for the throne itself. There is however evidence of politicking in other

---

47 *Paston Letters*, i. 339 misdated 1455. C.H. Williams, 'A Norfolk parliamentay election, 1461', *EHR* 40 (1925), 79–86 prints Howards's complaint.
48 *Paston Letters*, i. 162.

counties, admittedly most of it from Henry VI's reign, though not all from the 40s and 50s when dynastic and political issues were particularly at stake. The same names, rivalries and accusations understandably are to be found in Suffolk as in Norfolk.[49] In Buckinghamshire, Cumberland and Huntingdonshire in 1429 the sheriffs made false returns; in Buckingham the background was probably rivalry between the duke of Norfolk and the earl of Huntingdon.[50] The sheriff of Cambridgeshire failed to make a return in 1439 because, it was alleged, Sir James Ormond's men had ridden about the shire for three weeks before the election asking and threatening the commons to give their voices for Ormond's candidates, and on election day there were so many armed men and outsiders present that the election could not be held. This is the story of Ormond's rival in the county, lord Tiptoft, and it is possible that the latter's men had deliberately prevented the election taking place for at a subsequent court two of Ormond's men were elected.[51] In Huntingdonshire in October 1450 the return has a certificate attached sealed by a knight, eight esquires, ten gentlemen, and 105 forty-shilling freeholders testifying to malpractice at the county court. They alleged that considering the king's need they, with 300 more good commoners (presumably men without a vote), chose two esquires of the royal Household to be the members, but some gentlemen of the county and outsiders and 70 freeholders nominated Henry Gymber, who was not a gentleman as the writ required, to be one of the knights. After 48 of the Gymber party, in-dwellers and out-dwellers, had been examined to test if they were enfranchised, they would not permit their opponents to be examined and the latter retired lest the peace be broken. This is one party's account but it is plausible.[52] The reference to the esquires of the Household is intriguing for it has been suggested that the relatively large numbers of Household men in the parliaments of 1447 and 1453 was due to pressure from the Court, mainly on the small boroughs, and probably in the form of letters to sheriffs containing the names of approved candidates.[53] Earlier in 1450 one of the complaints of the Commons of Kent has a familiar and practical ring about it. The people in Kent, it said, do not have free election because 'letters have beene sent from divers estates to the great rulers of all the Countrey, the whiche enforceth their tenants and other people by force to choose

49 R. Virgoe, 'Three Suffolk parliamentary elections of the mid-fifteenth century', *BIHR* 39 (1966), 185–96.
50 Roskell, *Commons in 1422*, pp. 17–20.
51 R. Virgoe, 'The Cambridgeshire election of 1439', *BIHR* 46 (1973), 95–101.
52 J.G. Edwards, 'The Huntingdon parliamentary election'.
53 Roskell, *Commons in 1422*, pp. 136–7. See also B. Wolffe, *Henry VI* (London, 1981), pp. 216–19 and R.A. Griffiths, *The Reign of King Henry VI* (London, 1981), pp. 622–4 etc.

other persons than the common will is'. In 1455 a royal letter to the sheriff of Kent, only four days before parliament met, ordered him to ensure a free election because there is 'besy labour made in sondry wises by certaine persones' which is nothing to the honour of the 'laborers' and against their 'worship' and may lead to 'inconvenience' at the election.[54]

This is the best of the evidence. There is a little more, and biographical studies of members would probably suggest cases where magnates may have interfered in elections, but it must be admitted that the total is not large. On the other hand the Paston Letters is a unique collection; without it we would know only one of these incidents in Norfolk and that very imperfectly. It is also striking that most of the legislation about elections was passed before 1430 while most of the direct evidence about labouring and malpractice comes after 1430. Yet both types of evidence tell of the same kind of elections. It seems reasonable to conclude that in all the fifteenth century – we will return to the fourteenth century in a moment – there was an active interest in county elections on many occasions which led to labouring and sometimes to disorder and malpractice, and that this was not caused, though it may have been increased, by the political troubles of mid century. It is not possible to describe these elections as Neale and Namier have been able to do for the sixteenth and the eighteenth centuries. Practice must have varied from county to county according to the differing pattern of landowning, lordship and personalities. John Paston struggled to be returned two or perhaps three times for Norfolk but William Burley, a lawyer and steward, was returned 19 times for Shropshire between 1417 and 1455. Some lords intervened on some occasions, others apparently took little interest, but a powerful man's good lordship meant so much that his potential influence must have been considerable. Lords sometimes had an eye to the business of parliament when they intervened in elections, but probably as important, perhaps more important, was concern for their status. The studies that have so far been made suggest however that no lord determined or influenced many returns.[55] The king and his Council intervened in some mid century elections, but this was probably

54 John Stow, *Annales or a General Chronicle of England* (London, 1631), p. 389 – *Select Documents*, p. 291. *Procs. & Ords.*, vi. 246–7.
55 Neither John of Gaunt in the 14th century nor William, lord Hastings in the reign of Edward IV used their considerable influence widely, and in the third quarter of the 15th century Neville but not Percy laboured men in the north. H.G. Richardson, 'John of Gaunt and the parliamentary representation of Lancashire', *Bull. J. Rylands Lib.* 22 (1938), 172–22. W.H. Dunham, *Lord Hasting's Indentured Retainers* (Connecticut Acad. of Arts and Sciences, 39, 1955). P. Jalland, 'The influence of the aristocracy on shire elections in the north of England', *Speculum* 47 (1972), 483–507. I.G. Rowney, 'Government and patronage in the fifteenth century: Staffordshire, 1439–59', *Midland History* 8 (1983), 49–69 shows that while the duke of Buckingham could not force his choice on the county, no one unacceptable to him was likely to be chosen.

unusual. Nationwide issues did enter into some elections, but this also was probably unusual. It was the affairs of the county or rather the interests of leading landowners in the county which seem to have been at issue in most cases. Some of the county gentry sought election – the new desire for election is clear in the 'invasion' of the borough seats (p. 204). It was clearly a sign of status to be elected, and the Paston Letters show how much status meant, for example in the care taken not to reveal one's ambition until election was assured. A parliament was an opportunity for furthering one's interest and winning favour; there was clearly a sense that parliament was the centre of great affairs and that it was honourable to be there. Elections meant 'labouring', sometimes a turbulent poll with the gentry leading their tenants and unenfranchised commoners to the county court where the result was probably normally determined by 'voices', by shouts of acclamation, and sometimes malpractice in the form of overawing the court or manipulating the business or the return. More often though, if Tudor and eighteenth-century evidence is any guide, and I think it is, elections were probably agreed beforehand and not contested at a poll, though this is a matter on which there is no contemporary evidence.[56]

The men who were elected fit this conclusion well. Almost invariably they were county men, landowners, with experience in county office as commissioners, Justices of the Peace, sheriffs, or escheators. Some were lawyers or stewards, but men of status and experience in the county and normally with land there. The outsider was a rarity; the reaction to Howard's candidature in Norfolk in 1455 shows why. Members were often knights or esquires, and certainly gentlemen within the meaning of the statute of 1445. They were likely to serve more than once, though opportunity varied from county to county. As McFarlane emphasized, the gentleman could sometimes match the lesser nobleman in wealth, and though almost necessarily the retainer of a great man because that was the character of society, he was a man of status in his own right.[57]

I have made much of the fifteenth-century member because most of the evidence about elections and most modern biographical studies of members relate to the fifteenth century. The average fourteenth-century member was a man of the same type, a county man with the slightly different experience of the gentry of that century. Who else could have been chosen? It was never difficult to find men to serve;

---

56 J.G. Edwards, 'The emergence of majority rule in English parliamentary elections', *TRHS* 14 (1964), 175–196 considers the post-medieval evidence. Because of the great continuity in English government medieval and modern historians should make comparisons like this more often.

57 K.B. McFarlane, 'Parliament and bastard feudalism'.

statistical analysis of re-election has disproved the theory that it was, though it has not shown that they were eager to serve.[58] At all periods many men sat only once, some a number of times, some often. From the early fourteenth century, when meaningful statistics are first possible, members who had served before were always a majority in parliament, and there is little variation in the figures between 1310 and 1460 though there is a significant but not a dramatic rise in the later fourteenth century.[59] Statistical analysis is too blunt a tool to justify precise conclusions, but this rise may indicate a turning-point in attitudes. There are a few indications that early elections were conducted by restricted groups; in 1318 it was alleged that the selection in Devon was delegated to two great landowners (p. 189) and the Northumberland indenture of 1422 refers to the fourteen men who sealed it and others 'nominated by assent of the said community to elect the two knights'.[60] There are several cases of great landowners or their attornies being accorded a special place at elections; in Sussex in 1297 the election was postponed because the archbishop of Canterbury and other important men were absent; the sheriff of Oxfordshire and Berkshire sometime in Edward II's reign made a memorandum to summon the magnates or their stewards to make the choice; and in Yorkshire for a time after indentures were introduced in 1406 only the attornies of the major landowners sealed. John of Gaunt was able to nominate the members for Lancashire, but this was a special case and the duke or the king or their councils could probably always determine the result there.[61] More significant than these individual cases is the general evidence already cited, in 1376 the beginning of complaints about too many taking part in elections in contrast to the apparent indifference to the return of sheriffs and pleaders earlier in the reign;

58 J.G. Edwards, 'The personnel of the commons in parliament under Edward I and II' demonstrated this point and fought off a counter by A.F. Pollard in *History* in 1926. K.L. Wood-Legh, 'The knights' attendance in the parliaments of Edward III', *EHR* 47 (1932), 398–413 and N.B. Lewis, 'Re-election to parliament in the reign of Richard II', *EHR* 48 (1933), 364–94 analyse the evidence, and there are figures for the period after 1439 in Wedgwood and Holt, *History of Parliament, 1439–1509.*

59 Lewis, 'Re-election', pp. 372–3 gives comparative figures:

	1295–1307	1309–16	1316–27	1376–81	1382–88	1389–97
% of county members with prior experience	36.8	55.7	51.5	56.9	67.1	66.5
Average no. of elections of each member	1.60	2.32	2.26	2.30	3.16	3.29

The comparable percentage of prior experience in the 1450s was 61. The figures for borough members are similar.

60 Roskell, *Commons in 1422* p. 10.

61 L. Reiss, *Electoral Law*, pp. 52–3. Gooder, *Parliamentary Representation of the county of York*, p. 237. On Lancashire see Richardson, 'John of Gaunt', Roskell, *Knights of the Shire of Lancaster* and R. Somerville, *History of the Duchy of Lancaster* (London, 1953), i.

the accusations that John of Gaunt and Richard II had packed parliament; and above all the flood of evidence of the need to regulate county elections in the very early fifteenth century and the observable 'invasion' of borough seats at the same time, all suggest that there was a new interest in elections in the later fourteenth century, which of course coincides with a new assertiveness and importance of the Commons in parliament.

Citizens and Burgesses*

Borough elections and borough members were quite different from those in the counties – the townsman was distinctly the social and political inferior of the country gentleman – but their history reinforces some of the conclusions already advanced about the medieval parliament. From about 1300 burgess members were often summoned to parliament, but kings interfered strikingly little in which towns were represented or how the members were chosen. The distribution of seats was the result of practice over a long period and each borough devised its own methods of election. By the fifteenth century, and probably by the late fourteenth, however, a major change can be seen, the invasion of borough seats by lawyers, royal officials, and gentlemen which was such a feature of parliament until the nineteenth century, had begun. And with it came some of the politicking better documented in later periods.

Towns were represented in every parliament after 1325 but the number remained uncertain until the close of the fourteenth century. The writ ordering the sheriff to have two townsmen chosen in each city and borough in the county at first presented him with a problem for he had no accepted list of boroughs to follow, indeed the term 'borough' was not yet a defined one. He had to use his discretion and a long settling-down process began. This story has yet to be told in detail for the numbers are considerable and the evidence is incomplete, but the general pattern is clear. In April 1275 the summons was wide and was answered generously. Many small towns and villages were represented, Biggleswade, Shefford, and Odell in Bedfordshire for example, and there must have been more burgesses than for any other medieval parliament.[62] Thereafter numbers fluctuated from parlia-

---

* The key book on town representation is M. McKisack, *Parliamentary Representation*. Roskell, *Commons in 1422* surveys the change in the 15th century. See also K.N. Houghton, 'Theory and practice in borough elections to parliament during the later fifteenth century', *BIHR* 39 (1966), 130–40 and P. Jalland, 'The revolution in northern borough representation in mid fifteenth-century England', *Northern History* 11 (1976).

62 H. Jenkinson, 'The first parliament of Edward I', *EHR* 25 (1910), pp. 231–42.

ment to parliament but the general pattern was of experience win-
nowing out the smaller and less willing towns. During Edward I's
reign some 166 towns sent representatives at least once but the average
number represented in any one parliament was only about 86, each by
two townsmen. During Edward II's reign the number represented
dropped to some 110 and the average to about 70 a parliament. The
downward trend continued in the first part of Edward III's reign, and
by its close there was little variation from parliament to parliament,
the numbers in fact began to increase, and there were few cases of
towns making no return. The number of towns represented averaged
about 75 for the reign as a whole, over 80 in the last 20 years, and
about 83 in Richard II's reign. Numbers seem to have fallen back
slightly in the early fifteenth century though there is no obvious reason
for this and it may be an illusion created by incomplete evidence, and
the rise continued during Henry VI's reign when the average was 87
and the highest figure 96 in 1453. In 1478 the number was 101 and the
rise continued through the sixteenth century.[63] This is broadly the
time-scale found in most other aspects of parliamentary development,
origins about 1300, increasing regularization in the fourteenth century, and then evidence of growing interest in the later fourteenth
century, increasing in the fifteenth.

The distribution of the seats was distinctly fortuitous. Larger towns
tended to be represented but, for example, Plymouth and Coventry,
probably the fourth and fifth largest in the country, began to send
members regularly only from 1442 and 1453 respectively, and the
historic weighting towards the south, particularly the south-west, is of
early origin. The seven northern counties came to contain only six
parliamentary boroughs, Carlisle, Appleby, Newcastle, Scarborough,
York and Hull, while Devon, Cornwall, Wiltshire (with 16), Dorset
and Somerset had 41 by the end of the period. Riess suggested that the
major reason for this was that the sheriff sent the order to elect members to those boroughs which did not have the right of 'return of
writs', not to the town direct but to the hundred bailiff or the lord of
the liberty. In these cases the borough was more likely to escape the
obligation to send representatives. In the south-western counties however, because of pressure of time, the custom was to send the order
direct to *all* towns, more towns made returns, and the anomaly
appeared. This explanation seems to stand scrutiny though it requires
detailed examination.[64] Local circumstances everywhere played a large
part in the evolution of the electoral map. It used to be suggested that

---

63 The figures come from McKisack, *Parliamentary Representation*. The 15th century figures
   exclude the 14 'barons' who represented the seven Cinque Ports but who were in practice
   merely burgesses.
64 Riess, *Electoral Law*, pp. 32–6.

there was widespread opposition in the towns to representation and that many of those elected failed to attend, but this is unlikely.[65] It is probable that at first there was little enthusiasm to be represented, save perhaps in the larger towns; for one thing it meant paying wages to the members. Many towns quietly escaped the burden and a few such as Torrington in Devon in 1368 were formally excused by the king, or obtained permission not to send representatives for a few years on the grounds of poverty, but the remainder seem to have accepted the burden and in the fourteenth century there was a steady decline in the cases where the sheriff reported that a town had failed to reply to his order. The king for his part seems to have been content with a reasonable representation as long as unrepresented towns did not refuse to be bound by decisions made in parliament.

The growing interest in county elections in the later fourteenth century was reflected in complaints about malpractice and then in legislation. There was legislation about borough elections also but it was much less and much later and was primarily an appendix to legislation about the counties. The statute of 1406 (7 Hen. IV, c.15) which provided that county returns should be by indenture made no mention of the boroughs, but the writs of summons thereafter ordered the borough returns to be in the form of an indenture between the sheriff and the electors. The statute of 1413 (1 Hen. V, c.1) laying down that in the counties both the electors and those elected should be residents, adds that borough members must also be residents and enfranchised. The statute of 1445 (23 Hen. VI, c.14) was more specific though primarily a definition of existing practice with additional penalties. The preamble says that frauds had been committed by sheriffs and town officials and the statute provides that on receipt of the writ of summons the sheriff should send a precept under his seal to the mayor or bailiffs ordering an election by the citizens or burgesses, that their return must be in the form of an indenture with him, and that he must make an honest return of the writ and the indenture.[66] This legislation was much less substantial than the legislation about county elections. There was no established borough franchise and indeed there was none until 1832. In theory the electors were the citizens and burgesses but practice varied widely and in most towns elections were not surprisingly in the hands of the circle of prosperous townsmen who provided the mayors, bailiffs, aldermen and councils and con-

---

65 See p. 187, n. 23.
66 *Select Documents*, pp. 280–2. Towns incorporated as counties were special cases and the writs of summons were sent to the sheriffs, but in practice the election took place as in other towns. Only Bristol adopted the 40 shilling freehold franchise. McKisack, *Parliamentary Representation*, p. 51–2.

trolled the government of their towns (p. 154).[67] In the thirteenth and fourteenth centuries borough members were overwhelmingly townsmen, merchants and traders, drawn from the same circle. Many served only once, some a numbers of times, and there were old parliament hands such as Thomas But who sat 15 times for Norwich and William and Thomas Graa, father and son, who sat 14 and 12 times respectively for York in the second half of the fourteenth century. In the fifteenth century the pattern in the larger towns was much the same. In London there seem to have been more citizens anxious to be elected and re-election was slightly less common and the same was true in York. In Bristol re-election was more common than before. Thomas Yonge, Bristol's recorder, served nine times but he was more than a merchant. He was a lawyer, an active partisan of the duke of York in the 1450s, and eventually a judge at Westminster. The very major change was in the smaller boroughs where an increasing number of non-residents were elected. Professor Roskell has provided a statistical table based on his own work, on the pre-war *History of Parliament* and on Professor McKisack's study.[68] In the parliament of 1422 almost a quarter of the borough members, 23 per cent, were non-residents; by 1450 the figure was 50 per cent; and it rose further during the Yorkist period. By the end of the sixteenth century the figure was over 75 per cent.[69] The change clearly began before 1422, how far back is still unknown, but is must be associated with the growing interest in county elections and the increased status of the Commons itself in the later fourteenth century. The Commons in the fifteenth century always included a core of substantial merchants from the larger towns, men who might aspire to become landowners themselves, but increasingly county gentlemen, lawyers and officials, some of whom owned property there, were being elected for neighbouring towns and others, some of them royal Household men or Westminster officials, were being returned by smaller towns. There were a number of influences at work. The king sometimes had an interest in having support in the Commons. His knights and esquires would look to county seats, but lesser officials and members of the Household might obtain borough seats; in 1447 they formed 16 per cent and in 1453 17 per cent of the Commons and amended election returns and the fact that few of these men sat regularly indicates that their election was arranged from Westminster through the sheriffs.[70] The king as the lord of a number of boroughs had the means to influence returns directly. Magnates could gift or influence returns in

67 Roskell, *Commons in 1422*, pp. 33–7.
68 *Ibid*, p. 243.
69 J.E. Neale, *The Elizabethan House of Commons* (London, 1949), p. 147.
70 Roskell, *Commons in 1422*, pp. 136–9.

the same way, for example the duke of Norfolk at Reigate or Gatton or the bishop of Winchester at Taunton. Magnates could also 'labour' a town; Grimsby was 'laboured' (unsuccessfully) by letter about 1459 by John, Viscount Beaumont, in favour of his servant, Ralph Chandler, though Chandler was probably a burgess, and again, probably in 1460, by the earl of Westmorland who asked to have their writ so that he could nominate two of his councillors – he said it would save them money and further any causes they had.[71] The Paston Letters show John Paston in 1450 and 1455 being exhorted to 'labour' the mayor and aldermen of Norwich on behalf of friends and a letter of John Paston to his brother Sir John in 1472 reveals particularly clearly the new spirit about elections. If you don't get in for Maldon, he says, Lord Hastings could find you a seat. 'Ther be a doseyn townys in Inglond that chesse no bergeys whyche ought to do, and ye may be set in for one of those townys and ye be frendyd'.[72]

Evidence of this kind about borough elections together with the evidence about county elections already cited proves that a seat in parliament had become a desirable thing to an increasing number of people from at least the later fourteenth century, sometimes to the king to sustain his interest in parliament, to magnates to enhance their status and further their interests and to gentlemen and lawyers for the same reasons in their counties. The interest is often 'political' but the politics of the fifteenth century which we have seen in county affairs and county elections. The implications are considerable, for the continuity of 'politics' into the succeeding centuries and for the status of the Commons in parliament.

The Lower Clergy*

There was one further group of members, the lower clergy. They were first summoned in 1295 to the 'model' parliament; they were summoned to most of Edward II's parliaments; and from 1334 they were invariably summoned. The method was to include in the writs of summons to the archbishops and bishops or to the keeper of spiritual-

---

71 McKisack, *Parliamentary Representation*, pp. 62–3. In the 15th century the duke of Buckingham could control the election at Stafford and shared control of Newcastle under Lyme with the king. Rowney, 'Staffordshire', p. 56.

72 McKisack, *Parliamentary Representation*, pp. 63. *Paston Letters*, iii. 55.

* J.H. Denton and J.P. Dooley, *Representatives of the Lower Clergy in Parliament 1295–1340* (Royal Historical Society, 1987) and A.K. McHardy, 'The representation of the English lower clergy in parliament during the fourteenth century' in *Sanctity and Secularity: the Church and the World*, ed. D. Baker (Studies in Church History, 10, 1973), pp. 97–107 are the principal studies.

ities during a vacancy a clause, the *premunientes* clause, ordering them to 'forewarn' the dean or prior of their cathedral chapter and the archdeacons of their diocese to attend in person with one proctor having 'full and sufficient power' on behalf of the chapter and two on behalf of the clergy of the diocese. This meant 148 men from the 21 English and Welsh dioceses. The clergy maintained that they had no obligation to obey a secular order to attend a secular court or assembly and to give muscle to the polite form of the *premunientes* clause, on a number of occasions down to 1340 the kings also sent a writ to the two archbishops ordering them to instruct the bishops of their provinces to summon their clergy to attend parliaments. The abandonment of this writ after 1340 is an indication that Edward III had tacitly accepted a compromise with the clergy. The three Edwards had wished parliament to represent all sections of the community, primarily so that all taxation, lay and clerical, could be approved there. Clerical taxation was however a thorny subject (pp. 77–80) and the clergy were determined to maintain their special status in every respect. The higher clergy attended parliament as part of their traditional place in lay assemblies, sometimes justified, not quite accurately, because they were the holders of baronies. The lower clergy had no such justification but it seems that a fair number of them did attend early fourteenth-century parliaments. The problems of their status however remained, and in the 1330s a compromise emerged in practice. The clergy granted taxation to the king in time of need, but they granted it in the two provincial councils, coming to be called convocations, of Canterbury and York. The lower clergy continued to be 'forewarned' to come to parliament – the *premunientes* clause was removed from the writs of summons of the bishops in due time – in 1969! – but they were no longer a significant part of parliament though some were still being chosen to attend until at least the end of the fourteenth century.

There is a common time-scale to all these changes. Until the early years of the fourteenth century it was clearly not considered necessary to define membership at all closely. Then, in a remarkably short time, one generation, conventions firmed about the summons of the lay lords, the abbots and priors, the lower clergy and the towns. By 1340 the membership of parliament was largely established in its classic form and a hundred years later there were firm conventions about the rights and status of the lords and statutory regulation of the procedure for electing the county knights. What is striking is how little of this definition was on the initiative of the king. Definition came about because officials had to take decisions or because practice produced problems or because the changing society demanded it. Parliament was the king's creation but he did not deliberately create it in its classical form.

10
The Work of Parliament*

A recurrent theme in the last two chapters had been how radically parliament changed during this period, and not surprisingly the same radical change, with the same time-scale, is to be found in the work that parliament did. Down to the 1330s the evidence is slight and it is not possible to describe proceedings with any confidence. A great change must however have taken place about 1300 when parliament ceased to be an enlarged meeting of the Council and became increasingly the assembly of the whole community. Large numbers soon became normal, the balance of business altered and proceedings must therefore have changed. Moreover the change must have taken place remarkably quickly because by 1340 the broad pattern of parliamentary procedure during the rest of the Middle Ages – and beyond – including the division into two 'houses', was formed. By 1400 many of the classic features and rights of parliament were established, the Speakership of the Commons, for example and its rights over taxation. By 1461 parliamentary terminology and procedure had become surprisingly defined. Indeed there is a temptation to read too much of the later parliament into the fifteenth century because the terminology is so familiar. Medieval people however did not have the later sense of constitutionality; conventions and even statutes could be ignored; and, most important of all, the balance of authority between king, lords and Commons was different.

The Evolution of Parliamentary Procedure

The earliest parliaments of this period, those of Edward I down to the 1290s, were distinctly different from their successors. Regular Easter

* There is no comprehensive book on the work of parliament and specialized studies will be cited at the beginning of each section of this chapter. The articles by H.G. Richardson and G.O. Sayles republished in *The English Parliament* are important; there is a brief survey of parliamentary business after 1340 in J.G. Edwards, *The Second Century of the English Parliament* (Oxford, 1979); and J.S. Roskell, *The Commons and their Speakers in English Parliaments, 1376–1523* (Manchester, 1965) is always useful.

and Michaelmas parliaments were the ideal, often consisting of the king, councillors, officials and a limited number of bishops and magnates. There were no doubt full meetings in the presence of the king, but much of the business was probably done by small groups, for example considering petitions and the matters which the law book *Fleta* in the 1290s described as the business of parliament – concluding the doubts of the judges, providing new remedies for new injuries and doing justice to each according to his merits.[1] In the relatively well-documented large Lent Parliament of 1305 a group of councillors were told to deal with as many petitions as possible before the king arrived, important business was done in parliament after most of those summoned had been sent home and the Council was still the heart of parliament (pp. 167–8). Yet by 1305 parliament must already have changed greatly. It had ceased to meet on a regular basis; meetings were now summoned when the king required them or circumstances demanded. Numbers of spiritual and lay lords were invariably summoned by individual writs; county knights and townsmen were summoned more often and were soon to be summoned on almost every occasion. Parliaments were now large assemblies which must have required organization, and the balance of business was changing. Petitions were still received and legal and administrative business determined, but the writs summoned the lords to consult, treat and ordain and there is more evidence of 'political' debate, of complaints about royal misgovernment and taxation and discussion of royal policy. Evidence about proceedings is still slight but, taken with the account of parliament in the *Modus Tenendi Parliamentum* of the 1320s (p. 174), it suggests that the procedures documented in the 1330s and 1340s had been evolving since at least the beginning of the century. The *Modus* says that on the first day there was a proclamation about handing in petitions – which is true – though it is probably romancing when it describes the attendances of the several grades in parliament being checked over five days and fines levied on absentees, though checks were certainly made on at least some occasions.[2] It says that there was an opening sermon by a prelate and a statement of the reasons for the summons by the chancellor, the chief justice or a justice. A statement was made by a justice in the January parliament of 1316, the only parliament before the 30s for which a narrative-type roll was written, and this was normal in later parliaments. In 1316 the earl of Hereford and later the bishop of Norwich made statements on behalf of the king and it may be that it was already a convention that the king's dignity demanded that he often spoken

1 *Fleta*, ed. and transl. H.G. Richardson and G.O. Sayles (Selden Society 72, 1953), ii. 109.
2 N. Pronay and J. Taylor, *Parliamentary Texts of the Later Middle Ages* (Oxford, 1980), pp. 70–1 and 83–4.

through intermediaries. The *Modus* describes the seating arrangements. The king sat on his royal seat, even when speaking; to his right
sat the archbishop of Canterbury and the bishops of London and
Winchester and, beyond them, in due order the other bishops of the
Canterbury province, the abbots and priors; to his left sat the archbishop of York and the bishops of Durham and Carlisle and, beyond
them, in due order the earls, barons and lords; and at his feet sat the
chancellor, treasurer, justices and clerks. Significantly, this is the seating arrangements known in the lords at a later date and there is no
reason to doubt the *Modus*.[3] The knights and townsmen are not mentioned in this assembly; perhaps they stood at one end of the hall when
they were required to attend – as they did later and still do when called
to the House of Lords. The five grades, bishops and abbots, earls and
barons, clerical proctors, knights, and townsmen are said to meet
separately, each with a clerk assigned to it. The clerks are probably
fictional but there certainly were meetings of groups of members. In
the January parliament of 1316 there were meetings of all members, of
prelates and lay lords, possibly of the king and the prelates to hear his
answer to their petition, and the implication of the grant of taxation
by the citizens, burgesses and county knights and several petitions
from the commons is that they had met together.[4] The *Modus* contains
other details of procedure, many of them unlikely or at least incapable
of verification, but what is important is that it describes a manner of
proceeding which can in part be confirmed in records of the first two
decades of the century and which agrees broadly with the better
records of Edward III's early parliaments. The implication is that
procedure in the larger parliaments which were common after 1295
soon began to develop along lines which became traditional.

There are brief, narrative-type records of parliaments between 1331
and 1333 and a more or less continuous series from October 1339.
Evidence for the 30s is therefore slight but it is worth listing it in some
detail.[5] In September 1332 the chancellor explained the reasons for the
summons, the king's need for advice on the affairs of France and
Ireland, to the prelates, earls, barons and other *grantz*. They gave
their advice individually and collectively; the commons are not mentioned. In March 1332 there were three opening addresses to the lords;
again the commons are not mentioned. Law and order and therefore
the shedding of blood was an issue, so the prelates and clerical proctors met separately from the lay lords. The advice of the latter was
read to the king, the prelates, lay lords, county knights and townsmen

3 *Ibid.*, pp. 72–3 and 85–6. This is the arrangement in the drawing prepared for or by Garter
   King of Arms of parliament in 1523 and in the drawing of Edward I in parliament prepared
   at the same time. J.E. Powell and K. Wallis, *The House of Lords in the Middle Ages*
   (London, 1968) Plates XX and XXI and pp. 55–7.
4 Pronay and Taylor, pp. 74 and 86–7. *Rot. Parl.*, i. 351.
5 *Rot. Parl.*, ii. 60–1 (1331), 64–5 (March 1332), 66–7 (September 1332), 76 (December 1332),
   and 69 (January 1333).

(*gentz du commun*) and approved. On the sixth day the knights, townsmen and the clerical proctors were given leave to return home but proceedings continued in 'full' parliament. In September 1332 the chancellor explained the summons and three separate meetings took place – the prelates, the earls, barons and *grantz*, and the county knights. They advised the king to go to resist the Scots rather than to Ireland and with *tote la commune*, granted a tax. Parliament ended on the third day when the *grantz* and the knights advised the king to go north at once. In December 1332 at York Chief Justice Scrope asked all for advice on the king's policy towards Scotland and again three meetings took place – prelates and clergy; earls and barons; and knights and townsmen (*gentz du commun*). They replied separately that they could not give advice because so many prelates and lords were absent, and parliament was prorogued until January 1333 when three groups again met over several days – a committee of six bishops, two earls and four barons; prelates, earls, barons and clerical proctors; and knights and townsmen. On the sixth day the knights and townsmen were sent home while the lords remained one day longer. The evidence, slight as it is, suggests that the opening proceedings were already traditional. There were proclamations about maintaining peace and order during the parliament and about receiving and handling private petitions – though petitions were largely squeezed out in these parliaments by shortage of time (p. 217). There was a statement of the reasons for the summons from the chancellor or a justice, probably to all the members; the commons are not mentioned but they were probably there, crushed in by the door. The king sought advice – and military and financial support – and it was the advice of the lords which was important. The commons sometimes receive no mention; they may be sent home before the close of parliament; and the knights have more status than the townsmen. All lords meet together but they also meet in *ad hoc* groupings, and this had probably been the practice for decades. In the 1290s the four groups of lower clergy had each met separately (p. 78) and the same may have been true of other groups, for example the knights and townsmen. Significantly the knights and townsmen met together in the last two parliaments of the series and when narrative rolls began again in October 1339 separate meetings of *all* the lords and *all* the commons are the rule. The lower clergy are no longer mentioned. In October 1339 the reasons for the summons and a message from the king in Flanders were declared to the *grantz* and to those of the *commune*, it is not clear whether together or separately, but they must have gone on to meet separately because they replied separately in written 'schedules' to a request for taxation. The *grantz* made a grant and added some requests; the commons asked for another parliament so that the communities could be consulted about taxation and they presented two 'bills', the first answering the matters that had been put to them, the second containing a series of requests.[6] In the next parliament, in January 1340, *grantz* and *communes* met in the Painted Chamber at Westminster to hear the opening postponed. When it met the reasons for the summons were explained to the commons and they were reminded that they had promised a grant of taxation. They answered that they wished to speak and treat together about this, and almost three weeks later they offered a grant of 30,000 sacks of wool on conditions contained in indentures sealed by prelates and other *grantz*; there had clearly been discussions between the two groups.[7] While the matter was referred to the king in Flanders the commons were persuaded after long discussion to grants 2,500 sacks in another indenture as a conditional advance.

By 1340 there were therefore two group meetings after the opening proceedings, the *grantz* and those of the *commune*, the lords and what must now be described as the Commons, and the Commons were already taking a stand against burdens being imposed on their communities. These became the classic groupings. There was however nothing inevitable about them and they were unusual in the parliaments of other countries. The prelates and lower clergy might have met together; the knights and townsmen might have formed two groups; the knights might have met with the lay lords; all might have met together. Different groupings had met in English parliaments but, with hindsight, a number of things favoured two houses. Bishops, earls and barons formed an ancient grouping; they were the greater landowners, notionally the holders of baronies, and they came together in a privileged peerage in the early fourteenth century. The lower clergy had an obvious link with the prelates but they seem never to have been on important part of parliament, particularly from the 1330s when clerical taxation came to be granted solely in convocation (p. 79). The linking of knights and townsmen is the most surprising feature, and throughout this period the county knights were not only socially superior to the townsmen, they were often the only members of the Commons to receive mention. The determining factor in their union was taxation. Until 1297 Edward I had normally negotiated separately with the towns outside parliament about direct taxes but all later levies were with the consent of both groups in parliament. This probably gave them the community of interest and experience which led to what was probably at first an uneasy union in the 1330s.

After 1340 much of the earlier uncertainty is removed. There is an

6 *Ibid.*, ii. 103–5.
7 *Ibid.*, ii. 107–8.

almost unbroken series of narrative-type parliament rolls; from 1340, if not earlier, there is a succession of clerks of parliament and from 1363 there are clerks of the Commons.[8] Parliaments follow a standard pattern. Proceedings open, often some days late because the lords were slow in coming, with a meeting of all the members in the presence of the king or his deputy to hold the parliament. If the parliament was at Westminster, as most were, the place was the Painted Chamber in Westminster Palace, the lords seated in their already traditional order, the Commons presumably standing. In the 1340s a proclamation against disorder was read and this practice may have continued. The latest date for handing in private petitions was announced and receivers and triers appointed (pp. 216–17). Proceedings began with a speech by the chancellor, an archbishop or a justice explaining the reasons for the summons; it came to open with a text from scripture and often conclude, after a deal of circumlocution, with a request for a grant of taxes.[9] A check on who had come was probably made though this is mentioned only occasionally. The two houses then met separately, the lords traditionally in the White Chamber which remained their meeting place until 1801, the Commons in the Painted Chamber, the Chapter House or the Refectory in Westminster Abbey. Their later meeting place, St Stephen's Chapel, was a royal free chapel until it was dissolved in 1547, and only then did it become the 'Commons' Chamber with its facing benches.[10]

The meetings of the lords in the White Chamber must have been a relatively intimate gathering of men who knew one another well. Fifty was probably a typical attendance, sometimes it was perhaps no more than 30. Dukes and earls attended well, bishops and barons generally in middling numbers, abbots and priors in small numbers, and a declining number of ministers, councillors and judges were in attendance.[11] The same men discussed great issues in parliaments and Great Councils on average two or three times a year. Many of them had experience as military commanders, envoys, ministers or councillors. All had status and authority; they were considered to be the king's natural counsellors. The character of their meetings must have been very different from those of the Commons. The lords discussed issues such as military campaigns, relations with the papacy and other kingdoms, patronage, political rivalries and the like. They were the judges in parliament (pp. 230–1). They considered the requests that came

8 H.G. Richardson and G.O. Sayles, 'The king's ministers in parliament, 1327–1377', *English Parliament*, XXII, 337–8 and 396 (from *EHR*, 1932).
9 The texts from 1399 to 1485 are listed in S.B. Chrimes, *English Constitutional Ideas in the Fifteenth Century* (Cambridge, 1936), pp. 165–6.
10 Edwards, *Second Century*, pp. 4–7 etc.
11 J.S. Roskell, 'The problem of the attendance of the lords in medieval parliaments', *BIHR* 29 (1956), pp. 153–204.

from the Commons and grants of taxation. They had meetings with groups of members of the Commons or with the whole house. It was common for the members to give their opinions one by one as well as collectively. We must imagine them sitting in their respective grades, by the fifteenth century in a strict order of precedence within each grade. The king or his lieutenant might preside but this was not invariable and it is possible that the chancellor was already presiding on occasion; he certainly was often the royal spokesman. The lords however became much more than a council, in particular as the procedures for granting taxes and approving statutes became more and more formalized. This gave an order to the lords' business on at least some days. By 1461 bills were being considered article by article, every member present perhaps declaring his opinion. Committees might be appointed to investigate and report on issues. Communication in writing and by consultation was maintained with the Commons.[12] There was an established order to proceedings.

Proceedings in the Commons must have been distinctly different. It was a much larger body, well over 200, with a membership that changed considerably from parliament to parliament, and a different rôle.[13] The 'points of the parliament' were declared to the lords and the commoners and on occasion the latter were directly asked their advice on issues of policy, but the Commons were primarily 'petitioners and demanders'.[14] They presented common petitions; they came to have the right to assent to all statutes and all taxes; but they were not judges and though they protested about misgovernment they frequently, and I think genuinely, protested their inadequacy in great matters. The rolls of parliament never directly describe proceedings in the Commons but there is a unique account of them during the Good Parliament of 1376 in the Anonimalle Chronicle, an account clearly based on the evidence of a member of the house.[15] This was an unusually long, politically-charged, untypical parliament, but the Chronicle does prove that there was genuine 'debate' in the Commons. They met in 1376 in the Chapter House of Westminster Abbey – which still survives. They sat, shoulder to shoulder, round that octagonal building; at least the knights did, no townsman is

12 *The Fane Fragment of the 1461 Lord's Journal*, ed. W.H. Dunham (New Haven, 1935) is the major source of information on day-to-day proceedings.

13 The size of the Commons is uncertain because the numbers of townsmen can be known only from the returns which are incomplete and from casual references. There should have been 74 county knights and about 170 townsmen by the second half of the 14th century rising to about 200 by 1461. The *Anonimalle Chronicle* states that there were 280 members in 1376.

14 Rot. Parl., iii. 427 – *Select Documents*, pp. 198-9; *EHD*, iv. 185. This phrase come from a statement made in the king's name in 1399. See. p. 236.

15 *The Anonimalle Chronicle, 1333 to 1381*, ed. V.H. Galbraith (Manchester, 1927), pp. 79-94 – *Select Documents* (in full) pp. 93-104, *EHD*, iv. 117-21.

mentioned. They began to discuss the 'points of the parliament' and it was suggested that it would be wise first to take an oath together to keep secret what was said so that all could speak freely, and this was done. The Commons was already an institution with some experience and political perception. A knight rose and spoke from a lectern in the middle of the floor so that all might hear. He was critical of the request for taxes because previous heavy taxes had been wasted and misappropriated. A second knight went forward and agreed with this, adding further names and details to the charges; a third advised that the advice and help of a group of lords should be sought because lords were greater and wiser in such great matters; other knights also spoke. There is no mention of a chairman or Speaker but a knight representing Herefordshire in his first parliament, Sir Peter de la Mare, spoke so well in the debates which went on for several days, that he agreed to act as the Commons' spokesman in the 'great parliament' before the king's lieutenant and the lords. At this meeting Peter said that he had authority to 'speak' only for that day but in fact he became the spokesman for the Commons throughout the parliament and should be considered its first Speaker.[16] Before 1376 there had apparently been different spokesmen drawn from the small delegations which customarily represented the Commons before the king and the lords. After 1376 there was almost certainly a Speaker in every parliament. The parliament roll for 1376 does not mention Sir Peter, but the roll for the next parliament in January 1377 records that Sir Thomas Hungerford had *les paroles* for the Commons; six out of the following nine rolls mention a Speaker; and from 1398 the roll always records his name. The impression is of an office developing rapidly over a few decades. For example in 1384 the Commons were for the first time ordered at the beginning of parliament to chose their Speaker and this was certainly the custom by the turn of the century when it was also customary for the Commons to present his name to the king for his approval. The common title of the Speaker, *parlour*, first used in 1394, implies a duty to speak on behalf of the Commons as Sir Peter had done in 1376 but the indications are that he soon came to have a rôle in organizing the business of the house.

Sir Peter de la Mare's request when he first met John of Gaunt and the lords in 1376 was for a group of four bishops, four earls and four barons or bannerets to come to the Commons to advise and hear and witness what they said. This procedure, 'intercommuning', had been a common feature of parliaments since the 1340s.[17] Groups of lords

---

16 Roskell, *The Commons and their Speakers* is an important case-study of how and over what time-scale procedure developed.
17 J.G. Edwards, *The Commons in Medieval English Parliaments* (London, 1958) and W.N. Bryant, 'Some earlier examples of intercommuning in parliament, 1340-48', *EHR* 85 (1970), pp. 54–8.

might go to the Commons or groups from the Commons to the lords or groups from both houses might meet in another room. It had probably originated in the need for agreement on grants of taxation but it soon became a useful procedure for other purposes. It is last mentioned on the parliament rolls in 1407 but communication between the houses certainly continued. In 1461 groups from the Commons came to have discussions with leading members of the lords, but by then the business of the two houses, in particular on legislation and taxation, had become so formalized and customary, so much in writing, that communication between the houses may often have been arranged through the 'usual channels', the clerks, the Speaker, the chancellor.

One indication of how much proceedings must have changed and the time-scale involved is the length of sessions.[18] Some early parliaments lasted only a few days, others a few weeks; in the two decades before 1350 one or two weeks was normal, in the two decades after 1350 three weeks was normal. The Good Parliament of 1376 lasted an unusual 10 weeks and the 'crisis' parliaments of the following 30 years were often lengthy – the extreme was the parliament of 1406 which lasted 23 weeks. Henry V's parliaments were briefer; Henry VI's parliaments were fewer though most met over several sessions; but the normal session now lasted for a couple of months. The general pattern was for sessions to become longer with a distinct increase in the second half of the fourteenth century. Longer parliaments in which no group was sent home early must have had more corporate identity, more genuine discussion – for example on legislation – and more authority.

The rolls of parliament unfortunately do not tell much about how as distinct from what was done. But a great deal about the changing character of parliament's work can be deduced from the process of legislation and taxation.

Petitions and Statutes*

The early records of parliament consist almost entirely of petitions, not petitions to or from parliament but petitions from individuals or communities to the king or to the king and the Council seeking a grant, a grace or a remedy, and considered in time of parliament. For example the first half-dozen enrolled petitions from the Lent parlia-

18 *The English Parliament in the Middle Ages*, ed. R.G. Davies and J.H. Denton (Manchester, 1981), pp. 37–8 and 112–13.
 * This is a subject still unevenly and incompletely studied. H.G. Richardson and G.O. Sayles, 'The Early Statutes', *English Parliament*, XXV, 1–56 (from *Law Quarterly Rev.*, 1934), T.F.T. Plucknett, *Statutes and their Interpretation in the first half of the Fourteenth Cen-*

ment of 1305 are from a man seeking a pardon of 100 marks he had received to go on the king's service in Gascony; from a religious house to have a tenth of the rabbits in a warren gifted to it but denied by the keeper of the Isle of Wight; from a priory seeking support in a dispute with its bishop over an advowson; from the community of Cumberland asking that a forest justice cease infringing the Forest Charter; from the king's daughter, Mary, seeking to have the escheats, wardships and marriages in some manors granted to her; and from the burgesses of Cokermouth asking permission to levy pontage to repair their bridge.[19] There was nothing necessarily parliamentary about these petitions. Written petitions became a standard way at this period to approach the king at any time or indeed anyone in authority. It is possible that Edward I tried to 'methodize' the requests that came to him by laying down early in the reign that all petitions or, more likely, those presented at parliament should be in writing.[20] He was however soon complaining that petitions were threatening what he considered to be the important work of parliament. In 1280 he ordered that 'because people coming to the king's parliament are often delayed and disturbed by the multitude of petitions placed before the king, to the great grievance of them and the court (*curia*)', they should go first to the chancellor, the exchequer or the justices, and only those that were so important or touched the king's grace should then come before him and the Council. In this way, he said, 'the king and his Council may, without the charge of the other matters, attend to the weighty matters of his realm and his foreign lands'.[21] The solution was to have panels to receive petitions and panels to 'hear' them, so that

---

tury (Cambridge, 1922) and Chrimes, *Constitutional Ideas* are the major discussions. The rôle of parliament and in particular of the Commons is discussed in H.L. Gray, *The Influence of the Commons on Early Legislation* (Cambridge, Mass., 1932), a book considerably vitiated by its search for 'popular' initiatives in legislation and corrected by Chrimes, *Constitutional Ideas*, D. Rayner, 'Forms and machinery of the "commune petition" in the fourteenth century', *EHR* 56 (1941), pp. 198–223 and 549–70 (a striking article) and A.R. Myers, 'Parliamentary petitions in the fifteenth century', *EHR* 52 (1937), pp. 385–404 and 590–613. Edwards, *Second Century*, pp. 44–65 surveys 'petition and bills'.

19 *Memoranda de Parliamento, 1305*, ed. F.W. Maitland (Rolls Series, 1893), pp. 5–10.

20 The written petition to the king, the Council, officials and indeed to anyone in authority is a feature of the late Middle Ages, thousands come to be presented each year. There are some but not many from Henry III's reign, many from Edward I's parliaments but not very many at other times – perhaps because they have not survived so well, and they multiply in the 14th century. Probably the written petition was part of the growth in literacy and in the formality of government in the 13th century. A parallel development is surely the written plaints to the justices which became common in Henry III's reign. See *Select Cases of Procedure without Writ under Henry III*, ed. H.G. Richardson and G.O. Sayles (Selden Society, 60, 1941) and the essay on 'King's Bench Bills' in *Select Cases in the Court of King's Bench under Edward II*, ed. G.O. Sayles, vol. 4 (Selden Society, 74, 1957), pp. lxvii–lxxxvi. L. Ehrlich, *Proceedings against the Crown* (Oxford Studies in Legal and Social History, 6, 1921) draws parallels with other kingdoms and the papal court and suggests that the terminology of petitions, at first varied in form, became distinctly standardized by the last years of Edward I.

21 Printed in J.G. Edwards, ' "Justice" in early English parliaments', *Hist. Studies*, i. 284 (from *BIHR*, 1954).

only some petitions would come before the king himself. Receivers of petitions go back at least to the late 70s and soon it became customary to appoint panels of auditors to hear the petitions. In April 1290 there seem to have been separate panels for at least English, Irish and Gascon petitions and in Lent 1305 there were receivers and auditors for English, Scottish, Irish and Gascon petitions. It became normal practice to issue a proclamation at the opening of each parliament announcing the last date for handing in petitions and to appoint the panels. The number of panels continued to vary during Edward II's reign and then became standardized at two, the first for English, Irish, Welsh and Scottish petitions, the second for Gascon and other overseas petitions. The receivers were at first royal clerks and justices, then from Edward III's reign chancery clerks. The auditors were at first mainly royal officials and justices; magnates were increasingly appointed during Edward II's reign; and from then there were increasingly large and distinguished panels of prelates, lay lords and justices. Their task was to sort and answer as many petitions as possible, often by referring petitioners to chancery, exchequer or the courts for a remedy; the remaining petitions would then go, perhaps after consideration by a committee, to the Council or the king. Receivers and auditors of petitions continued to be appointed until the late nineteenth century! In practice they had comparatively little to do from early in the reign of Edward III. The enrolment of petitions on the parliament roll ceased in the 1330s and by the 1340s their numbers had declined to a trickle. They had been driven out by the king's business over a long period. In 1309 Edward II was accused of failing to appoint receivers. He promised to do so, and one of the reasons for the requirement of annual parliaments in the Ordinances of 1311 was to answer petitions. In 1325 the Council advised summoning a *tractatus* rather than a parliament, probably because there would be no petitions there, and in the early years of Edward III's reign there were a number of brief parliaments dominated by war and war-finance in which petitions are known to have been squeezed out. For example in the parliament of September 1332 the king was advised to go immediately to the North and to have the petitions dealt with at some convenient time, and in the following December no petitions were received or answered.[22] When parliament was an opportunity for the king, councillors, *curiales* and officials to meet and sort out problems – as well as consult about great matters – the private petition, though a nuisance, had its place; when it became an assembly of the kingdom, common business drove it out. Petitions continued in their thousands each year but most went directly to the king in his Court, to the Council, to the chancellor and to other officials.

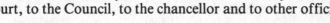

22 *Rot. Parl.*, ii. 67.

At the time private petitions were being driven out of parliament by common business, another type of petition, the common petition, the petition which concerned a number of people, perhaps the whole community, began to be a feature of parliament. These were presented in the name of the Commons and by the mid fifteenth century a written petition or bill – the words are interchangeable – became the necessary preliminary to the making of a statute, and a number of 'readings' of a bill in the lords and Commons became accepted practice. This development is worth discussing in some detail – because it is important and because it is documented in the petitions themselves. The context is a major change in the understanding of law and legislation in England which begins to be seen in the later thirteenth century. Bracton, writing about 1250, adheres to the older view of law as custom. England, he wrote, employs only unwritten custom, though he clearly did not consider that legislation was impossible nor that custom was necessarily ancient, unchangeable or unenacted. He knew that the law had been changed and he went on to say that what 'is justly defined and approved with the counsel and consent of the magnates and the engagement of the republic, the authority of the king or prince preceding' should have the force of and be called a law.[23] The thirteenth century indeed produced a significant body of written law and in the last years of Henry III's reign lawyers began to collect together some of the most important items for reference – Magna Carta, the Charter of the Forest, the provisions later called the Statute of Merton, the Provisions of Westminster republished as the Statute of Marlborough and the Edict of Kenilworth. The names, the forms and the methods of enactment varied but these did constitute a body of written, enacted law. Edward I in the first half of his reign added a further body of legislation which is arguably unequalled in importance down to the nineteenth century.[24] It was however a miscellany of pieces made in response to immediate problems, sometimes made formally, sometimes informally; sometimes in the form of a schedule or list of enactments, sometimes merely of orders to the justices. It was described by terms such as establishments, provisions, ordinances and statutes. It was enacted by the king with the assent of (some) magnates, sometimes in parliament, apparently twice with the approval of representatives of the commons. At first no official *corpus* of this legislation was maintained but about 1300 necessity

23 Henry de Bracton, *The Laws and Customs of England*, ed. S.E. Thorne (Cambridge, Mass., 1968–77), ii. 19.
24 See T.F.T. Plucknett, *Legislation of Edward I* (Oxford, 1949) and M. Prestwich, *Edward I* (London, 1988).

began to produce some order. A Statute roll was written in chancery from 1299, perhaps even earlier. It began with Magna Carta of 1225 and continued with other important texts taken from some private collection, and new statutes, though not all, were added as they were made.[25] The exchequer came to have its own, less complete collection and private collections began to be made.

The word 'statute' itself was slow to be defined. It was not used consistently even a century later, but in the fourteenth century distinctions and definitions began to be made between statute and common law, between statutes and ordinances, on the authority of statutes and how they must be made. They were not yet sharp distinctions and definitions. Plucknett wrote that though legislation took place 'fourteenth-century England was content to see the fact and leave the theory alone'.[26] A distinction between statutes and ordinances does however begin to be drawn from the 1320s and by mid century was well understood by members of parliament. In 1353 ordinances for the government of the Staple were agreed in a Great Council and published, but, because all wished the Staple to last forever, parliament was summoned the following year so that the ordinances could be read, amended if necessary, and be perpetual 'as statute in parliament' to be changed only in parliament. In 1363 the lords and Commons preferred to have an ordinance rather than a statute about dress so that any necessary amendments could be made in the next parliament, and in 1414 they authorized the king to make an ordinance about counterfeiting to be effective until the next parliament when it could be made a statute to last forever.[27] A statute was now considered to be a permanent though not unchangeable piece of legislation, and made only in parliament. An ordinance was less solemn and more administrative in character, dealing for example with defence, the constitution of the royal Household or the duties of customs' collectors; it might be made in parliament or with the authority of parliament but it was more often made by the king and Council. The supremacy of statutes was accepted in practice in the courts by the mid fourteenth century. Justices who had earlier exercised a wide discretion in interpreting statutes, became cautious about doing so. Shareshull, J. in 1346 for example said that justices should not take a statute further than its own words.[28] The theoretical possibility that it might

25 Richardson and Sayles, 'The Early Statutes', pp. 9–17. A new edition and review of Edward's statutes are badly needed.
26 Plucknett, *Statutes and their Interpretation*, p. 31.
27 *Rot. Parl.*, ii. 254 and 257 (1353–4), 280 (1363) and iv. 35 (1414).
28 Plucknett, *Statutes and their Interpretation*, p. 88. In the second half of the 15th century justices were certainly considering the intentions in making a statute when interpreting it.

be declared null by the justices because it conflicted with divine or natural law may be ignored. A statute was supreme over the common law. It overrode the royal prerogative for the courts declared royal patents issued contrary to statute, safeconducts for example, to be null – though the issue of necessity of state was not faced. The king could not alone annul a statute though he could, and frequently did, give dispensations from statutes such as Mortmain and Praemunire. Edward III's revocation of the statute of 1341 only months after it was made (p. 16) was an exceptional action. A statute bound all the king's subjects at home and abroad, inside and outside franchises, whether or not their community was represented in parliament – in Durham or Wales for example – and they were bound by it immediately it was made. All these things are vouched for by contemporary statements and were well understood but they were not brought together into a constitutional statement. One indication of the importance of the statute is how many privately owned collections of statutes still survive – Sir Peter de la Mare cited from a book of statutes to prove a point in a speech before John of Gaunt in parliament in 1376.[29]

The principle that the law should not be changed without consent goes back long before 1272 and counsel and consent, though not necessarily given in a parliament, are mentioned in some of Edward I's more wide-ranging legislative acts. Edward II's smaller body of legislation mentions the complaints of the 'people' or of the 'community' and the assent of the 'community' as well as of magnates. This was the time when the county knights and the townsmen in parliament begin to be recognized as the spokesmen and representatives of the community, the *commune*, and from the 1320s they quite often presented petitions to the king on matters of concern to the community as a whole. Some of these common petitions led to statutes. In Edward III's first parliament in February 1327 the commons presented a document of 41 items; 16 of these were the basis for 16 of the 17 articles of the statutes the king made; the 17th probably arose from a petition of the clergy. The statutes state that the king had granted the articles 'at the request of the *commune* of his realm by their petitions placed before him and his Council in the said parliament, with the assent of the prelates, earls, barons and other great men'.[30] Evidence is scarce over the next decade but in parliament in 1339 the king gave a significant answer to a commons' complaint that many petitions had not been fully answered; all the petitions of *la commune en parlement* in the past had been answered and auditors would be appointed to hear individual (*singuleres*) petitions before the end of parliament. The

29 *The Anonimalle Chronicle, 1333–1381*, p. 86 – *Select Documents*, p. 99.
30 *Rot. Parl.*, ii. 7–12. *Statutes of the Realm*, i. 255. Gray, *Statutes*, pp. 217–22 shows the relationship in detail.

distinction is between common petitions and the older private petitions.[31] From 1343 the roll of each parliament normally ends with a block of enrolled common petitions and the king's answers under the heading *communes petitions* or *petitions des communes* and some of these led to statutes. It was from these petitions, bills (*billa* or *billes*), that the classic legislative procedure in parliament developed.

This development took time and it was unplanned. It is a good example of how parliament evolved – and of the dangers of hindsight. For a start the petitions were 'common' because they concerned the community as distinct from an individual, not because they came from the Commons.[32] In fact, though few of the originals survive from the fourteenth century, the copies on the rolls show that though they came in the name of the Commons, they did not necessarily originate from the Commons as a body. Petitions from the same parliament are sometimes repetitive, petitions from one parliament may be contradicted by those from the next. The wording sometimes shows that they originated in petitions from local communities or their representatives. An ordinance of 1372 forbids the election as county MPs of lawyers with cases before the courts because they presented petitions on behalf of their clients in name of the Commons. Sometimes the Commons disavowed petitions presented in its name. Clearly, though common petitions were an accepted part of parliament from the 1340s and probably a generation earlier, and though some led to the making of statutes, they were not scrutinized carefully in the fourteenth century. They were probably not even read out before the Commons. On some occasions at least the Commons were given a time-limit in which to present petitions and they were probably handed in as loose documents before being edited into a schedule. Perhaps the under-clerk of parliament who became the clerk of the Commons about 1363 became the receiver. Unlike private petitions, common petitions passed directly to the king and the Council in parliament, in effect to the lords and the king who customarily announced his answers on the last day of the session. Lack of information may make the procedure seem less organized than it was and certainly it was normal for 20 or 30 common petitions to go forward in each parliament – in 1376 quite exceptionally there were 140. Some were of local concern and others which raised a general issue may have arisen out of particular cases aired by a few members, but many raised matters which may have arisen out of general discussion. Some complaints recur, about purveyance, about

---

31 *Rotuli Parliamentorum Anglie Hactenus Inediti*, ed. H.G. Richardson and G.O. Sayles (Camden Society, 51, 1935), pp. 270 and 272 – *Select Documents*, p. 48.

32 This was established by Myers, 'Parliamentary Petitions' for the 15th century and by Rayner, 'Forms and Machinery' for the 14th century. The latter is a particularly important article to which this paragraph is heavily indebted though it should be emphasized that the 'public interest' character of the petitions often meant 'interest to the locality'.

the conduct of royal officials, about who should be appointed as officials, about the raising of troops. Some required only a promise from the king, some were refused, but some required a change in the law and led to statutes. In the reign of Edward III most statutes originated in this way. Too much should not be read into this for the king rarely had a programme of legislation and most statutes merely amended the law, something which contemporaries considered should properly arise by way of request from the community, from the Commons which was now held to speak for the community.

There are a number of indications from the early fifteenth century that the Commons and common petitions had acquired an increased status and that formal procedures were hardening round them. Beginning in the last years of the fourteenth century an increasing number of important people were seeking Commons' sponsorship of their private petitions to the king. They were not common petitions but they went directly to the king and the lords; they were the ancestors of private bills and in the course of the fifteenth century it became increasingly common for private bills, for example from towns, to be introduced through the Commons and be lobbied there.[33] In 1414 the Commons presented a remarkable petition to Henry V. They claimed that they had always been part of parliament, both as assentors and petitioners, that it had always been their liberty and freedom that no statute or law should be made without their assent, and they asked that in future when they asked by the mouth of their Speaker or by written petitions for any remedy, the resulting statute or law should not change their 'sentence' and 'entente' in any detail without their assent.[34] The king's answer evaded the issue and conceded only that no enactment should be made contrary to their petition without their assent. The petition had arisen out of events in the previous parliament and not as a 'constitutional' issue, but it is remarkable that the Commons already believed this myth about their history and sought to define their right to assent to amendments to their bills. Their unfounded confidence reflected how much attitudes had changed. Officialdom also reflected it, for while in the early fourteenth century statutes might record the assent of the lords, by the later fourteenth century it was often the assent of the lords and Commons and by the early fifteenth century the almost standard phrase was 'by advice and assent of the lords spiritual and temporal at the instance and/or

33 Myers, 'Parliament, 1422–1509' in *The English Parliament in the Middle Ages*, ed. R.G. Davies and J.H. Denton (Manchester, 1981), pp. 168–73.
34 *Rot. Parl.*, iv. 22 – *Select Documents*, pp. 237–8; *EHD*, iv. 461–2. Chrimes, *Constitutional Ideas*, pp. 159–64 re-assessed this incident and destroyed earlier opinion that it marked a major constitutional advance.

request of the Commons'.[35] The procedures for scrutinizing 'bills' were apparently still haphazard in 1400 but by mid century they had firmed a great deal. The first bill known to have come down from the lords and bearing an endorsement of the Commons' assent comes from Henry V's reign and the classic endorsement on bills (which is still in use for public bills) 'soit baille as seigneurs' was in common use by the 1420s.[36] By the 1450s there is some evidence that bills were being 'read' three times in the lords and the same may have been true of the Commons.[37] In 1455 the clerk of the rolls of parliament, Thomas Kirkby, gave his opinion on the 'course of parliament' in relation to bills before the justices in the exchequer Chamber and this is reported in a Year Book.[38] He refers confidently to the passage of bills between the Commons and the lords, the proper endorsements, the enacting and filing, and he gives his opinion on the proper procedure where the lords amend a Commons' bill. They may limit the effect of the Commons' decision but if they enlarge it, the further assent of the Commons is necessary, and he cited as an example a grant of tunnage and poundage granted for a term of years; if the lords reduced the term, no further Commons' assent was necessary; if they increased the term, the assent of the Commons must be obtained.

Much of this evidence is about procedure. This is important in its own right but more important it is the best evidence of how much the working atmosphere in parliament and government had changed between 1300 and 1461. Statutes had become recognized as the supreme form of man-made law in England and their relationship to the law of God or the law of nature was not a practical issue. Statutes could modify or change the common law and judges would enforce them in this spirit though most statutes were of a limited, amending or administrative and often repetitive character. They could be made only in parliament, only with the assent of both lords and Commons and, by the end of the period, only by an established procedure. This procedure was by bill, often coming from the Commons, sometimes from the lords – and in either case sometimes originating in a decision of the king and the Council. The formalizing of endorsements and the practice on amendments and readings shows that proceedings in the two houses must have become more consciously formal in the fifteenth century. And, of course all these features are the essence of all later legislative procedure. But, and in every aspect of government there is the same reservation, the spirit of government could only be that of the late Middle Ages. For example, major government legisla-

35 The sanctioning clauses of statutes between 1377 and 1485 are listed by Chrimes, *Constitutional Ideas*, pp. 101–4.
36 Myers, 'Parliament, 1422–1509', p. 170.
37 *Ibid.*, p. 174 referring to *Rot. Parl.*, v. 264 and *The Fane Fragment*, pp. 19, 22, 25 and 71.
38 Chrimes, *Constitutional Ideas*, pp. 361–2 – *Select Documents*, pp. 302–3. See *The Fane Fragment*, pp. 80–4.

tion was uncommon. There is an insight in a decision of the Council a month after the end of the parliament of 1422. The acts of the parliament were to be shown to the justices of the two benches who were to draw up in proper form those which were to become statutes; they were then to be shown to the Council and sent down to the counties to be proclaimed in the accustomed manner. This was a long way from Chief Justice Hengham's cutting remark in 1305 – 'Do not gloss the statute; we know it better than you, for we made it' and a long way also from the time when parliament's precise words were what became law.[39]

Grants of Taxation*

The right to assent to all taxation became parliament's most powerful means of restraining a king, and one that soon became particularly that of the Commons. Already in 1272 there was no doubt that general taxation required the assent of those who paid it, though it was also understood that they had a duty to give their assent if the king's need was evident. In 1215 Magna Carta had stated the principle that common consent for scutages and aids must be obtained from the prelates, earls and the 'greater' and 'lesser' barons duly summoned. The re-issues of the Charter omitted this requirement but the principle was observed throughout Henry III's reign and from mid century wider consent began to be considered proper. In 1254 two knights from each county were summoned to an assembly which refused to grant taxation and in 1270 Henry III's first tax on movable property since 1237 was granted in a parliament which included county knights and some townsmen. Edward I observed and prudently expanded the principle. Assemblies, not all of them parliaments, which included county knights granted him taxes on movables in 1275, 1283, 1290, and 1294; townsmen also were present in 1283 but in the other cases there were separate negotiations with some towns to obtain approval. The 1290s was a time of direct taxation on an unprecedented scale and this led to a broadening of the practice of consent. It was the time when the writs of summons of the commons began to include the 'full power' clause binding the communities to the decisions of their representatives.[40] In 1295 and 1296 both knights and townsmen gave their

---

39 *Procs. & Ords.*, iii. 22 – *Select Documents*, p. 253. *Year Books*, ed. A.J. Horwood (Rolls Series, 1879), v. 78–82.

* The particular authorities are G.L. Harriss, *King, Parliament, and Public Finance in Medieval England to 1369* (Oxford, 1975) and J.G. Edwards, *Second Century*, pp. 17–43 with the general works already cited.

40 J.G. Edwards, 'The *Plena Potestas* of English parliamentary representatives', *Hist. Studies*, i. 136–49 (from *Oxford Essays in Medieval History* to H.E. Salter, 1934).

assent in parliament but in 1297 Edward I foolishly departed from customary practice and thereby raised the issue of consent directly. In the midst of financial trouble and about to depart on an unpopular campaign in Flanders he announced that a tax of an eighth and a fifth on movable property, an unusually heavy tax, had been granted by the earls, barons, knights and all the laymen of the kingdom, when in fact it had been granted by a gathering of his supporters. The earl Marshal and the earl of Hereford went to the exchequer and halted the levy, saying that it had not been granted by the community and that to pay it would be tantamount to accepting servile status.[41] A document, the so-called statute *De tallagio non concedendo* which was neither a statute nor accepted by the king, shows what the king's opponents thought was proper – 'no tallage or aid should be levied without the assent of the archbishops, bishops and other prelates, earls, barons, knights, burgesses and other free men of the kingdom'. The king's promise to archbishops, bishops, abbots, priors and other men of Holy Church and to earls, baron and all the commonalty of the land in the charter which ended the crisis was less specific but meant almost the same thing. Aids, mises and prises, that is direct taxes and seizures of goods, should be taken only by the common assent of all the realm, for the common profit of the realm, saving the ancient aids and prises due and accustomed.[42] The eighth and fifth was withdrawn and a parliament which included knights but not townsmen granted a ninth. London subsequently granted the same and this was held to cover all towns. After 1297 knights and townsmen were always summoned together to give their consent to taxes on movables, though not necessarily in a parliament; for example in 1327 a twentieth was granted in an assembly described as a *colloquium* and *tractatus*. There is therefore some significance in a statute of 1340 (14 Edw. III, st. 2, c.1) which promised that a new and heavy direct tax granted by the lords and commons in parliament would not be a precedent and that no common aid or charge should be imposed save 'by the common assent of the prelates, earls, barons and other *grantz* and commons of our said realm of England, and that in parliament'.[43] This statute must not be seen as a constitutional landmark; it was rather a record of what had come to be accepted custom for *direct* taxation, and the principle was never challenged again. The story of assent to clerical taxation is very similar, with a confrontation in 1297 and the principle of assent in convocations finally accepted in the 1330s (pp. 77–80).

---

41 *Documents Illustrating the Crisis of 1297–8 in England*, ed. M. Prestwich (Camden Series, 24, 1980), pp. 137–8. This is an exchequer report to the king of the eloquent statement by the earl of Hereford.
42 *Select Charters*, p. 491; *EHD*, iii. 486.
43 *Select Documents*, p. 54.

The case of *indirect* taxation was quite different. The three Edwards never claimed to impose duties on exports and imports without consent but they preferred to obtain this consent from assemblies of merchants who were more amenable to bargaining and who could pass on the duties they paid. This was for long acceptable. The 'old' and the 'new' customs on wool, skins and leather were agreed with native merchants in 1275 and foreign merchants in 1303, the former with a measure of parliamentary approval. A duty on cloth to compensate the king for loss of income caused by the decline in wool exports was granted in a large council in 1347. These were all thereafter permanent duties which required no further assent. It was the additional heavier duties called subsidies, mainly on wool and often called *maltolts* (unjust exactions), which raised the issue of consent. Between 1294 and 1297 Edward I imposed a substantial duty on wool with the assent of assemblies of merchants but in his charter which ended the 'crisis' of 1297 he promised that 'because the great part of the community feel themselves heavily burdened by the *maltolt* on wool . . . and have asked us if we would release them, we at their prayer have fully released them, and have granted that we will neither take this nor any other without their common consent and their good will'.[44] This was a less specific promise than that on direct taxation but it did promise wider consent than that of the merchants. It was not however, honoured. Edward I negotiated the 'new' custom of 1303 with foreign merchants and attempted to do the same with native merchants. Edward II levied subsidies with the consent of merchants. Edward III did the same on a large scale from the 1330s until the 1350s against a background of criticism from parliament. The story is instructive. In 1338 and again in 1339 the lords and commons protested at increasing subsidies agreed by merchants but they compromised in 1340 by granting a wool subsidy from Easter 1340 until Pentecost 1341 while the king promised that only the old custom would be levied thereafter. This was embodied in a statute (14 Edw. III, st. 1, c.21) and the lords promised to hold the king to it and to assent to nothing contrary without the assent of prelates, earls, barons and the Commons, and this in full parliament.[45] Despite this the subsidy continued to be levied and an assembly of merchants in 1342 agreed to a higher wool subsidy for a year. In 1343 the Commons protested that it was unreasonable that their goods should be taxed by merchants but, after new minimum prices for wool were laid down which safeguarded the wool producers, the lords and Commons assented to a continuation of the subsidy until 1346. In 1348 the Commons were again complaining

---

44 *Select Charters*, p. 491; *EHD*, iii. 486.
45 *Select Documents*, p. 54. The struggle over consent to subsidies is mentioned *supra* pp. 67–8 and discussed in the authorities cited there.

about subsidies granted by merchants or the 'privy' council but the issue was dying. Subsidies were granted in a parliament in 1351, in a representative Great Council in 1353 but from 1355 always in parliament. These are only the bare bones of a dispute which was more political and economic than constitutional. Edward III was exploiting the wool trade to pursue his war aims and the greater merchants could more readily be induced to co-operate; parliament, which contained wool producers and lesser merchants who believed with an element of justice that subsidies were passed on to producers in the form of lower prices, had an interest in asking that subsidies should cease or at least should require its assent. By the 50s Edward's war needs had changed, his foreign creditors were bankrupted and the major English merchants exhausted, and he was prepared to concede the freedom of trade parliament wished. The right of parliament to assent to subsidies was tacitly accepted from 1355 and it is ironic that after complaining so much, parliament in effect granted the subsidies continuously from this time onwards, and indeed preferred to grant subsidies rather than direct taxes from 1361 until 1370. Edward made a number of promises about consent during this period, some of them in statutes, but none of them should be regarded as a definitive statement. For example in 1362, in return for the subsidy for three years, he promised (36 Edw. III, st. 1, c.11) that it would then cease 'and that no subsidy or other charge should be placed on wool by merchants or others in future save by the assent of parliament' and in 1371 (45 Edw. III, c.4) that 'no subsidy should be placed on wool, skins or leather without the assent of parliament'.[46] All one can say is that parliamentary consent to wool subsidies became customary and was firmly established by the 1370s. The same happened with the other major subsidy, tunnage and poundage. It was granted by a Council in 1347, then for a time by merchants. In 1372 the town members and the lords in parliament granted it after the county members had been sent home; in 1373 the lords and *all* the Commons renewed it at the same time as the wool subsidy; and this became the practice thereafter.[47] In 1381 and 1385 the Commons enforced token breaks in the levy of subsidies – which the king circumvented – to make clear that they 'may not be claimed as of right and custom' but only by the grant of the lords and Commons.[48] Ironically, after all these struggles, parliament granted the subsidies for life to Richard II in 1398, to Henry V in 1415 and to Henry VI in 1453.

46 *Ibid.*, pp. 85 and 91.
47 *Ibid.*, pp. 70–1, 92–3 (1372) and *Rot. Parl.*, ii. 317.
48 *Rot. Parl.*, iii. 104 – *Select Documents*, p. 127, and iii. 204.

The middle years of the fourteenth century therefore saw the right of parliament to assent to all taxation accepted piecemeal and by the 1370s it had become an accepted principle, never again questioned. In 1379 a Great Council decided that taxation was necessary but that it could be granted only in a parliament.[49] Fortescue unequivocally says that the king may not impose any burdens on his subjects 'without the concession or assent of his whole realm expressed in his parliament'.[50] Moreover by the end of the fourteenth century it was accepted that this meant the assent of the Commons. The origins of this principle go back to the early part of the century when the Commons began to be accepted as the representatives of the community. The *Modus* gives them the greater voice in taxation for this reason and in Edward III's reign the theory becomes translated into parliamentary practice. In the 40s the Commons began to make grants of taxation in written schedules. In 1344 there was a significant division of respon- sibility – the lay lords promised to accompany the king to fight in France, the prelates and clerical proctors granted a tax on the clergy and the Commons granted two tenths and two fifteenths on certain conditions which the king accepted.[51] In 1352 Chief Justice Shareshull in the king's presence gave the lords and Commons a long account of the war and current problems, and thanked the Commons for their past grants. The Commons were told to choose 24 or 30 members to listen to the lords' discussion and report to their fellows; a group of lords subsequently came to the Commons to advise on taxation and drawing up petitions; and the Commons later presented the king with a roll containing a large grant of taxation and the conditions and petitions they had attached to it.[52] This probably fairly represents the new practice. The king had to 'sell' his case for a grant of taxation; the lords and Commons discussed the matter and exchanged views, the better-informed lords giving advice to the Commons; and finally the Commons representing the community announced their grant, often with conditions attached. In 1380 the Commons returned after a day's discussion to ask through their Speaker for more facts and figures about the grant they had been asked to make; the officers and the Council prepared a statement which showed that £160,000 was needed. The Commons considered this sum impossible and asked the lords to consider how a smaller sum might be raised; the lords suggested three ways but favoured a poll-tax. The Commons eventually offered a poll-tax of 100,000 marks if the clergy made a grant of 50,000 marks, and after further discussions made this grant in a written schedule.[53]

49 *Ibid.*, iii. 56 – *Select Documents*, p. 121.
50 Sir John Fortescue, *De Laudibus Legum Anglie*, ed. S.B. Chrimes (Cambridge, 1942), p. 87.
51 *Rot. Parl.*, ii. 148.
52 *Ibid.*, ii. 237.
53 *Ibid.*, iii. 89–90 – *Select Documents*, pp. 123–5.

This division of authority was recognized in 1383 when a direct tax was granted by the Commons with the assent of the lords and this became the standard form of words from 1391. An incident in the Gloucester parliament of 1407 shows how jealous the Commons were of this right. Henry IV and the lords had discussed taxation, the lords had answered one by one how much they thought was needed and a minimum figure had been agreed. A delegation from the Commons was then summoned to be told of the discussion with the intention of speeding up the grant. The Commons 'were greatly disturbed, saying and affirming it to be to the great prejudice and derogation of their liberties' and the king with the advice of the lords made a statement which is worth quoting in full.[54]

> It is fully permissible for the lords to discuss together in this present parliament, and in any other in the future, in the absence of the king, about the estate of the realm and the remedy necessary for it; and that in the same way it is permissible for the Commons on their part to discuss together about the estate and remedy aforesaid, provided always that the lords for their part, and the Commons for theirs, make no report to our said lord the king of any grant granted by the Commons and assented to by the lords, nor about the discussions about the said grant, before the lords and Commons are of one assent and one accord in this matter, and then in the manner and form accustomed, that is to say by the mouth of the Speaker of the said Commons for the time being.

Henry IV was being conciliatory but he was apparently only confirming existing practice. Discussions about taxation between lords and Commons had been going on since the 1330s, by intercommuning delegations (p. 215) and no doubt in other ways. The Commons had made their grant in writing from about the same time, first in a schedule or bill and later in an indenture, one part of which presumably remained with the Commons' clerk. It became common for the grant to be made at the close of parliament when the king gave his answers to common petitions. By the mid fifteenth century the grant was being made in a bill for in 1455 when Thomas Kirby, the clerk of parliament, gave evidence about parliamentary procedure he cited as an example a bill from the Commons granting tunnage and poundage being sent to the lords for approval in the same way as any other bill (p. 223).[55]

The right to assent to all taxes is one thing, the right to refuse or to impose conditions is another. Taxation was normally asked for war purposes and in most cases parliament did what was considered to be

---

54 *Ibid.*, 611 – *Select Documents*, pp. 228-9; *EHD*, iv. 460-1.
55 Chrimes, *Constitutional Ideas*, pp. 361-2 – *Select Documents*, pp. 302-3.

its duty and granted at least much of what the king claimed to need. It did however refuse a grant on some occasions, for example in the famous Good Parliament of 1376 when fraud at Court and treason in Brittany were alleged, but more commonly it acted as a restraint on the king. A popular and successful king such as Henry V was granted heavy taxes but even in his case by 1421 the Commons were making it clear that they expected the war to become self-financing and that they were not prepared to continue the heavy taxation. Henry VI had to face an increasing debt for the French war with no prospect of obtaining enough taxation to pay it off. Taxation had to be laboured for in parliament, and that meant particularly in the Commons. On a number of occasions, most of them in the unhappy 40 or so years after 1370, the Commons were conciliated by unusual concessions such as facts and figures to justify that king's requests. Both Richard II and Henry IV on several occasions even reluctantly allowed the Commons to have accounts of how taxes had been spent. Grants were given on conditions on a number of occasions, for example on condition that the war continued or that the tax was spent only on war purposes. Sometimes the Commons' suspicions went a stage further and they were able to insist that the revenue from a tax they granted was received and paid out by special war treasurers and not by the exchequer and that their accounts were scrutinized.[56] Incidents like these must not be seen in terms of the appropriation of supply or accountability; they are rather important examples of the Commons' determination to defend the communities they represented. They were the product of particular political and military circumstances not of any constitutional campaign.

The Court of Parliament

From its origins parliament was a court and in the fifteenth century it was often referred to as the 'High Court' of parliament (p. 233), though this referred to its status rather than its practical rôle as a court which by then was modest. In Edward I's reign it was still the great occasion for the king, his councillors and ministers to decide all manner of legal matters. The law book called *Fleta* from the 1290s set this out well – 'the king has his court in his council in his parliaments'

56 For example in January and October, 1377, October, 1375, January, 1380 and on a number of other occasions in parliament down to the reign of Henry IV the Commons granted taxes on condition that they were received by war treasurers and spent only on defined war purposes. *Rot. Parl.*, ii. 364, iii. 7, 38 and 75 – *Select Documents*, pp. 112, 116–17, 120 and 123. On several occasions they received information on how the money had been spent and in 1406 they were permitted to nominate auditors to hear the war treasurers' accounts. *Rot. Parl.*, iii. 577 – *Select Documents*, p. 220.

where judicial doubts are concluded, new remedies provided for new injuries and justice done to everyone according to his merits.[57] This included responding to petitions seeking a remedy as distinct from a favour, resolving difficulties that had arisen in other courts and hearing cases, important cases *ab initio*. The best evidence is the roll of the Lent parliament of 1305 but, as Maitland stressed, this was essentially the work of the king and his Council (p. 168). When parliament ceased to meet regularly and became the assembly of the community, its rôle as a court changed. The king, the Council and the chancellor came to handle most of the cases and petitions which previously had come to parliament and the common-law courts became more professional and self-sufficient. Parliament, or rather the lords which was now the Council in parliament, however, remained a court. The members of the Commons had no part in this and in 1399, in the aftermath of the state trials of Richard II's reign, they denied that they were party to judgements unless they were shown them by the king as a matter of grace.[58] Some petitions for remedy still came in parliament time; one group which stand out was from men disinherited for political reasons and seeking restoration. Appeals alleging error in King's Bench or the common-law side of chancery lay to the lords. The right to judgement by peers in cases of treason or felony had become the special privilege of lords and from 1442 of peeresses also (st. 20 Hen. VI, c. 9) and this included the right to be judged in the lords if it was sitting. In Edward I's time trials of great men or great cases, for example in 1305 of Nicholas Segrave for deserting a royal army, were often reserved for parliament but by the end of the fourteenth century this was coming to be seen as abnormal. For example in 1377 Alice Perrers was made to answer in parliament to charges of misusing her influence at Court when she was Edward III's mistress and was convicted. In 1378, in the next parliament, she and her husband pleaded error in these proceedings, basically because they had denied her the normal procedures of the common law, and she was given the right to return to the courts.[59] Later in Richard II's reign, in 1388 and again in 1397, there were political trials in parliament initiated by private 'appeals' of treason. The unease which these travesties produced led in 1399, after Richard had been deposed, to a remedy by statute (st. 1 Hen. IV, c. 14). This referred to the 'inconveniences' and 'meschiefs' that had resulted and enacted that appeals should in future be tried 'by the good laws of the realm' and never again in parliament – save appeals relating to acts committed abroad which would be heard before the Constable and the Marshal.[60]

57 *Fleta*, ii. 109.
58 *Rot. Parl.*, iii. 426 – *Select Documents*, p. 199.
59 *Ibid.*, iii. 40–1.
60 *Select Documents*, p. 200.

One new form of trial in parliament, impeachment, was created and remained a potent procedure for centuries (and potentially today) because it was appropriate to the new status of parliament. It was first used in 1376, probably without much forethought, when the Commons and some of the lords came to parliament indignant at the mis-doings and wastefulness of members of the Court circle. The Commons presented and proved their allegations before John of Gaunt and the lords, and they probably expected the king to punish the accused. He did nothing and the Commons pursued their accusations in common by the mouth of their Speaker, and a trial took place before the lords. The precedent for this procedure – and precedent was now very important – was the common-law procedure by which the accusation of a community could lead to a trial before the Council or a court.[61] The courtiers were duly convicted by the lords and though they were released by the king when parliament was dissolved, a new and important precedent had been set. It was used again in 1386 when the Commons impeached the chancellor, Michael de la Pole, earl of Suffolk, and again in 1450 against his descendant, William de la Pole, duke of Suffolk. It was a political weapon, significantly in the hands of the Commons speaking for the community, by which an offender could be accused and brought to answer before the lords. It was not often used during the Middle Ages but it was revived in 1621 and used on a number of important political occasions in the seventeenth and eighteenth centuries.

The Authority of Parliament

The last two chapters and the previous sections of this chapter have shown how much parliament changed in the course of the late Middle Ages, how its composition, its procedure and its rights developed and became defined. There were no clear-cut turning points but there was a clear difference between the parliaments of the late thirteenth century, often small gatherings of some prelates and magnates with the king and his Council, and the large parliaments which became customary in the first decades of the fourteenth century. These were understood to be gatherings of the whole community, the prelates and the hereditary lay lords coming as individuals, the lords of land and the accepted leaders of the community, together with the representa-

---

61 The impeachments of 1376 are reported in the rolls of parliament and in the *Anonimalle Chronicle – Select Documents*, pp. 104 and 107–10. The article by G. Lambrick, 'The impeachment of the abbot of Abingdon in 1368', *EHR* 82 (1967), 250–76 supersedes earlier articles on the origins of impeachment and G.A. Holmes, *The Good Parliament* (Oxford, 1975) explains the background to the charges.

tives of the communities of the counties and the towns. The former quickly became a privileged peerage, the latter quickly became recognized to have authority to speak for the community and to raise 'common' issues. By the last quarter of the fourteenth century parliament had become an institution with a self-consciousness and a status in English life and government which it has never lost. It was now more than a meeting, a treaty or a parley with the king. It had its own authority and indeed the phrase 'the authority of parliament' begins to be used about 1400 and became common in the fifteenth century. Contemporaries did not speculate much about this authority nor about parliament at all – no more than they speculated about the king and his authority. But references to it and this and other phrases indicate the assumptions that were being made. Acts were regularly made 'by authority of parliament' from the 1440s. The phrase 'the High Court of Parliament' began to be used in the 1380s and came into wider use in the fifteenth century. It was not a phrase with a precise significance; its most obvious meaning was that parliament made and unmade laws; it was a lawyer's phrase. It had the merit of conveying in traditional rather than political terms a sense of the authority and status which parliament undoubtedly now possessed. A similar but narrower view was expressed in very partisan circumstances in 1388 by the lords appellant when their proposed proceedings in parliament against some of Richard II's friends were declared by the lawyers to be proper by neither the common nor the civil law. This was answered by a declaration by the lords with the (undoubtedly unwilling) assent of the king that such a grave (*haute*) crime as this which concerned the king himself and 'the estate of all his realm' and perpetrated by peers of the realm, could be decided only in parliament according to the law and course of parliament – and not by the course, process and order of any lower court.[62] This was a 'lynching' occasion but it is nevertheless significant that the argument was used. In 1454 Chief Justice Fortescue declared that the justices should not in any way determine the privilege of the High Court of Parliament which was so high and mighty in its nature.[63] The source of this authority ultimately lay in the fact that parliament represented the whole community – in practice the 20,000 or so most substantial men in the community. Contemporaries did not say this explicitly but they assumed it. The rôle of the Commons in presenting common petitions assumes it and as early as 1365 Chief Justice Thorpe declared that everyone is held to

---

62 *Rot. Parl.*, iii. 236 – *Select Documents*, pp. 147-8.
63 *Rot. Parl.*, v. 239 – *Select Documents*, p. 296. This related to parliamentary privilege of freedom from arrest. Parliamentary privilege did originate in this period but not with its later significance.

know a statute made in parliament 'because parliament represents the body of all the realm'[64] The frequent references from the late fourteenth century to the three estates in parliament, the lords spiritual, the lords temporal and the Commons, imply the same thing.

Within parliament it was undoubtedly the lords who were the more important. Significant numbers of the lords often failed to attend but the more powerful and experienced men in the kingdom, the dukes and earls, the barons and bishops who were active in government, diplomacy and war, were good attenders. They were the men who were regularly summoned to Great Councils and who came about the Court. The lords itself was indeed sometimes referred to as the 'great council'. The status of the lords is shown in the declaration of the Council in 1425, admittedly in special circumstances, that when the king could not govern, the execution of the king's authority to rule and govern the land and ensure the observance of the law belonged to the lords spiritual and temporal in parliament or Great Council or to the lords of the continual Council. Lords are referred to as the king's 'natural' councillors; it was they who appointed and served on the Council if the king was a child; and it was they to whom the Commons turned to serve on the Council when things were going wrong. In the Ordinances of 1311 it was the baronage in parliament whose assent was necessary for foreign wars or the king's absence of the appointment of his leading officials. The lords were the leaders of society; they had wealth, status and authority in their own communities and they were at the heart of the politics of the day.

In practice the primary rôle of the lords in parliament was to discuss and offer the king advice on the great matters of the kingdom – as their writs of summons said. The opening address to the whole parliament normally gives some indication of what these issues were but the discussions are rarely reported in the rolls in any detail. The records of some Great Councils report discussions more fully and these must have been similar to discussions in the lords. Lords may give their opinions one by one. Discussions range over matters such as the defence of the kingdom and the seas, projected expeditions, the king's need for money and how it could be met, diplomatic negotiations, the regulation of trade and political issues such as the restoration of a deprived magnate, a restriction or resumption of grants or a magnate feud. In some parliaments lords' discussions were reported to the Commons through intercommuning or by emissaries to guide its deliberations. The matters most commonly mentioned are money matters but these normally required broader explanations of the king's policies and difficulties. The lords also give advice on common petitions and issues raised in parliament. The *Fane Fragment* of a lords' journal in 1461 records the lords setting up committees to inves-

64 Chrimes, *Constitutional Ideas*, p. 352.

tigate matters and meeting day after day to examine bills item by item, in some cases over several readings, amending them and sometimes rejecting them. The lords had over a long period become not only a council but a scrutinizing body working with some degree of order and method. The lords was a relatively small body, often with no more than 50 members with the great officials in attendance. It could readily be a working council as well as a gathering of the greatest in the realm.

The 'house' of Commons was a very different body with 200–300 members who did not have the status and experience of the lords, and always included a substantial number of newcomers. The best contemporary statement of its rôle was made in the name of Henry IV in 1399, in his first parliament. The Commons were anxious to affirm in the aftermath of the state trials of Richard II's reign, that they had no part in judgements in parliament. The king agreed and (through the archbishop of Canterbury) went on to say that they were 'petitioners and demanders' save that in making statutes and granting taxes and in things to be done for the common profit of the realm, he particularly wished to have their advice and assent.[65] This was a finely judged statement and essentially true. Henry could have been more positive about their rights to assent to taxes and statutes but he was not a constitutional lawyer. The Commons came to parliament to speak for the community, for all who did not sit in the lords, to assent on their behalf and to present their grievances. Common petitions were one way of doing so. Another was to voice their grievances and the Commons are recorded doing so from the 1330s, often on the theme of the waste of resources and the burden of taxes. The Good Parliament of 1376 is a prime example of this because the Anonimalle Chronicle reports some of the speeches in the Commons and before the lords (pp. 213–14). The parliament of 1406 is an even better example because there were no scandals alleged and no faction-fight among the lords as in 1376.[66] Members of the Commons were then vocal in their criticism of misgovernment and in demands for better government and the lords shared their views. The Commons' repeated request was for 'good and abundant governance'. They were primarily responsible for delaying the session from March until December and winning a number of detailed promises from the king. In both of these parliaments and in a number of other less dramatic ones the Commons were going beyond the obvious meaning of 'petitioning and demanding'.

The Commons were certainly not afraid to speak out on occasions such as this, but they were critics of misgovernment not seekers after a

---

65 Rot. Parl., iii. 427 – *Select Documents*, p. 199.
66 A.L. Brown, 'The Commons and the Council in the Reign of Henry IV', *Hist. Studies*, ii. 42–57 (from *EHR*, 1964).

share in government. In 1376 they declared eloquently that they were willing to give their lives and goods for the king, but it was obvious that if the king had loyal councillors and good officers around him, he would be rich and have no need to tax the commons.[67] They wished the evil-doers removed (and punished) and they wished the king *himself* to appoint new officers and councillors. They were petitioners and demanders though in this case they were obliged to become prosecutors. But they did not seek authority to govern. In 1376 even the lords had to be pressed to give advice on who should be appointed to the Council because, they said, this decision belonged to the king. The balance of councillors the Commons sought was three bishops, three earls and three barons 'who would not hesitate to speak the truth and act profitably'. Good examples of this same philosophy come from the parliaments of Henry IV where the Commons several times asked for the appointment of a strong Council. In some they asked only that the king should formally nominate his councillors who would then be 'charged' to do their duty and provide better, more economical and effective government; in others the king appointed new councillors but the Commons never asked for or had a hand in the appointment. Their ideal Council was invariably a strong, balanced body of lords to serve with the officials, never commoners whom they considered to lack the status needed to be effective. Their philosophy was the thoroughly orthodox one that governance belonged to the king with the counsel of the lords. The Commons were indeed chary of giving advice on any matter of government. They sometimes declared that they were too simple to do so and sought the advice of the lords. In some cases they were merely anxious to avoid being bound by giving advice to vote the money to give it effect. But not infrequently they were provoked by the strength of their opinions or their prejudices to give opinions on war or foreign policy. The lords and Commons were understood to have different rôles but in practice they shared a common outlook.

It is difficult to assess the authority of the medieval parliament with confidence because opinions have differed so much in the past and every generation sees it with its own hindsight. It must certainly be seen in the context of government and society as a whole and of all their parts. The king governed and parliament was first of all *his* parliament. It normally met when he chose to summon it – despite the statutes of 1330 and 1362 requiring annual parliaments.[68] In practice it was often his need for taxation which determined when he summoned it. Most parliaments voted taxation and proceedings normally followed, more or less, the course he and his advisers had envisaged. But

---

67 *Rot. Parl.*, ii. 323 – *Select Documents*, pp. 106–7.
68 Statutes 4 Edw. III, c. 14 (1330) and 36 Edward III, c. 10 (1362) – *Select Documents*, pp. 44.

parliament was more than this. The king in parliament had an authority which he did not otherwise possess, in particular to tax and to make a statute. The members of parliament also had authority. God had given the king authority to rule his kingdom, but he had also given the lords rule and power under the king. It was therefore to the lords that the king first turned for advice. And when the greatest political decisions had to be taken, a deposition or the issue of the succession or the form of government during a minority for example, the lords decided while the Commons had at best a nominal, assenting rôle. Parliament became the place where political conflicts were determined, for example in 1340–41, 1388 or the late 1450s, and it was the lords, who were the great politicians, who determined them. The Commons had an important rôle, but it was a different one. They came to speak for the community in granting taxes and assenting and requesting statutes, in petitioning and demanding, and, when necessary, criticizing the conduct of government and demanding changes. In practice it seems to have been the county gentlemen who always took the lead. Townsmen are rarely mentioned in parliament save in connexion with trade and finance; none was Speaker of the Commons during the Middle Ages. This is not an unfair reflection of the status of the gentry who were well on the way to become the 'lesser nobility' and who in practice had become the governors of their counties under the king and the lords. It is not surprising that the evidence of complaints and legislation about county elections and then the evidence of elections themselves suggests that interest in county elections grew rapidly from the late fourteenth century onwards and led to the 'invasion' of borough seats by gentlemen and lawyers in the fifteenth century. In parliament there were members who slept or stammered and mumbled or pursued their own advantage but there were others who spoke out bluntly[69] – but loyally – men such as Speakers Sir Peter de la Mare in 1376 or Sir Arnald Savage in 1401 and 1404 or Sir John Tiptoft in 1406. Significantly the last two were the king's own men who did not consider it disloyal to speak out before their lord.

---

69 The members of the Commons are caricatured in a poem written in the 1390s – *Mum and the Sothsegger*, ed. M. Day and R. Steele (Early English Text Society, 199, 1936), pp. 24–6 – *EHD*, iv. 435–4.

Conclusion

The late Middle Ages did not see a new beginning to the governance of England. They inherited a tradition and a structure of government going back to the early Anglo-Saxon kingdoms and in particular to the great extension of royal government that had taken place in the twelfth and thirteenth centuries. But there were so many major changes in government about the end of the thirteenth century and so many more by 1461 that the period deserves to be considered distinctive – within the long continuity of English government. Moreover the form of English government until the nineteenth century and to an extent until the present day was in significant part the creation of this period, certainly much more so than of any earlier period. The most striking example is the representative parliament. Its composition, its electoral practice and its form of proceedings were largely determined between 1300 and 1461. It was for example in large part a statute of 1430 and the practice of late medieval elections which were reformed in 1832. The offices of administration, the courts and their practices which were investigated by reforming commissions in the late eighteenth and nineteenth centuries were also in large part creations of this period. Innovation and change did not of course end in 1461. Major change took place in each succeeding century but often within the late medieval framework of institutions and practices. The most important parts of this legacy were, I suggest, the increased range and quantity of royal government, its greater professionalism and bureaucracy, the increased rôle played by 'middling' people, the county gentry and wealthy townsmen, in the king's government of their communities and the authority of parliament which now represented the whole community of the kingdom, in the affairs of the kingdom.

The marked expansion in royal government continued a development begun in the twelfth century. By 1200 for example both chancery and exchequer were established offices, keeping elaborate records, by 1300 both had finally cast off their connections with the Household and by 1400 they were busier, more highly departmentalized and more independent offices. The quantity of their records is evidence of the growing amount of government. By the mid fourteenth century the number of letters issued in the king's name by chancery and the other offices and courts was probably in excess of 100,000 a year. Chancery enrolments of letters under the great seal peaked in the mid fourteenth century but by then many more letters were being issued under the privy seal and the signet, and chancery was turning to other work in particular as a court. The records of the exchequer were multiplying, not on the traditional county side of its business, but on the 'foreign accounts' side, the accounts relating to the new activities of government. The records of the Westminster common-law courts and of the visiting justices were now 'monumental'.[1] There was more government, more record of government and more than growth in quantity. In chancery most letters were now issued on the authority of the chancellor himself, in practice on the authority of his senior officials. The same was true of the day-to-day business of the exchequer. Both had become administrative offices, taking the decisions and holding the information without which the government of the day could not have functioned. They may, anachronistically, be called 'government departments' and they were normally to be found at Westminster (where else!) which by the fourteenth century had become the administrative capital of the kingdom. This had come about because the range of royal government had expanded. For example from the late thirteenth century there were for the first time both regular customs duties and the staff to collect them in the ports and frequent direct taxation and the experience to collect it readily. Kings relied on heavy taxation to pay for the greater costs of their own life-styles and in particular because war became much more expensive. From the reign of Edward I armies became larger, the men serving for pay and raised and supported in new and more expensive ways. There was also significant expansion in the royal courts. The roots of the common law were in the twelfth century but in the late thirteenth century both King's Bench and Common Pleas ceased to have any connexion with the Household and became Westminster courts staffed by professional, lay lawyers with their own professional literature and a century later their own system of professional education. In the counties and towns the old grand, infrequent inquisition of the eyre and irregular visits by justices were replaced over a period by the new Justices of the Peace backed up by regular visits of justices of assize and gaol delivery and by *ad hoc* commissions. The procedure of the law also changed,

1 There is an indication of the scale of legal records of this period in J.C. Davies, 'Common law writs and returns: Richard I to Richard II', *BIHR* 26 (1953), 125–56 and 27 (1954), 1–34 which refers to hundreds of thousands of documents – still largely unused.

for example the bill changed it fundamentally. Medievalists have been too inclined to see the changes of Henry II and the treatise of Bracton as the culmination of medieval English law – even Maitland was guilty of this.

There is a good example of the character of these changes in the conduct of government at the highest level of executive government at Court and the Council. The king himself governed the kingdom, and his successors continued to do so until the eighteenth century. But the manner of his government was changing. It was no longer Household government of the old style. The great offices and courts had been born in the Household to be near to the king, but by 1300 they had gone 'out of court'. They were no longer part of the Household. It continued to serve the personal needs of the king and his Court and it was used extensively at times for some governmental purposes, in particular in wartime. It could hold money to pay troops; it could assemble and supply them; it could write letters. It was certainly extensively used by Edward I on campaign, but it was never used on this scale again and it became largely a domestic institution. Those close to the king, his friends, his courtiers and the members of his Household continued to be important – because they had access to him and because he continued to rule personally. He had a great deal of patronage in his own hands. On most days he would receive requests for graces, pardons, gifts of offices, lands and goods, church preferment, timber and so on – from the reign of Edward I most of them in the form of written petitions. Only the king himself could grant them though his Court officials methodized the work for him – and used their good offices for their friends. In the same way, though the evidence is less abundant, more of the issues of state now came to the king in writing in the form of memoranda, draft documents from his officials and letters from the Council, foreign rulers, noblemen and others. There were discussions with ministers, sometimes formal Council meetings at Court and undoubtedly a great deal of informal talk but it was the king himself who was responsible for the more important decisions and for a surprising number of the less important ones as well. This was not however in any meaningful sense 'Household government'. It was personal government, government by the king in his Court, sometimes in his Council, taking decisions which were implemented mainly outside the Household. This was the form of government for centuries. Court ceremony and state became more elaborate but the king had to face bundles of papers every day. He still ruled and decided issues himself.

The king could not however deal with the increasing burden of government without advice and help. The other aspect of central government was at Westminster, at the Council and in the great offices. The Council is the best documented example of change. There was no Council in the twelfth century; it is mentioned frequently only in the reign of Henry III and it was then more a meeting of counsellors than an institution. Even in Edward I's reign it met on a very *ad hoc* basis though letters were now sometimes exchanged between the king and his Council. In the course of the fourteenth century, probably by mid-century, the Council became an institution – a working body, of limited membership, meeting frequently, almost daily, normally at Westminster in the Star Chamber. The king directed government but the Council took many of the complicated, difficult decisions and investigated issues with which he did not have the time nor the inclination to deal. If offered him advice and to some extent at least acted as a friendly restraint on his decisions. At the highest level government was a matter of co-operation between an active king, his Council and the three great officers who came about Court, sat in the Council and had a great deal of independent authority in their own departments.

The day-to-day conduct of government became more bureaucratic and parchment-bound. Matters and requests could come before the king verbally but increasingly they came in writing. Even the queen and their children often approached him in writing to seek favours. When the king made his decision it might be transmitted in the form of a signet letter to the privy seal and then a privy seal warrant to chancery before the grant was given effect in a patent. This became a 'restrictive practice' to maintain the fees of the clerks. Records of the transaction were kept in the privy seal, in chancery and probably in the signet office as well. This was an age of files of documents, enrolments and multiple copies. The exchequer was particularly addicted to copying and re-copying and rolls in triplicate were commonplace – not unreasonably in a department which handled money. In the 1290s chancery began the practice of noting the authority for its action on the letters it issued and on the copies it kept. Proper procedures and proper records were not novelties but there were undoubtedly many, many more of them and almost all survived for centuries. The men who served in the offices were increasingly making life-long careers there. They were almost career 'civil servants'. In the fourteenth century they were still mainly clerics but often in minor orders only to acquire a source of income. In the fifteenth century an increasing number of 'clerks' were laymen, and even a devout clerk such as Thomas Hoccleve, who gave up his orders to marry, had a distinctly materialistic view of his career. Money, he thought, could cure all ills. The clerks worked in a professional, greedy, gossipy world where Pepys would have felt at home.

This was also the first period when it became respectable and common for the nobleman and the gentleman to become an office-holder and even build a career upon it. The first lay chancellor was Sir Robert Bourchier in 1340, and the first lord and the first earl had served as chancellor by 1400 though most chancellors were archbishops and bishops with experience in government behind them. The first lay treasurer was also appointed in 1340 and in the fifteenth century the office became almost the preserve of knights, lords and noblemen. Laymen became much more prominent at the Council and when the Council became a political issue, the ideal composition became a balance of bishops, earls, and barons or bannerets. In practice lay lords were often irregular attenders but there were always a few who found service at the Council attractive. Service in office was one way in which a gentleman could make a career and found a family. John Tiptoft served the three Lancastrian kings as a Household man, in Household office, as a councillor and as treasurer; he became a lord and his son became an earl, and there were others who rose in a similar but less dramatic way. It is noticeable from the early fifteenth century how many senior offices in the Household and in the Westminster departments begin to be held by laymen. The justices in the Westminster courts were entirely laymen by 1340 and the common law became a wholly lay profession. There was a decisive shift in the balance between clerics and laymen in government.

In the counties and town a different though related change took place. Lawyers became ubiquitous, in the courts and in private and royal service as advisers and administrators. In the parliament of 1422 between a fifth and a quarter of the MPs the counties and towns sent to Westminster were men of law. The others were county gentry and the 'better' townsmen, most of them men with considerable experience of administration in their own communities. Landowners were not newcomers to this; they had been attending the county and hundred courts and serving as jurors for centuries; some had served as sheriffs, coroners or keepers of the peace in the thirteenth century. This period however saw a great extension of their rôle as royal officials, as commissioners to assess and collect taxes, array soldiers and conduct enquiries, as escheators, sheriffs and, above all, as Justices of the Peace, and largely without payment. The knights, esquires and gentlemen in the counties and the better townsmen, with due deference to the nobility and the social customs of their communities, enforced the king's laws and carried out the orders he gave them subject to little direct control from Westminster save through the law and the justices. They had their clerks to assist them but many, by the fifteenth century almost all, were literate and capable of understanding papers themselves. This is the classic manner in which the counties were governed for centuries.

The driving force of all these changes was a change in society itself.

Land remained the fundamental and respectable source of wealth but wealth from trade and service was increasingly important. Paid service became normal in every aspect of life. For example feudal military service ceased to be demanded; services on the land and serfdom were in rapid decline. Feudal taxes, feudal courts, feudalism itself, became obsolete. The old, largely feudal, social hierarchy was replaced and the higher nobility as we know it, the peerage, with its right to be summoned to parliament was created. So too was the lesser nobility, the (landed) gentry, of knights, esquires and gentlemen, accustomed to taking an active part in the administration of their own lands and their own communities as royal officials. The supreme example is the office of Justice of the Peace created in the fourteenth century, held by local landowners, lawyers and backed up by royal justices from Westminster, which for centuries dominated government in the localities.

The gentry and the lawyers were the members who represented their counties in parliament and began to invade the town seats. They had been on the fringe of the 'political nation' in the thirteenth century but it is the archbishops, bishops, abbots, priors, earls and barons who are mentioned in documents such as Magna Carta and who could still speak for the community. Knights and townsmen were summoned to a few parliaments before 1295; by the second quarter of the fourteenth century they were an essential part of parliament. Soon there are references to the the whole community represented there and to the Commons not the lords as its voice. Parliament consists of the king and the three estates, the lords spiritual, the lords temporal and the Commons. It is important not to read this with hindsight but it is remarkable that within half a century, between the 1290s and the 1340s, parliament changed from a relatively small and normally regular gathering of magnates and officials to the large, representative assembly meeting in two houses that it has remained ever since. And that by 1461 it had the right to assent to all taxation and to all statutes and that its business was conducted in ways that are still basic to its procedure today. The weight of political power of course lay with the king and the lords. The Commons were not seeking the rôle which their successors in the seventeenth century began to seek with reluctance. Parliament is however the classic example of how much government and attitudes to it changed between the late thirteenth and the mid fifteenth centuries and of how long these changes lasted. This was not a revolution in government. It was a major, and not well-appreciated change in the long list of changes which make up the essential continuity in English government.

Index